FOUR CITIES

A Study in Comparative Policy Making

FOUR CITIES

A Study in Comparative Policy Making

by

Oliver P. Williams and Charles R. Adrian

Philadelphia

UNIVERSITY OF PENNSYLVANIA PRESS

Note

Portions of Chapter One have been published in the *Midwest Journal of Political Science*. In slightly altered form, Chapter Four has been published in the *American Political Science Review*. Both are here used by permission of the publishers.

FELS INSTITUTE SERIES

ISBN: 0-8122-7381-8

Printed in the United States of America

Preface

We have attempted in this study to make a comparative analysis of the political process in four cities, holding certain factors constant and seeking to find explanations for policy variations over the same time span and in communities of similar size, which were faced with essentially the same issues. We have not by any means completely isolated the significant variables, but we believe that the analytical framework developed is a useful one and that the product of our efforts provides a first approximation that will lend itself to further development.

Our work was financed principally by the Institute for Community Development and Services at Michigan State University. The Institute was founded with generous support from the Kellogg Foundation. It has a central interest in the problem-solving process in communities. We believe that this study will provide local decision-makers with insights into community policy-making techniques in both their healthful and morbid aspects. If it does this, it will have contributed to the purposes of the Institute.

In its early stages, the study received some support from the Bureau of Social and Political Research at Michigan State University, and its publication was made possible in part through assistance from the Fels Institute of Local and State Government at the University of Pennsylvania.

We wish to extend out thanks to the many anonymous persons in four anonymous cities who cooperated so generously and helpfully. They know who they are, even though our promises to them make public identification impossible. Responsibility for the data as interpreted remains, of course, with the authors.

Oliver P. Williams

Charles R. Adrian

Contents

Part I

Introduction

Chapter I

The Study Approach

The casual observer of the political landscape in America's middle-sized cities will initially receive the impression of sameness and monotony. Viewed against a background of innovations by the national governments, our cities give scant evidence that they are furnishing "laboratories for social experimentation." The services, the problems, the limitations, and the preoccupations are similar the country over. However, an intimate look by an interested observer does reveal variations in accomplishments; while these are not of great scope, they do indicate that distinct sets of values appear to guide the individual civic spirits. It takes a person familiar with the possibilities of civic enterprise to begin drawing the distinctions between sets of community politics. The "laboratory" element is present, but it often operates within a narrow framework.

The appearance of sameness is partially created by the similarity of the problems which the cities face. The dissimilarity begins with the varied responses of cities to these problems. In this study, four cities of similar size, location, and economic base were observed. In all four, the record-setting postwar sale of automobiles had made it impossible for the downtown areas to serve the flood of shoppers demanding space to drive and park their cars. The alarms of the downtown merchants, fearful of peripheral shopping plaza developments, led to pressures on the city governments. The four city governments responded in programs ranging from a $15,000,000 downtown rebuilding program to a near denial that the city government had any obligation to handle the problem.

Fringe matters offered another common problem. The unincorporated fringes were developing land-use patterns that promised to warp the character of urban development for generations to come. The city stakes in the fringe policies included coordination of planning, utility and street expansion, and tying the increased tax base derived from new industrial development to the deteriorating base of the core city. In the four cities the response varied from the development of regional planning authorities and large annexations to complete opposition to annexation by the core city with little extraterritorial planning.

Each of the four cities had some Negroes in the work force. In one city discrimination was virtually eliminated in production lines of the larger firms, while in another little attention was given to the matter and many major production lines had no Negro workers. One city became concerned with discrimination in housing locations and another city did everything possible to prevent the dispersal of Negroes.

Running through the gamut of civic activities, the responses varied with respect to urban renewal, park systems, pay scales for city employees, inspection services, and sewage disposal systems. All this raises the question as to whether the cities behaved differently because of variation in local resources and wealth of the community, the ownership pattern in industry, and composition of the population, or whether the differences occurred as a result of "political" factors.

By "political factors" we refer to the process of choosing between alternative resolutions of issues. In this sense the "political factors" or the "political process" includes not only the legal requirements pertaining to decisions, but also the total complex of customs, systems of deferences, traditions of influence, and patterns of formally and informally organized pressures. Obviously there may be a connection between the political process and the general composition of a community. But there is also the possibility that each set of general community characteristics does not in itself define the political process. An examination of the relationship between policy, the policy process, and general community characteristics provides the central focus of this study.

At the outset of the research project this was not the central purpose of the study. Instead it was an investigation into the function of size of place as a factor in the political process. There is currently a gap in the professional literature regarding the political process in the middle-sized United States city. While many generalizations are made concerning the function and importance of the size of place as a variable in the urban political process, existing studies usually neglect the middle-sized city in favor of the extremely large and the very small urban places.[1] Our Jeffersonian-rooted preoccupation with grass roots democracy perhaps explains the latter tendency, while the drama of the great metropolis has proved to be a magnet drawing scholarly inquiry. The Lynds' pioneering venture into Middletown did explore the middle ground, studying a city of about 35,000, but this effort dates from a day when local preoccupation with welfare functions gave a different caste to the nature of the political process.[2] This case study of four cities, while somewhat diverted from the original intent, still provides some probes into the unexplored politics of cities between 50,000 and 70,000, while also inquiring into the reasons lying behind the differences in their behavior.

Although we refer to the cities in this study as middle-sized, we realize that the term is without precision. Some may want to call them small cities. Whatever they are called, communities between approximately 25,000 and 250,000 persons remain the most unexplored terrain in local government. We suspect that it is within the limits of this range that urban places lose the face-to-face style of politics peculiar to small towns and yet retain some central system of communication in political and social affairs that is often lacking in the very large population centers. While again the point is by no means precisely known, as cities increase beyond this range the local political processes become compounded around multi-nuclear centers and politics becomes increasingly a function of formally organized interest group activities.

THE POLICY PROCESS

This study places emphasis on the process of policy formation and is not centrally concerned with power relationships. We recognize, however, that the institutions of policy formation are not neutral vessels, which are equally accessible to and can be equally exploited by all citizens. The very nature of the process by which policy is promulgated in many respects shapes the ultimate choices made by the process. While the data are organized around a description of the traditional formal political institutions—elections, city councils, citizen boards, and the administrative bureaucracy—an initial goal is to identify the benefactors of the particular behavior of these institutions.

Class stratification has been the traditional concept employed by sociological studies to classify the community membership, which in turn provides a framework for describing the system of rewards and deprivations emanating from the entire social system, including the political system. Such studies as the one by Hunter have concentrated on the political forms of social control, and in doing so have been preoccupied with the identification of the most powerful.[3] These approaches are useful for certain purposes, but they both have their shortcomings in illuminating the role and operation of local government. Indeed Lynd, Warner, and Mills, each of whom employs a hierarchical model, have stressed that the most powerful upper stratum in our society has little interest in local government.[4] The selectivity of Hunter's account of local issues leaves at least some doubt as to how completely the power leaders control local government.[5] Both the power structure thesis and the class stratification studies uphold the validity of their claims by endeavoring to show that whatever is not controlled by the elite groups is not important. Few such studies concern themselves with developing a satisfactory standard of what constitutes importance.

Another difficulty with class or elite analysis is the limitations in the use of social concepts for political analysis. As Howard Brotz has pointed out, social stratification cannot be directly translated into political stratification.[6] The politician is typically not of the social four hundred. The persons who hold the formal symbols of political power frequently come from lower strata. This has long been recognized by the sociologists, for as the Lynds said, "the man whom the inner business group ignores economically and socially [they] use politically." [7] The politician had no real power; he was but a lackey. However, Brotz points out that such a generalization is too neat. A Boston Curley did at times sell out to the business elite and short-change his own supporters, but to describe him either as powerless or as a lackey would not offer an accurate account of political life in Boston during the Curley regime. In our study of the four cities, the politicians were often something other than pliable tools for local wealth.

Dissatisfaction with the power structure approach to the study of local political systems has led some political scientists to present alternative models. The pluralist approach is a recent alternative that is employed in the New Haven studies. [8] In asking "Who governs?" Dahl and his associates have rejected the use of social stratification as the starting-point of their analysis. They endeavor to answer their question by finding who is actually involved in making important local decisions. Through a case study approach, the decision-makers are isolated and the answer to who governs is deducted from the character of the decision-maker group.

Our study employs neither the method of Dahl nor of Hunter, but is probably closer in spirit and approach to the work of Dahl. It asks two related questions: Who governs? *and* What values prevail? Ostensibly, cliques and classes exist because of shared values; hence, our two questions may appear to be redundant. Whether they actually are is a function of specific local situations. Government by Main Street merchants may frequently mean the prevailing values of economic boosterism, but sometimes it may not.

The earlier part of this study is mostly concerned with who governs; the latter, with prevailing values. The "who" is identified by asking who elects whom and how interested parties make claims for public approval. Prevailing values are identified by a scrutiny of governmental actions and nonactions.

In controlling for size of place, we are asserting that a New York City is not simply a Roxborough projected onto a wide-angle screen. Large urban places have problems that are nonexistent in smaller places. The stakes, the issues, the rank order of political anxieties, the character of efforts, all differ qualitatively. As obvious as this fact is, we have no clear picture of the differences between the interests that make claims in various-sized places. Consequently, it is proposed to start with the interests, the basic and all-pervading ingredient of politics. We shall ask what the interests are and how their claims shape the institutions of the political process. What interests do the existing institutions favor?

Through what institution does initiatory leadership arise and from which does the general supporting leadership come? Are there significant differences related to types of issues? Are there particular types of issues that involve one institution more than another? Are there particular institutions that have become submerged or dominant in the total political process? Does any pattern appear at all?

A preoccupation with structures of government has entertained many students of urban affairs. It appears that the above questions should be prerequisites for their concern. Until we can develop a system of weighting the importance of institutional components in the policy process, efforts at structural manipulation will achieve their objectives only by accident.

In our study we asked specific questions about each of the institutional components. As each of the cities employed nonpartisan elections, the success of this device in insulating local politics from party politics generally was gauged. Additional propositions about nonpartisan elections assert that they favor incumbents, encourage issueless politics, make collective responsibility by the council more difficult, and frustrate protest voting.[9] While a testing of some of these generalizations must await a comparative study with partisan cities, our data furnish introductory information on these matters.

Questions concerning councilmanic and administrative roles pertain to the function of leadership. Who initiates, who gives continuing support, and who finally disposes of city policies? As each of the cities employed the city-manager plan for administration, consideration of these questions was not confused by variations in the formal arrangements. While some attention was given to the contrasting roles of the council and the administration implicit in the theory of the council-manager system, stress was given to the institutional roles in relationship to the size of place.

Discussions of the council-manager plan and the companion feature, nonpartisan elections, assert that these devices prove most satisfactory in small cities, but least so in the very large cities. Some of the most ardent supporters of the council-manager plan do not press the scheme for the large metropolis. Part of the professional lore is the story of the new charter in Philadelphia. The "civic leaders" of that city reportedly sought advice concerning governmental structure in Cincinnati, one of the large cities in which the plan was supposed to be working with success. Mayor Taft, a man whose very name symbolized the Cincinnati experiment, advised them that the plan was not suitable in large cities.[10]

The size of the city at which this breaking point appears between successful and unsuccessful manager plans is a matter of dispute. Furthermore, it may be that size is an important, but not the most important variable. The manager plan appears to demand an established consensus of general community goals. Ostensibly this consensus is more likely to be present in smaller and more homogeneous communities than in the larger and more heterogeneous ones. However, before approaching this problem of consensus, it is necessary to establish a standard of success for council-manager governments. What are the characteristics of a successful and an unsuccessful plan? The mere acceptance of the plan in its formal sense is not sufficient. The Stone, Price and Stone studies documented that manager plans often existed in name but not in spirit.[11]

The concluding work of this same study series summarized the fundamental principles of the city-manager form in the following manner:

First, there was the idea that the most capable and public-spirited citizens should serve on the governing body as representatives of the city at large, to determine policies for the benefit of the community as a whole, rather than for any party, faction, or neighborhood. This idea was embodied in the nonpartisan ballot and in the system of election at large of a small council.

Second, there was the idea that municipal administration

should be delegated to a thoroughly competent, trained executive, who should get and hold his job on his executive ability alone and should be given a status and salary comparable to that of an executive in charge of a private corporation. This idea was embodied in the concentration of administrative authority in the city manager.

Third, there was the idea that the voters should hold only the councilmen politically responsible and should give the city manager a status of permanence and neutrality in political controversy. This idea was embodied in the unification of powers in the council as a body comprising the only elected officials in the city government.[12]

However, this passage is less a statement of the objectives of the city manager plan than a statement of the necessary conditions for objectives that remain undefined. Indeed, the objectives of the plan must remain nameless, for the city manager plan is avowedly only a legal form and consequently one which can serve various ends. Thus, our considerations of the manager plan revolve around two questions: What are the community conditions that permit the realization of the three principles quoted above? Does the manager plan appear to be associated with any specific set of community objectives in fact?

A parenthetical note must be added here concerning the third "principle." The old policy-administrative dichotomy still lurks within the phraseology of the Stone, Price, Stone quote, though it was not embraced by the authors in their subsequent discussion. It is not our intention to review a question that has received a sufficient airing in the last decade. The 1952 version of the city manager's Code of Ethics takes cognizance of the postwar theoretical revision when it refers to the manager as a "community leader" who submits policy proposals to the council." The code appears to be developing a concept of neutrality akin to that of the higher civil service in Great Britain. The city manager is a kind of municipal permanent secretary who is capable of serving various masters, but who draws on his expert knowledge and personal prudence in attempting to guide the policies of the elected official.

Finally, we will undertake to examine the role of organized interest groups. While a rich literature has developed on this subject at the national and to a certain extent at the state level, interest groups in local policies have been largely ignored by political scientists.[13] We have asked: What are the interests affecting city governments? Which of these interests operate through fomal organizations? What are their techniques for achieving goals? What are the principal points of access? Do any interest groups have a stake in particular institutional arrangements?

Having answered all the foregoing questions it will still not be possible to state finally what is the function of size of city in determining the nature of the urban political process. All that is possible in a study of this scope is to state hypotheses, which are suggested by the data on four cities.

A TYPOLOGY OF LOCAL POLITICAL VALUES

As work progressed in gathering data on the political institutions, the differences among the four cities became as striking as some of the similarities. These differences were articulated by the way in which the political institutions were used, the activity and organization of particular interests, the types of persons holding public office, and the general pattern of citizen participation.

While observable conditions, such as economic conditions and tax load, help to explain a number of the varied responses to similar problems, they were inadequate in many respects. In addition, our data suggested that the differences in community responses took on certain discernable patterns which, when made explicit, clarified the nature of policy conflict and dominance in the cities. It also made apparent the absence in political science of any typology of local political values. Without a coherent statement on this subject, it is difficult for the observer of local politics to communicate his findings other than through detailed description by means of discreet case studies. This situation frustrates communication of an essential aspect of comparative local government. In an attempt to overcome this important obstacle, a typology of local political values has been formulated, based upon our findings in the four cities and those reported by other students of government.

As most case studies are comparative only in a prospective sense, systematic distinction between different sets of policies has presented no problem. But when we begin to investigate panels of cities or to discuss the character of local governments generally, random description becomes unmanageable. The need for systematic distinctions is further emphasized by the fact that policy differences among cities are often inconspicuous. Momentary reflection on extremes indicates that there are, in fact, real differences between communities. The few remaining company towns stand in contrast to the middle-class suburb. Vidich's village can be contrasted to Warner's Jonesville and Dollard's Southern town.[14] The National Municipal League is able to make distinctions in enumerating its annual "ten best." The question may be raised whether the local governments, which have distinct political qualities, are merely extreme manifestations of tendencies that are present generally in communities. If this is true, conceptualization of the different values will enable us to focus more sharply on the community components that lead to the elevation of one set of values over another.

Initially let us consider differing roles of local government. The concept "role of government" may be given at least two interpretations. It may refer to images of the *proper* role of government or to the *actual* role of government. A typology of roles based on the first interpretation will be outlined initially. Conversion of the typology for the second usage will be discussed subsequently.

The typology characterises four different roles for local government: (1) promoting economic growth; (2) providing or securing life's amenities; (3) maintaining (only) traditional services; (4) arbitrating among conflicting interests. The development of the typology will proceed as follows: First, each role will be described, followed by a discussion of the relationship between the roles and forms of governmental structure; second, the convertability of the typology for different uses will be suggested; finally, the operational character of the typology and criteria for its application will be discussed.

The first type characterizes government as *the promotion of economic growth*. The object of government is to see that the community grows in population and/or total wealth. Born of speculative hopes, nurtured by the recall of frontier competition for survival, augmented by the American pride in bigness, the idea that the good "thriving" community is one that continues to grow has been and still remains a widely held assumption in urban political thinking. It is essentially an economic conception drawing an analogy between municipal and business corporations. Just as the firm must grow to prosper, so must the city increase in population, industry, and total wealth. But the parallel is not simply an analogy, for according to this view the ultimate vocation of government is to serve the producer.

Although this image is endorsed most vigorously by those specific economic interests which have a stake in growth, its appeal is much broader. The drama of a growing city infects the inhabitants with a certain pride and gives them a feeling of being a part of progess: an essential ingredient of our national aspirations. The flocking of people to "our" city is something like the coming of the immigrants to our national shores. It is a tangible demonstration of the superiority of our way of life in that others have voluntarily chosen to join us. Growth also symbolizes opportunity, not only economically, but also socially and culturally. Large cities have more to offer in this respect than smaller ones.

Certain groups have such concrete stakes in growth that they are likely to be the active promoters of this image, while others in the city may give only tacit consent. The merchant, the supplier, the banker, the editor, and the city bureaucrats see each new citizen as a potential customer, taxpayer, or contributor to the enlargement of his enterprise, and they form the first rank of the civic boosters.

The specific policy implications of this image of the role of government are varied. Historically, local government was deeply embroiled in the politics of railroad location, land development, and utility expansion. But today city government is more handicapped than it was in the nineteenth century as an active recruiter of industry, for the vagaries of industrial location are determined more by economic market considerations than by the character of locally provided services. Although a number of ways exist in which economic growth may be served, producer-oriented political activity often expresses itself negatively; that is, nothing should be done that might hinder the community's growth. The city should have "a good reputation." Politics should be conducted in a low key. The image of stability and regularity in city finances must be assured. Friendliness toward business in general should be the traditional attitude of city officials.

But to some, growth itself is not a desirable goal for a community. Indeed, it is the very thing to be avoided. Growth breeds complexities which, in turn, deny the possibilities of certain styles of life. For some the role of local government is *providing and securing life's amenities.* "Amenities" is used here to distinguish between policies designed to achieve the comforts and the necessities of life as opposed to only the latter. Both comfort and necessity are culturally defined attributes of living standards, but the distinction is useful. Most communities recognize the demand for amenities in some fashion, but only an occasional community makes this the dominant object of collective political action. Many cities have their noise- and smoke-abatement ordinances, but the idea of creating a quiet and peaceful environment for the home is hardly the central purpose of government.

The policies designed to provide amenities are expressed by accent on the home environment rather than on the working environment—the citizen as consumer rather than producer. The demands of the residential environment are safety, slowness of traffic, quiet, beauty, convenience, and restfulness. The rights of pedestrians and children take precedence over the claims of commerce. Growth, far from being attractive, is often objectionable. That growth which is permitted must be controlled and directed, both in terms of the type of people who will be admitted and the nature of physical changes. It is essentially a design for a community with a homogeneous population, for civic amenities are usually an expression of a common style of living. Furthermore, because amenities are costly, the population must have an above average income. All expenditures for welfare are unwanted diversions of resources. Those asking for public welfare assistance are seeking necessities which other citizens provide for themselves privately. Consequently, this image finds expression chiefly in the middle- to upper-income residential suburbs.

However, as we descend the scale from larger to smaller cities, middle-class consumers are not necessarily isolated in a self-imposed suburban exile and their demands may become channeled toward the core city itself. In other places, a fortunately located large industrial facility may allow a city of persons with modest means to enjoy costly amenities. The Ford Motor Company's tax base supplies Dearborn, Michigan, with sidewalk snow removal and a summer resort. There are villages with iron mines within their limits, located in the Upper Peninsula of Michigan, which have free bowling alleys in the city hall and other rarely found city services.

Amenities are also likely to become a dominant concern of local government in the traditional small town threatened by engulfment from a nearby major urban complex. Such a town will not be characterized by the homogeneity of the suburb, nor will its particular kind of amenities require costly expenditures, for the amenities being secured are simply those which are a function of small-town life. Because growth of the town was slow, the necessary capital investments for urban life were amortized over a very long time. A sudden population influx threatens both the styles of life and the cost of maintaining that style. However, all small-town civic policies can hardly be characterized as the desire to preserve amenities, for conditions in many small towns make a mockery of that term. This leads us to our third image of the role of local government: that of *maintaining traditional services* or *"caretaker government."*

Extreme conservative views toward the proper role of government can be more effectively realized at the local than at any other level. The expansion of governmental functions often can be successfully opposed here by the expedient of shunting problems to higher levels. Such evasions of difficult problems give the appearance of successful resistance to the extension of government and thus reinforce the plausibility of maintaining a caretaker local-governmental policy.[15]

"Freedom" and "self-reliance of the individual" are the values stressed by this view. Private decisions regarding the allocation of personal resources are lauded over governmental allocation through taxation. Tax increases are never justified except to maintain the traditional nature of the community. This substitution of individual for public decisions emphasizes a pluralistic conception of the "good." The analogy to *laissez faire* economics is unmistakable. The caretaker image is associated with a policy of opposition to zoning, planning, and other regulations of the use of real property. These sentiments are peculiarly common to the traditional small town.

Among the individuals most apt to be attracted by this view, especially in its extreme form, are retired middle-class persons, who are homeowners living on a very modest fixed income.[16] Squeezed by inflation and rising taxes, it is not surprising if they fail to see the need for innovation, especially when it means to them an absolute reduction in living standards. The marginal homeowners, the persons who can just barely afford the home they are buying, whatever its price, are also likely to find the care-taker image attractive. They must justify a low-tax policy.

Finally, the fourth image sees the purpose of local government as *arbitrating among conflicting interests.* Emphasis is placed upon the process rather than the substance of governmental action. Although the possibility of a "community good" may be formally recognized, actually all such claims are reduced to the level of interests. The view is realistic in the popular sense in that it assumes "what's good for someone always hurts someone else." Given this assumption, government must provide a continuous arbitration system under which public policy is never regarded as being in final equilibrium. The formal structure of government must not be subordinated to a specific substantive purpose; rather the structure must be such that most interests may be at least considered by the decision-makers.

That the proper role of government is to serve as an arbiter is held most logically by interest groups that fall short of complete political control, including, especially, the more self-conscious minorities. The numerical or psychic majority does not have to settle for a process, but can act directly in terms of substantive conceptions of the community good. The minority can only hope for access.

The most conspicuous interests that self-consciously

espouse an arbiter function for government are neighbor-hood and welfare-oriented groups. Ethnic blocs reaching for a higher rung on the political ladder, and home owners and businessmen with stakes in a particular neighborhood, especially one threatened by undesired changes, make claims for special representation. The psychological minorities—persons low on a socioeconomic scale—also stress the need for personal access. In the four cities it was found that welfare matters were high among the subjects about which city councilmen were personally contacted. This was true even though welfare was entirely a county function. Welfare is a highly personal problem, at least from the viewpoint of the person in need. Perhaps personal access is desired because welfare, received in exchange for political support, is viewed as more legitimate—more nearly "earned"—than that which is received by merely qualifying under bureaucratically defined standards.

Government-as-arbiter does not mean a neutral agency (government) balancing diverse pressures with mathematical precision. The accommodation envisioned is not one that operates according to a fixed standard of equity or political weighting. Rather it is a government of men, each with weaknesses and preferences. It is just this human element in government which opens up the possibility that the imbalance between the majority and the minorities may become redressed.

The four types of images may be classified into two groups: those implying a unitary conception of the public "good" and those implying a pluralistic conception. The unitary conceptions are stated in substantive terms: i.e., "promoting economic growth" and "providing or securing life's amenities." The types which incorporate a pluralistic notion of the "good" stress a procedural role for government. "Arbitration among conflicting interests" clearly denotes this procedural emphasis.

The third type, "maintaining traditional services," presents a special problem with respect to the unitary-pluralistic dichotomy. A policy favoring a limited role for government seems to constitute a unitary conception of the good; however, the premise of this view is that the public good is achieved by maximizing the opportunity for individuals to pursue their private goals. The role of government is held in check so that a greater range of choices may be retained by individuals. Hence, this third type is essentially pluralistic in its objectives.

This unitary-pluralistic distinction is important to an understanding of the relationship between attitudes toward governmental structure and those toward the proper role of government. The formal structure most consistent with arbiter and caretaker government is one which includes a plural executive, ward elections for councilmen, and other decentralizing devices. These arrangements provide multiple access to policy-makers and, by decentralizing leadership, make programmatic political action more difficult.

Centralization and professionalization of the bureaucracy are attractive to those who can control and who desire to exploit control to achieve specific substantive goals. While it is true that the early advocates of civic reform acted in the name of economy, most successful reforms have been followed by action programs. Promotion of economic growth or increased amenities have formed the inarticulate premise of most of these efforts, even though the more neutral language of procedural adjustments has often been employed. Centralization, through strengthening the office of mayor, the appointment of city managers, and the institution of at large elections, usually leads to a reduction in the political strength of certain particularistic interest groups or minorities. Professionalization of the personnel in a city bureau may achieve some economies, but it also creates a political force pressing for the extension of the services performed by that bureau. Thus the reform devices are most consistent with the two types of unitary views of the community good.

It should be stressed at this point that the prime concern here is with the development of the typology and not with the implicit hypotheses regarding the groups which support each type. The foregoing references to group interests are used only to suggest the plausibility of the types by citing the relationships among them and familiar forces within communities.

The typology has been elaborated in terms of images of the proper role of local government. The necessary data for verification of the types would include some kind of opinion sampling. However, the typology may be used for other purposes and differing kinds of data. It may be converted into a typology of *actual* roles of government or even prevailing norms among all community policy-making institutions.

This study uses the typology in the second sense: as a classification for the actual role of government. For this purpose the emphasis in data collection must pertain to prevailing policies. For a policy typology, the fourth category, arbitration between conflicting interests, poses a problem. Arbitration is not, strictly speaking, a policy in the same sense as promoting economic growth, providing and securing life's amenities, or maintaining traditional services. However, in classifying prevailing governmental policies this fourth type may act as a useful category for characterizing cities in which the policy complexes embodied in the other three types are continuously compromised and no one or even pair of the other policy types epitomizes civil actions over any substantial period. However, in some cities the arbiter type, as first defined, will be useful as a completely parallel policy category. This will be where the process of adjusting claims among various and disparate interests becomes the all-pervasive preoccupation of officials and the norm for policy determination generally.

In the literature of case studies in community decision-making there are illustrations of each of the four types. Springdale village, described by Vidich and Bensman, is nearly a complete prototype of caretaker government.[17] Whyte reports the preoccupation with amenities in the politics of Park Forest.[18] The government of Middletown as described by the Lynds was primarily concerned with the interests of the producer.[19] Perhaps the best illustration of arbiter government is found in Meyerson and Banfield's study of public housing site choices in Chicago;[20] their study pertains to only one governmental policy, and is, therefore, not an accurate characterization of Chicago government generally. But with regard to policy formation in this one area, Meyerson and Banfield stress the way in which the political party, working through the city government, acted as an arbiter compromising the aims of all claimants in the political struggle.

APPLICATION OF THE TYPOLOGY

The usefulness of the typology is dependent upon developing satisfactory criteria, which provide the basis for distinguishing the policies of the various cities. As the very character of the types discourages the use of any rigorous mathematical measurement, primary reliance must be placed on descriptive material. In the final summary an attempt is made to assess comparatively the content of municipal politics, according to the subtle factors as well as the more obvious ones set forth in the above description of the types. However, primary emphasis will be on the following criteria.

A commitment to *economic growth* was gauged primarily by two standards: (1) policies designed to recruit industries or business that would increase employment or the total wealth of the community, and (2) policies that endeavored to preserve the fruits of growth for core-city interests. The problems attached to industrial recruitment will not be elaborated here, but under certain circumstances they involve annexation, utility expansion, zoning policies, and tax rates. Efforts to preserve the fruits of growth usually related to policies that favored central business interests as opposed to commercial developments on the city fringes.

An assessment of a city's interest in providing life's amenities was made according to the range and the levels of services provided. A fuller range of services represented a greater commitment to this standard. Evaluation of professionals was relied upon to determine service levels in many functional areas where city policies are related to citizens as consumers. It was assumed that a city which professionals judged to have superior service would rank high in terms of the amenities on the ground that professionals generally favor increased emphasis on their particular specialties.

The *caretaker* values were defined by an emphasis on private as opposed to public allocation of goods through the maintenance of only traditional services and consequently, a low tax rate.

Arbiter government implies freedom of access for all groups and specifically for minorities. Access is maximized when the city councilmen are willing to act as delegates for particular constituencies. Thus the measure of arbiter government rested largely on whether a city council was dominated by individuals who become advocates for various claimants or by persons who reject the legitimacy of this conception of representation, and guided their decisions by a unitary conception of the community's interests.

While the possibility of a rigorous quantitative scale has been denied, at least, with the data to be presented, a scale of sorts is developed. Consequently, in the interest of candor, as well as a means of presenting a brief visual capitulization, the Figure 1 is offered. In it the cities have been placed on a subjectively derived scale showing

Figure 1. A Typological Profile of the Four Cities

	Low ➡	Medium ➡	High
Economic Growth	Delta		Beta Alpha Gamma
Life's Amenities	Delta	Beta	Gamma Alpha
Caretaker	Alpha Gamma		Beta Delta
Arbiter	Alpha Delta		Beta Gamma

graduations of commitment to each of the four policy types. In doing so the universe of comparison is confined to the four cities. Undoubtedly, there are other cities which would scale higher and lower in each category. Secondly, each set of values is considered independently of the others. An amalgamation of the separate elements will be attempted next.

Several questions may occur as a result of this chart. (1) Are some of the types merely the reciprocal of others and therefore not truly distinct types? (2) If not reciprocals, are not some pairs more apt to be incompatible than are others? (3) If the categories are truly distinct, is not the chart inconsistent in showing a given city high on the scales of two or more mutually exclusive sets of values?

The answers to all these questions lie in the fact that the types are empirically, not logically, derived, even though the underlying assumptions of each of the types are logically distinct. The confusion stems from the fact that in actual behavior it is possible for a city simultaneously to follow contradictory policies. Only under certain conditions of duress are such conflicts forced to the surface. Thus, we would assume that none of the types is a complete reciprocal. For example, even though a city's leaders may place a low priority on amenities, they will not necessarily be committed to a caretaker government. This implies the answer to the second question. Within the experience of these four cities, there appears to be a pattern of disparity between certain pairs of types. It certainly seemed so for the caretaker and amenities types. However, it is conceivable to have nearly any possible combination. The answer to the third question has also been implied. Policies contradictory with regard to underlying principles are not necessarily perceived as contradictory in an actual political setting. Furthermore, in any given universe of a limited number of examples, cities may be found that stress both of two distinctly different sets of values in comparison with other cities. Our experience with the four cities indicated that sufficient slack existed between areas of possible choice for most cities to have the luxury of pursuing quite diverse goals.

There is one further apparent difficulty associated with applying each of the four types separately to the four cities. Preferences are shown only in relationship to choices in the other cities. Alpha is rated high in terms of amenities and low in terms of caretaker principles because other cities, especially Delta, rate in the opposite fashion. Similarly, Alpha rates high in terms of both amenities and economic growth because no other city rated higher. As a result there is no indication as to how Alpha behaved when the values of consumers clashed with those of producers.

To a certain extent this difficulty is a function of the fact that our universe is small. If we had some measure of value preferences in all American cities, our scale would expand revealing difference more precisely in a comparative fashion. There probably are prototype cities which subordinate most policy to a single standard. The company towns, the upper middle-class suburbs, and the isolated village provide examples where policy is dominated by producer interests, consumer interests, or *status quo* interests. Inclusion of such varied places would give greater polarity to a scale.

SOURCES OF DATA

The period of time selected for study was the same for each city, the decade of 1948-57, inclusive. Some events which took place prior to as well as following this period are mentioned when they appear essential. The first research step was to read the daily newspapers for the entire ten-year period in each city. (Each city had one daily newspaper). The purpose of this persual was to identify key issues, assemble an initial cast of persons and organizations who appeared to be involved in these decisions, to gather general background material on the communities, and to document the position of the newspaper on community affairs.

An objection may be made that the newspapers are a biased source for the selection of key issues, for this necessarily limits us to issues the newspaper saw fit to publicize. While it may be possible that the papers would ring down a cloak of secrecy around a significant public controversy, our subsequent interviews revealed no cases of this. Thus the key issues were those which received most prominent coverage and which, judged by the news reports, enlisted the most public interest. Given the nature of politics in cities of this size, there really is not a great variety from which to choose. It is an unusual year that produces two substantial issues. The more usual pattern was for an issue such as a proposal for bonding, annexation, capital improvements, or urban renewal to extend over two, four, or even ten or more years.

Following the newspaper digest, extensive interviews were conducted with several types of persons in the community. First, persons were sought who were both knowledgeable in local affairs and with whom it was easy for the authors to establish rapport. The basis of rapport was varied and led to talks with personal friends of the authors, university professors, political acquaintances, and others who shared a sympathetic concern for the kind of study we were making. Secondly, a panel of knowledgeables was constructed of active participants in the issues. It was often possible to interview the same individuals concerning a number of different issues. This second group led us to interview realtors, businessmen, labor leaders, bankers, and trade association professionals in each city. Lastly, a number of councilmen and administrators were interviewed in each city. If the council had visible factions, interviews were distributed among them.

The interviews depended on no structured questionnaire. The questions were directed toward determining the role performed by various institutions in regard to initiation, promotion, mobilization of public opinion, or veto action. Secondly the objectives of groups and individuals were delineated. Information regarding objectives often yielded the most productive information from these sources, as some group objectives were by no means predictable. Lastly, questions were asked pertaining to strategy and techniques of obtaining group objectives.

Because of the nature of some of the data presented all names of persons and places are fictitious. The cities have been named Alpha, Beta, Gamma, and Delta. There is no significance to the order of these alphabetically derived names. While the names are neutral symbols, we hope that they will acquire meaning and identity as the study progresses.

An attempt is made in the presentation of the data to segregate the treatment of the two separate themes of this study. Part II is devoted to the analysis of the political process in the middle-sized city. It must be kept in mind, of course, that we are discussing a selected type of city in the size range. Part III is primarily concerned with the application of the typology. Because it has not been always possible to keep these two themes separate, a dual set of conclusions is placed at the end in Part IV. Thus findings are reported after all data have been presented. Chapter

XII addresses itself to the considerations in Part III and Chapter XIII to those in Part II. The remaining chapters in Part I consist of a cursory introduction to the four cities. Detailed documentation of the characteristics of each of the cities has either been placed in the Appendix or is introduced later where more precise statements are required by the character of the analysis.

NOTES

[1] Some of the more prominent small town studies include: Albert Blumenthal, *Small Town Stuff* (Chicago: the University of Chicago Press, 1932), population 1,410; Elin C. Anderson, *We Americans* (Cambridge: Harvard University Press, 1937) population 25,000; John Dollard, *Caste and Class in a Southern Town* (New Haven: Yale University Press, 1937), population 2,500; W. Lloyd Warner and Paul S. Lunt, *The Social Life of A Modern Community* (New Haven: Yale University Press, 1941), population 17,000; James West, *Plainville, U.S.A.* (New York: Columbia University Press, 1945), population 275; Granville Hicks, *Small Town* (New York: The Macmillan Company, 1946), population 836; Walter Goldschmidt, *As You Sow* (New York: Harcourt, Brace and Company, 1947), populations 6,400, 7,000, and 7,500; W. Lloyd Warner and associates, *Democracy in Jonesville* (New York: Harper ad Brothers, 1949), population 6,100; Solon T. Kimball and Marion Pearsall, *The Talladega Story* (University, Alabama: The University of Alabama Press, 1954), population 13,200; Arthur J. Vidich and Joseph Bensman, *Small Town in Mass Society* (Princeton: Princeton University Press, 1958), population 3,000.

Major studies of the larger cities include the many early "boss" or "machine" case studies: Charles E. Merriam, *Chicago, a More Intimate View of Urban Politics* (New York: The Macmillan Company, 1929); Harvey Zorbaugh, *The Gold Coast and the Slum* (Chicago: the University of Chicago Press, 1929), Chicago; Harold Zink, *City Bosses in the United States: A Study of Twenty Municipal Bosses* (Durham, N.C.: Duke University Press, 1930); Charles P. Taft, *City Management: The Cincinnati Experiment* (New York: Farrar and Rinehart, Inc., 1933); George M. Reynolds, *Machine Politics in New Orleans, 1897-1926* (New York; Columbia University Press, 1936); Harold F. Gosnell, *Machine Politics: Chicago Model* (Chicago: University of Chicago Press, 1937); Floyd Hunter, *Community Power Structure* (Chapel Hill: The University of North Carolina Press, 1952), population 330,000; Martin Meyerson and Edward Banfield, *Politics, Planning and the Public Interest* (Glencoe: The Free Press, 1955), Chicago; Ralph A. Straetz, *P. R. Politics in Cincinnati* (New York: New York University Press, 1958); James Reichley,

The Art of Government: Reform and Organization Politics in Phila-delphia (New York: Fund for the Republic, 1959) ; Wallace S. Sayre and Herbert Kaufman, *Governing New York City* (New York: Russell Sage Foundation, 1960).

In addition to these larger studies, many articles also show a similar bias to extremes in size of place.

2 Robert S. and Helen M. Lynd, *Middletown* (New York: Harcourt, Brace & Co., 1929; and *Middletown in Transition* (New York: Harcourt, Brace & Co., 1937). Two other exceptions should be noted. Kenneth Underwood, *Protestant and Catholic: Religious and Social Interaction in an Industrial Communty* (Boston: Beacon Press, 1957) is a study of Holyoke, Massachusetts; and Seymour L. Wolfbein, *The Decline of a Cotton Textile City* (New York: Columbia University Press, 1944) concerns New Bedford, Massachusetts, with a 1940 population of 110,341. See also C. Wright Mills, "The Middle Classes in Middle-sized Cities," *American Sociological Review*, Vol. II (December, 1936) , 520-529.

3 Hunter, *op. cit.*

4 Lynd and Lynd, *Middletown in Transition*, p. 89: C. Wright Mills, *The Power Elite* (New York: Oxford University Press, 1956) , Chapter 2; W. Lloyd Warner and associates, *Democracy in Jonesville, op. cit.* While Warner devotes a chapter to politics, it is nearly exclusively confined to political parties, and this control system in his community seems un-related to political stakes in local government.

5 Hunter, *op. cit.* See especially Chapter 8, where issues germaine to local government are discussed.

6 Howard Brotz, "Social Stratification and the Political Order," *American Journal of Sociology*, Vol. 64 (May, 1959) 571-578, presents a scheme for analyzing the relationship between the two. See also Eugene Burdick, "Political Theory and the Voting Structure," in Eugene Burdick and A. J. Brodbeck, *American Voting Behavior* (Glencoe: The Free Press, 1959), pp. 136-149; Talcott Parsons, *Structure and Process in Modern Societies* (Glencoe: The Free Press, 1960), Ch. 6, "The Distribution of Power in American Society."

7 Lynd and Lynd, *Middletown in Transition,* p. 321.

8 Robert A. Dahl, *Who Governs?* (New Haven: Yale University Press, 1961) and a "A Critique on the Ruling Elite Model," *American Political Science Review,* Vol. 52 (June, 1958), 463-469 by the same author. See also Nelson W. Polsby. "Three Problems in the Analysis of Community Power," *American Sociological Review,* Vol. 24 (December, 1959), 796-803.

9 Charles R. Adrian, "Some General Characteristics of Nonpartisan Elections," *American Political Science Review,* Vol. 46 (September, 1952), 766-776.

10 Seymour Freedgood, "New Strength in City Hall" in the Editors of Fortune, *The Exploding Metropolis* (Garden City, New York: Doubleday Anchor Books, 1958), 76-77.

11 Harold A. Stone, Don K. Price, and Kathryn H. Stone, *City Manager Government in Nine Cities* (Chicago: Public Administration Service, 1940).

12 *Ibid.*, p. 236.

13 Among the exceptions are Meyerson and Banfield, *op. cit.*, and Sayre and Kaufman, *op. cit.*

14 Vidich and Bensman, *op. cit.;* Warner and associates, *op. cit.;* and Dollard, *op. cit.*

15 Vidich and Bensman, *op. cit.*, Chs. V, VII; esp. pp. 113-114.

16 See Amos H. Hawley and Basil G. Zimmer, "Resistance to Unification in a Metropolitan Community," in Morris Janowitz (ed.), *Community Political Systems* (Glencoe, Illinois: The Free Press, 1961) pp. 173-175.

17 Vidich and Bensman, *op. cit.*

18 William H. Whyte, Jr., *The Organization Man* (New York: Simon & Shuster, 1956).

19 Lynd, Middletown in Transition, *op. cit.*

20 Meyerson and Banfield, *op. cit.*

Chapter II

The Four Cities

Case studies always labor under a cloud of doubt that the particular series of events being recorded may be unique or fortuitous. However, any study in depth in local government that endeavored to overcome this obstacle would tax the abilities of even the largest and most generous foundations. In recognition of the need for controls and for acceptance of the resources available, the authors chose to study four cities simultaneously. Moreover, in choosing the four cities it was determined that they should be as much alike as possible, so that the generalizations might apply to a particular type of city.

The cities were alike in the following respects: populations were numerically similar, ranging from 50,000 to 70,000; each was the core city of a standard metropolitan area, as defined by the United States Bureau of the Census, yet each was outside the immediate economic orbit of larger metropolitan centers. The cities were in the same state and consequently operated within the same legal framework, and all were governed through home rule. All four were essentially manufacturing cities, as opposed to being centers of government or the extraction industries. In addition, the formal structures of government were similar. Each employed the nonpartisan municipal ballot and the council-manager form. Both of these devices had been in use for approximately the same length of time, having had their origins in the early twenties.

Obviously, no two cities are exactly alike; consequently, a more detailed analysis was made of the economy, social characteristics of the population, community history, and cultural traditions. Some differences emerged. And as was stated above, real differences in political behavior were exhibited. The question immediately arises as to whether the differences in the political process were a reflection of the differences in the basic character of the community. Answers to this were sought and some sets of impressive if inconclusive evidence were unearthed. Therefore, the reported association between political behavior and certain community characteristics must share all the infirmities of a case study and must "await the results of further studies" as the conventional jargon cautions.

THE SEATS OF GOVERNMENT

One of our first contacts in each of the four cities was a visit to the city hall. Although the researchers were not aware of it at the time, the physical appearances of these civic monuments were rough indicators of the prevailing civic values to be uncovered later.

The city of Beta owned no city hall, but conducted its business from rented quarters over a downtown drug store. In many respects the Beta city government was also figuratively homeless. The officialdom had many critics and few supporters. The search for a permanent home, in the form of a city-owned structure, provided Beta's most celebrated political controversy of the ten-year period.

Eventually the city did acquire a home through the renovation of an old school building.

In Gamma the city hall was a nondescript masonry building with badly peeling paint, indistinguishable from the buildings surrounding it. There was no identifying sign on the door. A stranger might pass the building several times not realizing that this was the seat of local government. After entry, the first impression was of having mistakenly walked into a vacant warehouse. However, the inhabitants of this building were cordial, desirous of pleasing, and hard at work. The combination of the physical appearance of the building and the attitudes of incumbents befitted a city ambitious for civic progress but continually penalized by repeated economic reversals.

One found the civic building in Delta in a deteriorating section off the main business district. Its location had been central when it was built, some seventy-five years ago. As we shall see, not only had the city hall been separated from the central business district, but there was a similar chasm between the city officials and the downtown interests. In wintertime one approached the building by mounting worn and crumbling steps and entered via a storm door hanging precariously on one hinge, the loser to a generation of irate citizens who had stormed in and out. Inside one discovered a relic of a bygone day— cavernous, ponderous, ornate in architecture, and spartan-bare in furnishing. This was the only city hall where a coterie of loungers was present, obviously seeking warmth and sociability within. One had the feeling of stepping into the past.

By contrast, Alpha's building was neat, newer than the others, and well maintained. It stood overlooking a pleasant downtown park, complete with fountain. In the same block one could find a new library built through public subscription. Nearby was an auditorium where the local theater company, symphony orchestra, and string quartet entertained the cultural elite. A short distance down the street was an art museum (soon to be replaced by a new structure). Further on were several new municipal buildings under construction and a new auditorium. A projected downtown renewal plan was designed to extend the parklike amenities of this civic center into the commercial core itself. Symbolic too, perhaps was the building of the Rank Club, the inner keep of the city's elite, situated equidistant from the library, the central business district (CBD), and the city hall. This old and conservative structure was the social home of those who contributed most of the funds and the leadership which had made the various civic monuments possible.

ALPHA WAS DIFFERENT

While the cities resembled each other in many respects, there were also differences that appeared to have real consequences for their political behavior. Economically, Alpha stood in contrast to the other three cities. While all four were manufacturing centers, Alpha was the only one importantly engaged in making nondurable rather than durable goods. As a result, Alpha had less unemployment and less general economic fluctuation. Beta, Gamma, and Delta experienced many economic ups and downs both before and during the study period. War production made the economies in these three cities boom, but the aftermath of World War II and the Korean conflict caused them to plunge. At the time this was written, Beta had made some recovery through the entrance of new industries, but Gamma and Delta continued to be left behind in the prosperous period of 1959-60.

Alpha was also different in several other respects: it had a higher percentage of large firms owned by local people than the other cities did. It was also the city with the highest percentage of nonunion shops in manufacturing firms employing 100 or more persons. These two facts may be related.

Alpha, furthermore, had a reputation for being a low-wage city, and, indeed, it ranked third among the four cities. Delta had the distinction of having the lowest wages per manufacturing employee of the four cities, while Beta was the highest, and Gamma second. Between 1947 and 1954 the wage scale in Alpha had increased at a more rapid rate than in any of the other cities.

Finally, in terms of recent growth, the city of Alpha had the greatest population increase, largely a function of annexation. The population growth rates in the metropolitan areas were roughly comparable during the postwar period, though again Delta lagged a little behind the others. A similar pattern existed in the value added to manufactured products. The growth rates since 1940 were, by this measure, comparable in Alpha, Beta, and Gamma, but Delta, was again a slight laggard.

Thus, economically speaking, Alpha had a stable economy, one of moderate growth and moderate wage scales. Beta and Gamma had fluctuating economies with higher real wages than in the other two cities, but with over-all growth comparable to Alpha. Delta had the greatest fluctuations and the lowest wages and general growth rates.

Alpha was different in several noneconomic respects also. It was the most homogeneous city in terms of religious, racial, and ethnic composition. Each of the other cities had minority blocs, which had some impact on the political pattern. Lastly, Alpha had three institutions of higher learning, which contributed leadership to local affairs. The other three cities had no such institutions, though they each supported junior colleges.

While these brief facts give but modest knowledge of the gross characteristics of the four communities, perhaps they can serve as introductory pegs upon which to hang the succeeding political events.

Part II

The Political

Process

Chapter III

Nonpartisanship: The Recruitment
of Elective Officials

Of all the links in the total political process, the recruitment practices pertaining to elective officials provided the
best index to the differing character of politics in the four
cities. While these practices were often merely symptomatic of more deeply imbedded political arrangements, they
reflected the pattern of political differences among the
cities that is to be elaborated in the succeeding chapters,
particularly those in Part III. Because the legal arrangement for local elections in each case was the nonpartisan
form, some exploration of the assumptions of this device
is necessary before describing actual practices.

Nonpartisanship was one of the devices developed by
the municipal reform movement. It was advocated in the
late 1880's at the very earliest meetings of the groups that
later became the National Municipal League. The principal rationale was its use as a weapon against the political
parties, which were often corrupt and nearly always more
interested in organizational success than efficiency, economy, or standards of service. Reformers also felt that the

parties were more concerned with state and national than with local matters. The choice of local officials was often determined, they believed, by the length of the coattails of the national candidates, and electoral success was frequently unrelated to the actual issues that could confront the local official in office. Some advocates hoped that nonpartisanship would deal a crippling blow to the national parties. It was felt that if local government could be wrested from the parties, they might die from lack of patronage. Thus, nonpartisanship was born of the same outlook that spawned such other antiparty measures as the direct primary, the initiative, the referendum, and the recall.

Of the claims that have been made over the years on behalf of nonpartisan elections, three stand out: (1) That removal of the party label from the ballot would insulate local politics from national and state politics, thus permitting local elections to be determined by local issues. It was believed that national party labels invariably introduced irrelevancies into the elections. (2) That higher caliber candidates would be attracted to public office if the parties were eliminated from the nominating process. Persons interested in local problems alone would become available for office. (3) That nonpartisanship would be conducive to prefessionalization and greater honesty in government. National parties would no longer control local patronage or other rewards of municipal office, and prestigeful citizens of the community would be more willing to serve if they did not have to bear the onus of "partisan politicians."

These assertions are matters for empirical verification, and the best procedure for examining the claims would be to compare the results of partisan and nonpartisan elections. Short of that, however, some tentative observations can be made on the basis of the experience of these four nonpartisan cities. No attempt to verify the third claim regarding honesty and integrity will be made. Although extensive interviews were conducted in the four cities, there were very few allegations of dishonesty on the part of the officials. In the next chapter we shall consider the first claim: the insulation of local politics under nonpartisan elections. Here, we shall concentrate on the second claim, that the nonpartisan election encourages candidates of higher caliber to run for office.

As one of the authors has pointed out elsewhere, there is a variety of kinds of nonpartisan political systems.[1] Consequently, part of the task in describing the effect of nonpartisanship on recruitment is to specify the particular type of nonpartisanship under question. In many so-called nonpartisan cities, the national political parties are active and the only thing that is nonpartisan is the printing on the ballot. This did not characterize any of the cities in this study. There was no evidence that the local organizations of the national political parties played a role in local politics. Therefore, the question is whether any groups stepped into the breach and performed the functions normally performed by parties. That is, did any groups take responsibility for recruiting candidates and promoting their election in order to take control of the government?

Eugene Lee's analysis of California city elections is the only other study concerned with similar questions with respect to nonpartisanship.[2] His study of 192 municipalities in California was confined largely to general characteristics of nonpartisanship, but he also asked several questions that are close to our concern. His survey of the backgrounds of city councilmen revealed that the vast majority of them were from the "professional, managerial and sales" occupations and were "living in the better part of town." In general, Lee felt that the absence of formal political organizations caused election information to be exchanged through a communication net centering around the service and fraternal clubs. The result was a heavy Main Street influence.

A number or case studies particularly concerned with the role of economic dominants reveal different recruitment practices by these groups. In some communities economic dominants directly controlled the recruitment process; in other cases pressure was exerted on public officials only in reference to specific policies, usually without any attempt to control the selection of office-holders. Generally, direct recruitment is reported as a practice in the smaller communities (examples include Goldschmidt in Wasco, Arbin, and Dinubia; Warner in Jonesville; Vidich and Bensman in Springdale).[3] On the other hand most investigations of large metropolitan centers (examples include Hunter in Regional City, Gosnell in Chicago, Meyerson and Banfield in Chicago)[4] characterize the recruitment process as being outside the immediate concern of economic dominants in most instances. In two studies of cities of comparable size to our four (Underwood in Paper City and the Lynds in Middletown)[5] the pattern was mixed and uneven. Based upon these studies, there appears to be a definite correlation between size of place and recruitment practices. Our data generally support this size-of-place theory. In the remainder of the chapter, we shall consider not only the existence of organized recruitment and general election involvement but also the occupational representation and general characteristics of council candidates.

While the cities all employed nonpartisan elections, each city had minor variations in the provisions governing the selection of elected officials. (See Table 1.)

Table 1.
Legal Provisions Governing Elections in the Four Cities

	Alpha	Beta	Gamma	Delta
Size of council	7	9	7	10
Term	2 years	2 years	4 years, staggered	2 years
Constituency	At-large	Ward nomination, At-large election	At-large	Ward
Primary	No	Yes	Yes	Yes
Method of choosing mayor	Highest vote for councilman	Separate At-large	Chosen by council	Separate At-large
Time of election	Nov. odd years	Nov. odd years	Nov. even years*	April odd years†

The authors felt prior to the study that minor structural differences were insignificant but the data have indicated that this was not so in all situations. Indeed, most structural features appeared to affect in some way the access or influence of particular groups. The ward system especially appeared to increase the influence of lower socioeconomic groups. In contrast, the absence of a primary

* Coincided with state-national general election.
† Coincided with election for several minor state officials.

in Alpha may have aided the higher socioeconomic groups. The timing of elections, staggered terms, and method of choosing the mayor, in combinations with specific circumstances also had some influence, but these all must be explained in the context of the narrative.

OCCUPATIONAL REPRESENTATION

In order to compare the character of the city councils in the four cities, occupations of all candidates were compiled. It was recognized that occupational profiles of representative bodies are fragile tools for analysis. Persons serving on city councils do not necessarily act as delegates for the particular interests of their occupational groups. However, by using broad occupational categories, the receptivity of the recruitment systems to particular economic statuses or broad interest groups may be identified.

The occupations were divided into seven general classifications. The seven classes were (1) owners and executives of nonretail firms, (2) owners and executives of retail firms, (3) salesmen, (4) professionals, (5) middle management, (6) labor, and (7) miscellaneous. Owners included all entrepreneurs except small operators where the owner actually was engaged in performing the service. Executives included all officers whose functions involved firm-wide activities of a general policy nature. Thus the production manager of a firm was classified as an executive, but the production head of plant division was considered to be in middle management. The top officers, such as president, vice-president, secretary, treasurer, sales manager, or legal counsel were considered executives, but a holder of a more technical position, such as chief accountant or personnel director was placed in middle management. Middle management generally included positions between the executive group down to the foremen in industrial concerns. Foremen and below were classed as laborers. White-collar workers in substantial supervisory positions or who were engaged in skills demanding college training, such as that of an engineer, were classed as middle management; others in more routine positions, such as shipping clerks, were classed as labor. Retail pertains to the selling of both goods and services and to allied businesses. Thus an advertising executive or an accountant whose firm had a retail clientele was placed in the retail category. Professionals were comprised of lawyers, physicians (all types), and teachers. Salesmen were restricted to insurance and real estate, two occupational groups with a peculiar affinity for local politics.

The seven categories constitute only a very rough socio-economic status scale. It is not more precise because the groupings were designed to serve two ends. One objective was to classify the councilmen according to economic status. The executive and professional groups, middle management, and labor form a three-tiered stratification for that purpose. Salesmen do not fit this scale. At the same time we were interested in identifying some large interest blocs, especially the retailers and the property representatives, which are frequently comprised of the realtor-insurance combination.

There are several flaws in the classification, but these can be remedied by description. The chief of these is the inclusion of many different types, sizes, and locations of retailing enterprises in one group. Similarly, in the non-retail category, there is a great spread in the size of firms involved. However, the numbers involved are sufficiently small that individual interpolation is possible. In brief, the tabulations are less statistical compilations than shorthand means of describing observed data.

Table 2 shows the percentage of city councilmen (plus mayors) in each city as they were distributed among the seven categories. Interpretation of these data must await description of the recruitment process in each of the four cities.

THE CIVIC TRADITION OF ALPHA

The single most important force in the electoral politics of Alpha was a group we shall call the Citizen's Com-

Table 2.
Occupations of Council Members in the Four Cities, by Percentages*

	Alpha	Beta	Gamma	Delta
Owners and executives (non-retail)	39	15	29	6
Owners and executives (retail)	14	15	38	31
Sales	8	15	21	10
Professional	22	11	4	19
Middle management	0	32	0	12
Labor	8	4	8	23
Miscellaneous	8	9	0	0
Total	99	101	100	101

* Each selection calculated separately, consequently those re-elected are counted more than once.

mittee. This was a self-selected and self-perpetuating body of business and professional men who took an active interest in most civic affairs. It originated with the adoption of the manager plan itself and had continuous existence over two generations. Its members recruited and financed the campaigns of a slate of candidates that was usually successful in controlling the city council. The Committee was active in most important referendum elections and it backed the council's stand in every such campaign.

Membership in this body was by invitation only. However, "membership" is used loosely because this group at times resembled an informal clique. Most of the major financial interests of the community were represented, including the banks, some of the largest industries, and the largest retail firm. Some individuals from smaller enterprises were also included. While most of the members belonged to the city's most important social club, membership in the club did not bring membership in the Citizen's Committee. Nearly everyone in the organization was a Republican.

The Committee operated by consensus and mutual confidence in all matters. A long-time member indicated in an interview, for example, that the Committee treasurer, the only formal officer, never had to account for any expenditures. He would only indicate whether he needed more money or had sufficient funds for a given campaign. If he was short, the word was passed around and funds would start to come in. The organization was not publicly conspicuous and had no publicly known title. One of the members could not even think of its official name (though it had one). Various pseudonyms were used to sign advertisements and they were chosen to fit the issues of the moment.

In candidate selection, the Committee made an attempt to recruit members from its own ranks and from those who were closely identified with some of its membership. Sponsored candidates included the presidents of some of the city's leading firms, the secretary-treasurer of an industry employing over three thousand persons, the president of one of the state's largest construction firms, and leading realtors. However, some of the candidates were smaller businessmen, lesser executives, and professional persons in whom the Committee had confidence.

The Committee was very successful in its recruitment operation. The very tradition of success, once established, made it possible for the Committee to "tap" nearly any citizen. When a leading firm was pressured into supplying a candidate, contacts were made between persons of equal status. One informant described how he went about a recruiting operation. He felt the council needed a financial expert among its members, so he went to the president of one of the city's largest industries. He described the plight of the council and its need for a certain talent. The president squirmed during the conversation anticipating that he was about to be drafted. When the informant asked that the treasurer of the firm be made available, the president heaved a perceptible sigh of relief and quickly replied he would think it over. The next day the treasurer of the firm announced his candidacy.

One professional, a college professor who had been successfully sponsored by the Committee, stated that the Committee exacted no commitments from its candidates. There was no doubt that sponsorship would be dropped if someone displeased the members, but apparently they always chose wisely, for there was no record of any candidate suffering this fate. The criterion for qualification, other than general ability, was a commitment to the general values of the efficiency-in-government movement. It was not necessary for a candidate to be a Republican to receive endorsement, though a large majority of them were. The Committee members took pride in the city and were not interested in low taxes as a goal of intrinsic worth. They were more interested in securing a council that would decide on behalf of the business community what were necessary expenditures. Once the council arrived at a policy that called for tax increases, the Committee members backed the council. However, it should be added that while the council maintained a policy of an orderly improvement schedule, a careful attitude of parsimony was present in budget policy-making.

Occasionally allied with the Citizen's Committee but independent in membership was a women's group, which had as its aim the election of one woman to each council. This was a surviving feminist group, which drew its members largely from among the wives of some of the wealthier businessmen and women associated with the local universities. Some of the husbands of these women were active in the Citizen's Committee. As the group was well financed, it was able to make a concerted effort on behalf of its candidate. In three of five elections studied, the Citizen's Committee also endorsed the women's candidate. In four out of five elections, the women were successful with their candidate.

There was organized opposition to the Committee slate occasionally, but most of the nonendorsed candidates were independents. As in many at-large nonpartisan elections, persistence on the part of a candidate paid dividends. One candidate ran three or four times unsuccessfully before being elected. Several retired businessmen with time and a little money to spend were successful, even though they had no organized support. One man was probably elected by fashioning Catholic bloc support (the city was less than 20 percent Catholic). However, the main concerted opposition to the Citizen's Committee was supplied by one man, Geoffrey Post.

Mr. Post, a prominent local businessman and a Democrat, was a city councilman and mayor at various times over several decades. During the study period, he headed the only two slates in opposition to the Citizen's Committee. In 1948, a coalition which claimed a broad community base—representing labor, veterans, small business, and large business—formed an opposition five-man slate. It had good financing, with the unions making a large contribution. The effort failed, however. Only Mr. Post, an incumbent, was victorious. On a second occasion, Mr. Post headed the opposition slate formed around a specific issue, the sale of the light plant, and this time even he went down in defeat.

In a sense, Mr. Post perfomed a service to the Citizen's Committee by providing it with an opponent who could arouse the emotions of the membership and thus encourage contributions. Being a wealthy businessman, but also a Democrat and an advocate of public power, he was viewed as an apostate to his own group. One Committee member reported that when Mr. Post announced his slate for the retention of a municipally owned light plant, the funds started flowing into the Committee treasury without solicitation. The interviewer had the impression that Committee members rather enjoyed the fact that Mr. Post put up a fight, thus making their own victory sweeter and more deserving of self-congratulation.

Of all the cities, Alpha had the greater representation

of industrial executives on the city council and the least labor representation (see Table 2). Although one union man sat for a number of terms on the council, he was repudiated by his own union. Despite this, he claimed to speak for "the little people." He was frequently in the opposition and voiced objections to most proposals for change. He was generally opposed to zoning, one-way streets, capital improvements, and urban renewal. This became a recurring theme in all four cities as many objections to changes were made in the name of defending the "little man." Judging by the voting patterns both for election of officials and in referendums, his was a fair representation of the views held in the lower-income areas of the cities.

Among the four cities, Alpha had the highest percentage of industries owned by persons residing in the community. The names that adorned the factory gates were still carried by the occupants of the local executive suites. Most of these individuals were of the second generation, but they retained active control of the family enterprises. Their names were household words in the community, and they were also magic at the polls.

The city had achieved a number of national awards over the years and these achievements were frequently brought to the attention of the interviewers. Both pride in the city and paternalism were expressed in several other ways. This was the least unionized of the cities. The nonunion shops were especially numerous among the home-owned industries, which incidentally included the city's largest employer. The nonunion status of several firms was preserved in part by a generous program of fringe benefits for the employees. Business leaders also pointed with pride to cultural facilities, which included

a theater group, a good small-city symphony, an art
museum, a new public library, and a civic auditorium.
While the local universities may have provided some
talent and catalytic action in realizing these accomplishments, the costs were underwritten by generous local
contributions from business and industry. The city also
had two industry-sponsored research organizations, which
gave attention to the problems of the area. Such facilities
were nonexistent in Beta and Delta, and were only faintly
approximated in Gamma. Thus the interest of the business community in local government must be viewed in
the context of tradition which encouraged a remarkably
high level of interest in all local affairs. In many ways, local
government elections were treated in a fashion similar
to that of community chest drives or the building of a
new hospital. Local political participation was a fashion-
able obligation.

While the Alpha city council was clearly dominated by
recruits from the larger business enterprises of the city,
these representatives did not act as delegates of specific
firms or businesses. This probably resulted less from
altruism than from the fact that most firms, especially
the industries, required no specific representation. City
policies rarely impinged upon individual industrial enterprises. However, general business interests were served in
several ways. Through an orderly improvement program,
the city was saved from sudden tax increases to remedy
capital improvement deficiencies. Over a long period, the
businessmen in office had been able to pursue a fiscal
policy that eschewed borrowing. Local tax dollars had not
gone into interest on bonds. When downtown merchants
considered redevelopment, they were assured of cooperation and aid. When the state was placing pressure on local

industries to cease polluting the river, the mayor pleaded, though unsuccessfully, with the governor to make some concessions. When the utility companies filed for rate increases, Alpha was not conspicuous as a spokesman on behalf of the consumers (except for the individual effort of Geoffrey Post). When the question of selling the municipal light plant was raised, the decision mirrored the views of the Citizens' Committee. When public housing and rent control were at issue, the outcome was never in doubt. But perhaps as important as anything, the council was simply a standby resource which the business community knew it could call upon when an issue did arise in which it would have an interest.

A CASE OF CIVIC LEADERSHIP

Some of the complexities of councilmanic behavior in Alpha can be illustrated by describing a particular issue: the decision to sell the municipal light plant. The case illustrates the kind of personal resources Alpha councilmen were willing to spend on a civic issue, the intensity of local politics, and the relationship between the Citizens' Committee and the council.

During the 1920's when municipal light utilities were in vogue, Alpha had constructed an electric power plant. Leading businessmen, including early leaders in the Citizens' Committee, were among the sponsors of this enterprise. As the city developed, the facility was not expanded at a rate equal to increasing demands for power, although the private electric utility grew apace. As a result, a smaller and smaller percentage of the city was being served by the city plant. Geoffrey Post, whom we have already introduced, had long been identified with the cause of publicly owned power in general and the Alpha light plant in particular. He held essentially the "yardstick" view of such operations, whereby government-owned utilities should be kept in operation as a check on the cost and, consequently, the rate claims of privately owned utilities.

Among the customers of the municipal light plant was the city water department, which needed the power for its pumping stations. Upon the expansion of the water system it was apparent that the light plant had insufficient power to supply the new pumping station. A private utility was asked for a bid, and its rate proved to be lower than the city power plant was charging for supplying existing pumping stations. Someone on the council or in the administration asked the private utility to suggest rates for other city agencies. The rate schedule submitted was one that would have saved the city over $30,000 annually. When the report failed to spur the council to action, one of its newer members, another businessman whom we shall call Derek Lane, began to investigate past financial statements and reported that the plant was losing money, that its true financial position had been obscured by its accounting methods, and that it was being subsidized by water users through high water rates. Mr. Post took violent exception to Mr. Lane's report and later issued his own statement attacking it. Both Lane and Post were men of strong personal convictions. They enlivened the politics of the city, and of the council in particular, for over three years with their battles, which included charges, countercharges, voluminous reports sponsored by both sides, referendums, feature stories, and a wealth of proposals. The city council itself became divided, the newspaper reported the matter prominently, and the whole community took sides.

The plant had actually been a matter of controversy intermittently for several decades for there had been a number of unsuccessful attempts in the past to expand its facilities. The controversy, however, resolved itself into a question of whether or not to sell the plant. An outside engineering firm, chosen by a neutral panel of prominent industrial executives and bank officers (both Lane and Post approved its composition), was called in to make an independent study. Both Derek Lane and Geoffrey Post claimed that the resulting report vindicated their respective positions. In a final effort to extricate itself from the deadlock, the council referred the matter for an advisory vote, a rare move for the Alpha council. The outcome was extremely close, but the majority favored selling the plant.

Both sides spent substantial sums on the election. Post personally financed his campaign. Many businessmen associated with the Citizens' Committee favored sale of the plant. Some of these men were ideologically opposed to municipally owned electric utilities. Others were merely pragmatists who preferred to buy electricity for the city as economically as possible.

The city council accepted the outcome of the advisory vote and decided to sell the plant, although Geoffrey Post dissented to the end. He would not accept defeat and ran a slate for city council in the following election, dedicated to the retention of the light plant. The Citizens' Committee slate was composed of men on record in favor of the sale. Post's entire slate, including himself, went down to defeat. (He had been on the council for about 25 years.) The campaign was a bitter one. Expenses by both sides for this city election were between $15,000 and $30,000. The cost of the total light plant retention campaign was in the neighborhood of $50,000, most of which was spent by Post and his allies. Derek Lane's personal contribution of time and money nearly bankrupted his business.

In many ways this issue was a highly personal one. It cannot be explained in terms of pecuniary interests. The total annual savings to the taxpayers, according to the sale proponents, was only about $35,000. A few hundred families had to pay increased electricity rates as a result of the sale, for private utility household rates were higher than those of the city. Neither Mr. Post nor Mr. Lane had any immediate monetary stake in the issue. They both spent a great deal of money which could not be recouped regardless of who won or lost.

Long before Mr. Lane's accession to the council many leaders of the Citizens' Committee had been opposed to municipal ownership of the light plant. However, there was no evidence that the Committee requested a statement of position on the matter by prospective candidates for endorsement. This was confirmed by several "independents" who received Committee endorsement. While Mr. Lane was associated with the Committee he disclaimed that his actions were promoted by Committee members or any other persons. In fact, he maintained that he had really never considered the issue previously. Although a nominal Republican, Mr. Lane admitted that he agreed with the Democrats on many state and national issues. He also maintained that he was not opposed to public ownership of utilities in principle, but through study of the issue had concluded that there was an economy of scale in electric generating facilities. While a large city might be able to finance a large enough facility to be efficient and competitive with private utilities, Alpha could never raise the necessary capital to be truly competitive.

When Mr. Lane first raised the issue, Councilmen endorsed by the Citizens' Committee were divided. One councilman supported Mr. Post and at least one other was on the fence. (All Committee-endorsed incumbents did eventually abide by the referendum decision.) Two of the incumbents on the Citizens' Committee slate who opposed Mr. Post's pro-retention slate in the showdown election were really indifferent on the issue. While the Citizens' Committee would probably not have continued the endorsement of a candidate who sided with Mr. Post, wholehearted dedication to the Committee's light plant cause was not demanded.

The light plant issue indicates the type of individuals who serve on the Alpha council and the kind of dedication to "civic duty" of which they were capable. It also suggests that the Citizens' Committee representatives on the council were not simply delegates taking orders directly from the sponsoring organization. Thirdly, and perhaps most important for gaining an insight into Alpha politics, the case portrays the intensity of involvement in local issues of which members of the business community were capable.

THE UNSTRUCTURED POLITICS OF BETA AND GAMMA

The recruitment patterns in Beta and Gamma were in many ways similar. In both cities a few business interests, both retail and industrial, made sporadic attempts to recruit councilmen. The organization in Beta was an Association for Sound Government. Unlike the Alpha Citizens' Committee, the Beta group had an open membership and a nominal membership fee. It was a rather large and unwieldy body, which operated through a board of directors. Its membership did not include many executives of the larger firms but was dominated by persons from middle management and small businesses. It came into being shortly before our study period began and dissolved shortly after it ended. Its open membership and broad base resulted in a lack of the intimacy and consensus that was possible in the Citizens' Committee. In recruiting and endorsing candidates internal differences were not really resolved. Instead a large number of candidates with diverse qualifications received Association approval. The Association was especially fearful of being accused of trying to control city hall. It was dedicated to a simple set of democratic principles including the maintenance of a free electoral choice. It tried not only to assure the electorate a selection in each ward, but a choice between two or more Association-endorsed candidates. Consequently, sometimes three or four candidates for the same ward post would carry its endorsement in the primary. This gave the appearance of a lack of standards and its endorsement was not coveted by candidates after the first few elections in which it was active.

The Association was also handicapped by the ward system, which made it difficult to find acceptable candidates in certain jurisdictions. Given the general middle-class orientation of the Association, the problem wards were in working-class residential districts. But the tendency was to endorse someone so the Association at times supported candidates in one ward who differed substantially in viewpoint, education, and training from those in another ward. This further reduced its identity.

Little was done to elect the candidates once they were endorsed. The Alpha Citizens' Committee spent as much as $15,000 in one campaign, though its average expenditure was much lower than this. The Association in Beta went no farther than sponsoring a one-half page newspaper ad on each election eve. As campaigning was in a very low key in Beta, the Association merely conformed to the prevailing pattern. Of the councilmen interviewed, both endorsed and nonendorsed, few made speeches or did much beyond printing a few cards and placing an election-eve ad. When a service club invited the candidates to speak before it on one occassion, only one of eighteen appeared at the meeting.

Despite the organizational shortcomings of the Association, as a political force it could not be dismissed. Its strength lay in recruitment, not in endorsement or promotion. It convinced a number of men to run for office and many times the reluctant volunteers were elected. A number of officers of the organization were interviewed to determine the criteria of recruitment and endorsement. The initial replies alluded to "efficiency," "good government," and "honesty." Because these are standards that are as widely embraced as they are vague, our questioning turned to why certain individuals (including some incumbents) had not been endorsed. The core of the reasoning in the response centered around the concept of "city-wide views" as opposed to "ward-mindedness." In terms of the typology, the Association affirmed a unitary concept of the civic good and specifically opposed the use of government as an arbiter between competing claims.

This dichotomous concept of the nature of ends in politics was repeated in each city. The Alpha Committee members and the industrialists in Gamma, along with the Beta Association members, alluded to the city council as a Board of Directors and likened the city manager to an industrial plant manager. The content of their unitary goals included an identification of city interests with vaguely defined business interests and a willingness to commit the city to limited capital improvements.

As can be seen from Table 2, Beta recruited its councilmen from more random occupational sources than did any of the other three cities. It might be said this was an ideal ward city from the standpoint of the distribution of representation. However, this distribution took place as a result of the Association's efforts and not through an automatic process. A probable effect of this activity was the larger number of councilmen from middle management. Many candidates from this occupational category were recruited by the Association to represent lower-middle-class wards. But as we shall see in Delta, the ward system under different conditions of organized recruitment may encourage greater representation from the lower-middle-class sector.

Gamma had no formal or continuous informal group performing an effective job of recruitment, endorsement, or promotion of city candidates. There were sporadic attempts. Two years prior to our study period, a group originating from three or four Protestant churches entered city politics in reaction to an incident in which a councilman told ribald stories at a public gathering while under the influence of alcohol. This momentary uprising of moral indignation resulted in the election of three small businessmen to the council. In addition, the local banks had informally and successfully sponsored one candidate for the council over a period of ten or twelve years. During the study period another group, largely associated with the chamber of commerce and the manufacturer's association, began activity in electoral politics. At two elections during the period this group sponsored a slate of three and were successful each time in electing them. With few exceptions, the Gamma group was unsuccessful in recruiting candidates from the top executives in the community. However, the group was very conscious of the successes obtained in Alpha and was deliberately attempting to emulate the Citizens' Committee. Several informants who were active in this recruiting activity felt confident that progress was being made and that within a few years more top executives would be willing to run.

In both Gamma and Beta, independent candidates were active and often successful. The self starters who were elected represented diverse groups. The city employees in Beta and Gamma were active in local elections. The firemen were especially active in Gamma, where they conducted house-to-house canvasses for some candidates in every election. However, employee activity was on an *ad hoc* basis.

In Beta, many persons with laboring occupations ran for city office, but they received no labor-union backing (see Table 3). Organized labor was practically inert in city elections. On the other hand, labor furnished one of the more important organized forces in Gamma election politics. It suffered many defeats in trying to elect men from union ranks, but nevertheless there was always at least one man on the council who was elected with union support and reflected the views of organized labor.

THE WARD POLITICS OF DELTA

Delta offered a distinct contrast to the other three cities in terms of candidate recruitment and election politics. In this city, the most powerful political force was the city employees' union. Working through an effective organization, this group was always able to elect a council majority. While it could never control the office of mayor, this was no threat to its political hegemony. The mayor had little power. One who held that office reported that he was able during a two-year span to oppose successfully only one measure that was favored by the union bloc, an anti-fluoridation effort.

In Delta candidates for council conducted vigorous door-to-door campaigns. This was almost unheard of in the other three cities. While campaigning was real and vigorous in Alpha, it was in the form of general appeals and publicity through the mass media. Candidates in Beta and Gamma prided themselves on doing little to gain election. They preferred to treat an election as if it were a draft. The net effect was that candidates did not feel they had been elected for a purpose or program, and interpreted the job as one of sitting in judgment of issues offered to them. In Alpha and Delta campaigns were much more programmatic. However, the content of the "program' in the two cities differed profoundly. The Delta councilman was a delegate from his ward. He was interested in its streets, its sewers, its children who got into trouble, and most of all in its tax assessments and levels. Strange as it may seem, the dominant bloc, which was sponsored by the city employees' union and generally supported working people, prided itself on economy in government. In fact, the wage scale for city employees was not particularly high. The union objectives were chiefly realized in controlling personnel and working conditions. The patronage system had probably resulted in an inflated payroll in terms of the number of city employees. This unquestionably had some impact on the tax rate, but in other areas the union organization was

parsimonious with the taxpayer's dollar. The union bloc
also specialized in providing a variety of personal services
to citizens.

The surprising factor in Delta was the absence of
organized electoral activity by business groups. While
businessmen did not have to fear high taxes from the
union group, they did face the usual threat involved in
assessment practices: the possibility of relatively higher
rates on commercial as against residential property. The
danger from this direction was minimized, however, by
the high level of confidence businessmen had in the assessor, who was a former officer in the county Republican
organization. Political effort from the business sector was
confined to sporadic resorts to the referendum, and the
election of the powerless mayor. Even the councilmen
from the upper-middle-class wards were poor representatives of business interests. In some cases, they were
idealistic individuals who were unable to deal effectively
with the shrewder politicians representing the union
faction. Perhaps these council positions were not exploited
because there appeared to be little possibility of electing
a business-oriented majority. Several respondents interviewed declared that some businessmen contributed to the
union election campaign funds, perhaps with the purpose
of assuring a more favorable hearing if they happened to
have business before the city council—as some of them
were certain to have.

The union organization, entrenched by personnel patronage and favors and equipped with a campaign fund,
presented a formidable foe for anyone challenging it in
its own constituencies. As the union was not controlled
by Federal law, union dues could be used for campaign
purposes. The union also had the strategic advantage of

being the group in power. Its efforts could be safely confined to one or two crucial races each election—in wards
where opposition had developed or an incumbent was
becoming uncooperative and was slated for replacement.

Thus the four cities present distinctly different sets of
recruitment practices. If it is true that these cities are
controlled by economic dominants, the system of control
did not express itself uniformly through actual selection
of candidates. Only in Alpha did we find a situation in
which an economic elite heavily influenced the selection
of city councilmen. While some similar attempts were
made in Gamma, the efforts were sporadic. Here the
absence of a pyramidal power structure apparently did
not result from public opinion or competitive organization, but rather from the unwillingness of businessmen
to act in concerted fashion, for the two slates that generally
represented the chamber of commerce and the industrial
association were reasonably successful at the polls. The
same pattern of experience was not evident in Beta. It was
by no means certain that if prominent businessmen had
been willing to run they would have been successful. On
one occasion, an eminent executive was defeated for the
mayoralty nomination by a house painter who specialized
in bizarre comments on local affairs. On another occasion
an incumbent mayor, supported by some of the large
economic interests of the community, was rejected by the
voters and replaced by a man with a long-established
reputation for opposing nearly every civic project, including such salient items as a public parking ordinance and
a bond issue for storm sewers, which engineers regarded
as urgently needed.

The most obvious explanation of the greater willingness and ability of the economic dominants to control electoral choices in Alpha and Gamma and their relative lack of interest or success in Beta and Delta was the contrast between ward and at-large elections. The residential requirements of the ward system meant that not all representation could be drawn solely from business executives and close associates. But there appears to be a further implication, which can only be suggested here and developed later: The ward system opened the council to small businessmen, clerical workers, lower middle management, and even laborers. While an astute economic interest group, such as industrialists or downtown merchants, might recruit obsequious representatives from these groups, this was not a regular practice in either Beta or Delta. Once in office all councilmen were courted by specific interests, often successfully. Furthermore, the lower-middle-class and working-class representatives were the most conservative groups in their attitudes toward expenditures and innovations. Consequently, when a mayor was elected in Beta or Delta with the support of downtown merchants, industrialists, and the banks, he often appeared too ambitious, with too many costly ideas, for the tastes of middle- and lower-income group representatives. Perhaps an able, forceful mayor could have operated successfully in this enviroment, but most of the incumbents did not prove to be adroit. Frictions developed and council-mayor relations deteriorated. The mayor's efforts to aid business groups or to raise service levels were often the cause of friction with the recalcitrant city council. Men representing the lower-income neighborhoods often showed a fascination for small details, which drove persons with high executive experience to exasperation.

Table 3.
All Candidates for Council Classified by Occupation

Occupation	Alpha*		Beta			Gamma			Delta		
	Elected	Not elected	Elected	Nom. not elect.	Failed nom.	Elected	Nom. not elect.	Failed Nom.	Elected	Nom. not elect.	Failed nom.
Owner & executive (Nonretail)	14	7	7	1	3	7	1	4	3	0	2
Industrial	7	6	7	1	2	3	0	0	2	0	2
Building contractors	1	0	0	0	1	0	0	4	1	0	0
Others	6	1	0	0	0	4	1	0	0	0	0
Owner & executive (retail)	5	12	7	14	17	9	7	10	16	6	12
Retail	1	10	4	9	14	6	6	8	9	3	9
Service	4	1	3	5	3	2	1	2	2	3	3
Allied	0	1	0	0	0	1	0	0	5	0	0
Sales	3	4	7	9	3	5	2	5	5	2	2
Insurance	0	0	3	5	2	2	2	0	0	1	1
Real estate	3	4	4	4	1	3	0	5	5	1	2
Professional	8	9	5	2	0	1	0	0	10	2	1
Attorney	4	5	4	1	0	0	0	0	2	2	0
Phycisian & dentist	0	2	1	1	0	1	0	0	0	0	0
College professors	4	2	0	0	0	0	0	0	0	0	0
Pub. school teacher	0	0	0	0	0	0	0	0	8	0	1
Middle management	0	3	15	10	7	0	0	2	6	11	10
Engineers	0	0	3	3	2	0	0	0	1	1	2
Jr. executives	0	1	3	3	3	0	0	0	3	5	4
Others	0	2	6	4	2	0	0	2	2	5	4
Labor	3	11	2	3	17	2	4	1	12	13	21
Clerk	0	0	2	1	2	0	0	0	0	1	1
Production workers	0	2	0	0	6	1	3	0	8	9	16
Foremen	0	0	0	1	1	0	0	0	2	2	1
Others (incl. independent craftsmen)	3	9	0	1	8	1	1	1	2	1	3
Miscellaneous	3	2	4	2	2	0	2	2	0	1	2
Housewife	3	1	0	1	1	1	1	2	0	1	0
Unknown	0	0	0	0	1	0	1	1	0	3	4
Total	36	48	47	41	50	24	17	35	52	38	55

* No Primary.

ACCESS AND OCCUPATIONAL REPRESENTATION

Principal attention in the forgoing section has been given to the representation of business interests on the city councils. A more complete breakdown of occupational types indicates a number of patterns of occupational access. Table 3 tabulates the occupations of all candidates for council according to their degree of success at the polls. The candidates are classified as (1) elected, (2) nominated but not elected, and (3) also ran. Each election is tabulated separately, so individuals running more than once are counted separately for each candidacy. As a result an incumbency bias is projected into the total. A five-term incumbent can grossly inflate an occupational category given the smallness of the numbers. However, the distortion would be even greater if individuals were counted singly. A five-term banker would then be made equal to a one-term factory worker in our tabulation. We have chosen the shorter horn of the dilemma.

Table 3 enables us to inquire whether the representation of certain occupational groups was a function of the availability of candidates. It also gives a more discrete breakdown of the major occupational categories than was given earlier. For the first purpose, the information in this table has been reformulated in Table 4 to show the percentage of candidates in each category who were successful in being elected.

Table 4 indicates that the nonretail and professional groups had the best record for electoral success of any of the occupational categories, with records of 63 per cent successful candidacies each. Nearly all the individuals in the nonretail executive category were candidates as a result of some type of organized recruitment or sponsorship. In Alpha only three men from this category ran

Table 4. Percentage of Candidates Elected in Each Occupational Category

	Alpha		Beta		Gamma		Delta		Av. %	Total Candidates
	%	No.*	%	No.	%	No.	%	No.		
Owners & Executives, Nonretail	67	21	63	11	58	12	60	5	63%	49
Owners & Executives, Retail	24	17	16	38	35	26	47	34	32%	115
Sales	43	7	37	19	42	12	55	9	43%	47
Professional	47	17	71	7	100	1	71	14	63%	38
Middle management	0	3	48	32	0	2	22	27	33%	64
Labor	21	14	9	22	12	17	26	46	19%	99
Miscellaneous	60	5	50	8	0	4	0	3	35%	20
Total	† (36)	84	† (47)	137	† (24)	74	† (52)	138		

* Total number of candidates.
† Total of candidates elected.

without the sponsorship of the Citizen's Committee and only one executive in Beta failed to carry the endorsement of the Beta Association for Sound Government. In Gamma only two individuals, both building contractors, were outside sponsored slates or did not first receive office by appointment. In Delta, five persons from this occupational class ran for office and three of these sought to become mayor. One of the two remaining was again a building contractor, an occupation with definite interests in city policies. Local politics apparently affected most nonretail businesses in such a marginal fashion that few executives of these concerns would consider allocating part of their time for city service on a voluntary basis. They served only as representatives of community-wide groups which presented to the public the image, and perhaps the substance, of broad community interests.

To a certain extent professionals were similarly reluctant to offer their services for city offices, unless organized backing was present. However, of the seventeen Alpha professionals who were candidates only seven were recruited by the Citizen's Committee. A number of young professionals sought election to this more highly regarded council, but they usually failed to gain organized backing and also failed at the polls. Five of the seven Beta professionals carried endorsement by the Association. The professionals of Delta fell into two distinct categories—attorneys and public school teachers—of which the latter was numerically the more significant. The public school teacher, with a generally lower socioeconomic status than the lawyer and physician, was only prompted to run in the ward situation of Delta. The lawyers in Delta usually ran for mayor.

In summary, the involvement of professional persons in city politics was aften encouraged by the organized groups, with the exception of Alpha where independent professional candidates were common. The candidates of both the professional and nonretail executive groups proved to be attractive to the voters. Perhaps this was a function of the "disinterested" posture of the professionals and executives. That is, given the present content of city policies, these persons often have no direct personal monetary interest in city government.

Numerically, the most overrepresented specific occupational groups on the councils were the real estate and insurance salesmen. There was a total of forty-seven candidates from these occupations, approximately 40 percent of whom were elected. While this record was not as impressive as that established by the nonretail executive and professional categories, it was better than that of any other occupational group. The interest of realtors is clear enough, for the bulk of the activities of city government affect their income potential. They are concerned not only with the general property tax levy, but also such matters as zoning, subdivision regulation, planning, parking, capital improvement schedules, extension of services, and downtown redevelopment. All these affect property values or the salability of property and hence the interests of realtors. The interests of insurance salesmen are not as direct. (The two businesses are frequently allied, and several of our insurance men were part-time realtors.) The city is an insurance customer, but sitting on the city council may be more of an impediment than an aid in selling insurance to the city, as several insurance salesmen in Gamma discovered. However, personal advertising is important to the insurance man and perhaps this is a prime motivation for candidacy. Finally, it should be pointed out that the salesmen fared equally well under each of the different political systems. One interpretation of this might be that they were equally motivated in all cities and, with or without endorsement, they expend a special effort to gain office.

The middle-management candidates were largely confined to the two cities employing a ward system of representation. As can be seen from Table 3, no person from this category was elected in Alpha and Gamma and few offered their candidacy. Apparently, the middle-range white-collar worker is not given sufficient status by his employment to run for office in a city-wide constituency. Only in the ward city, where neighborhood reputations become significant, did this group secure a role in local politics. The same might be said of the laboring group, except that the labor organizations gave a potential backing to its candidates that was lacking for the white-collar people. By contrasting the data of Table 2 and Table 4 we see that labor had significant representation only in Delta where the highest percentage of labor candidates were elected and the highest percentage of the councilmen were from the laboring class. The efforts of these candidates were backed by an effective organization. In the other ward city, Beta, there was no political activity on behalf of the labor candidates, and the two councilmen elected from the labor category were numerically insignificant. The Beta Association dipped into the middle-management ranks for fourteen of its endorsees and elected six of them. (There were thirty-one total candidates from middle management, of whom fifteen were elected.) Of the nine successful middle-management candidates that did not have Association endorsement, five were represented by one man, a long-time incumbent whom the Association steadfastly refused to support.

There is a widespread popular belief in America that

downtown merchants dominate the political life of American cities.[6] Judging from our sample, it cannot be maintained that they do so by direct representation. (Forms of indirect influence will be discussed below, especially in Chapter VI.) Table 2 indicates that the total retail group had 14, 13, 38, and 31 per cent of council posts in Alpha, Beta, Gamma and Delta respectively. From Table 2 we see that the candidates from this classification had a poorer record of success than any other group except labor. The retail category should not be equated with one of the central business district merchants. There were only two downtown merchants in the entire period who sat on the city councils, one in Alpha and one in Gamma. There were few cases where downtown merchants ran for office and those who did were all from small enterprises. The business representatives included in the retail "executive" category included a number of gas station operators, dry cleaning establishment managers, a milk distributor, a grocer, a produce wholesaler, an advertising executive, jewelers, a barber, a paint store manager, a fruit company manager, a coal dealer, and a professional member of an accounting firm. Thus, the occupations and businesses represented in the retail class were such that the title "executive" is somewhat misleading. This group consisted largely of small entrepreneurs.

The question remains why were central business district merchants unwilling to run for office, while the neighborhood merchants supplied a large number of candidates. The most probable hypothesis is that neighborhood merchants are able to identify their customer-constituents with greater assurance. The merchant of the central business district has a far-flung clientele. On any controversial issue, his customers are likely to include persons on both sides of the question. To the extent that city issues divide the citizenry along either geographic or economic lines, the neighborhood merchant is more able to take a position without offending any large segment of his customers and furthermore can be the advocate for the interests of most of them. Thus he can at least hope that political activity may help his business.

Educational data were available on the councilmen in three of the cities. The pattern was largely a reflection of occupational representation. In Alpha it was unusual to have as many as two councilmen who did not have a college degree. Of the forty-seven persons who sat on the Beta council in the ten-year period, ten had college degrees, six attended college, and thirty-one had a high-school education or less. No data were available for Gamma. The Delta council never had more than one incumbent with a college education.

SUMMARY

Earlier it was stated that we would consider in this chapter the premise that nonpartisan elections raised the caliber of council candidates. Nonpartisanship was a product of middle-class reform movement, and probably the leaders of the movement have used a self-image as the proper measure of what constitutes "higher caliber." Considering the great variety in the composition of the city councils in these four cities, our investigation would point to the conclusion that virtually any type of council was possible under the nonpartisan ballot. Perhaps a more important factor in determining the character of the council was the formal arrangement providing for at-large as opposed to ward representation. Our investigation of the councils has gone somewhat beyond the question of caliber; consequently, we summarize the findings of this chapter as a series of propositions:

1. The economic dominants had the greatest propensity to guide the recruitment process under at-large elections.

2. In contrast, the cities using ward representation recruited a higher proportion of city councilmen from occupational groups on the lower end of the socioeconomic scale.

3. Any control that Main Street exerted over the city council was not through direct occupational representation.

4. In our four middle-sized cities, continuous organized efforts directed toward electoral politics were not universal and a condition in which there existed competitive organizations seeking to mobilize support in order to control the city government was rare.

The foregoing gives some indication of the success of recruiting groups in electing their candidates, but nothing has yet been said about the sources of electoral support. While elaborate research was not necessary in order to uncover some of these sources, actual analysis of voting records revealed some subtleties in the patterns, which were not anticipated.

NOTES

[1] Charles R. Adrian, "A Typology for Nonpartisan Elections," *Western Political Quarterly*, Vol. 12 (June 1959), 449-458. See also J. Leiper Freeman, "Local Party Systems: Theoretical Considerations and a Case Analysis," *American Journal of Sociology*, Vol. 64 (November, 1958) 282-289.

[2] Eugene Lee, *The Politics of Nonpartisanship: A Study of California*

City Elections (Berkeley: University of California Press, 1960).

3 Walter Goldschmidt, *As You Sow* (New York: Harcourt, Brace and Company, 1947); W. Lloyd Warner and Associates, *Democracy in Jonesville* (New York: Harper and Brothers, 1949; and Arthur J. Vidich and Joseph Bensman, *Small Town in Mass Society* (Princeton: Pirnceton University Press, 1958).

4 Floyd Hunter, *Community Power Structure* (Chapel Hill: the University of North Carolina Press, 1952); Harold Gosnell, *Machine Politics— Chicago Model* (Chicago: University of Chicago Press; 1937) and Martin Meyerson and Edward Banfield, *Politics and the Public Interest* (Glencoe: The Free Press, 1955).

5 Kenneth Underwood, *Protestant and Catholic* (Boston: Beacon Press, 1957); and Robert S. and Helen M. Lynd, *Middletown in Transition* (New York: Harcourt, Brace and Co., 1937).

6 See, for example, Alfred de Grazia, *The Western Public* (Stanford: Stanford University Press, 1954), p. 185.

Chapter IV

Nonpartisanship: Electoral Patterns[1]

The term "nonpartisan" has frequently taken on misleading connotations. Ostensibly the term means "without reference to party." The definition has, however, been extended to imply "without reference to policy." In this chapter, both usages will be applied to politics in the four cities.

As for nonpartisanship in the first sense: Were the municipal elections in these four cities insulated from partisan politics? The "insulation" theory of nonpartisanship holds that the two national parties inevitably introduce irrelevancies when they are active in local elections. The party labels stand as symbols of traditions and policies largely national in meaning and the presence of these names on the local ballot prevents local officials from being chosen for local reasons alone. In essence this view of the nonpartisan idea is based upon the idea of improving the democratic process by rationalizing the levels of political participation. The voting decisions pertaining to various levels of government, it is thought, need to be segregated. As with many of the other reform devices, this idea is predicated upon a faith that the cure for the evils of democracy is more democracy.

In actuality there are many gradations of nonpartisanship, for national parties are only in part removed from local influence by elimination of the party label. In our four cities, however, the nonpartisan ballot was formally successful in that the national party organizations played virtually no role in them. In Alpha and Beta, the separation was emphasized by holding city elections on a separate day. Not only was there organizational separation but generally separate sets of persons engaged in the two political arenas.[2] This was especially evident with respect to candidates. Only one of all the councilmen during the ten-year period successfully ran for a partisan office following tenure in a nonpartisan one—a Delta mayor was elected to Congress—and a few councilmen made abortive attempts to win partisan county offices. Judged by these four cities, it appears clear that one effect of the nonpartisan ballot has been to eliminate city office as a step in the career ladder for aspiring party politicians. While this helped assure the nonpartisan objective of enlisting as candidates for city council only those persons interested in local affairs, it also eliminated the politically ambitious who were looking for local stepping stones to move on to higher levels.

The insulation theory of nonpartisanship implies that the separation of elections will extend to the actual voting behavior. Ostensibly, local and state or national issues are qualitatively so distinct that significantly different voting patterns will occur if local elections are effectively insulated. Partisan and nonpartisan voting behavior can be compared in two ways: correlation of some form of partisan vote (1) with the vote of individual nonpartisan candidates, or (2) with some identifiable blocs of candidates. The first of these approaches is the more hazardous methodologically. In city elections, many half-serious or self-advertising candidates appear on the ballot. Many other candidates run but once and are virtually unknown. While significant correlations may be found, it is difficult to interpret data resulting from such a polyglot source. Consequently, the second approach, using identifiable blocs or slates of candidates is preferable, since it provides a more reliable basis for correlation. This method has been followed where possible in our analysis.

PARTISAN AND NONPARTISAN PATTERNS

Correlation of local slates with partisan voting patterns was possible only in the three cities having at-large general elections; namely, Alpha, Beta, and Gamma. In each of these cities correlations were calculated between the votes for the "prevailing slates" and the Republican vote for governor in the state election nearest in time to the local elections. "Prevailing slates" refers to the candidates of the Alpha Citizens' Committee, the Beta Association for Sound Government, and the groups of candidates who banded together on two occasions in Gamma under the unofficial sponsorship of the Chamber of Commerce. The term "opposition slate" is used in reference to the opposing groups appearing in Alpha, which were described in the last chapter.

A simple correlation was computed between the percentage vote for the Republican candidate and the average percentage support for the "prevailing slates." The results are shown in Table 5, Columns 1, 3, and 5.

At least two hypotheses are possible to explain the relationship. First, it may be that the political affiliation of slate sponsors is not easily hidden in cities of this size,

Table 5. Alpha, Beta, and Gamma: Correlation Between "Prevailing Slate" Support And Republican Vote For Governor, By Precinct Percentages; And Resulting Slope of the Least-Squares Line

	Alpha			Beta*			Gamma	
	N†	Pear-sonian r	Slope	N†	Pear-sonian r	Slope	N†	Pear-sonian r	Slope
Year	1	2		3	4			5	6
1949	32	.928	.94	20	.777	.33			
1950							18	.919	.47
1951	32	.879	.62	20	.857	.26			
1952									
1953	32	.769	.52	20	.965	.37			
1954									
1955	32	.852	.72	20	.824	.23			
1956							21	.788	.26
1957	32	.832	.64	24	.847	.21			

	Critical Values‡ at .001		
N		N	
18	.708	24	.652
20	.679	32	.554

† N-Number of precincts.

* Beta Council elections are paired contests, consequently only those where an endorsed candidate was opposed by an unendorsed candidate are included.

‡ The critical value represents the figure that would result from chance one time in 1000. Higher values could also result from chance, but even less often. Statistically, a high correlation appears in each election, with the coefficient of correlation well above the value of chance at the 0.1 per cent level.

and the voters simply characterized the slates according to the party of the sponsors and voted accordingly. Secondly, general political values and preferences (whether conditioned by income, social position, education, or other influences) that mold the electorate into blocs supporting different political parties also furnish a meaningful basis for consensus in city politics for many citizens. If the first were true, that the slates were mere transparent appendages of a party, we would expect not only a high correlation, but a definite similarity in percentage votes for slates and parties. Less than complete coincidences in voting patterns would support the second hypothesis.

The parallels between the actual percentages for slate and party voting may be indicated by measuring the slope of the line summarizing the relationship between party support and slate support in all the precincts in a given election. (Technically, this is called the *slope of the least-squares line.*) If voters in every precinct voted in the same proportion for Republican gubernatorial candidates and for all members of a slate, we would have a least-squares line rising at a 45° angle, or having a slope of 1.000. (For each 1 per cent rise in Republican vote there would be a corresponding one per cent rise in slate support.)

Table 5, Columns 2, 4. and 6, gives the slopes for each of the correlation figures computed for Columns 1, 3, and 5.[3] As can be seen, there is a great variation in the slopes. In all the Beta elections, and in the one in Gamma in 1956, the slopes are indeed flat: These figures qualify considerably the correlations of Columns 1, 3, and 5. For example, in 1956 in Gamma, for every 4 per cent rise in the Republican vote, there was only a 1 per cent rise in the support of the "prevailing slate." But, on the other hand, the slopes describing the Alpha elections range more steeply, thus reflecting more nearly the Republican percentages.

The calculations of the angles of the slopes lead us to reject the hypothesis that voters perceive the slates as adjuncts of national parties. The variations in slope are sufficient evidence. But these variations themselves invite explanation: What distinguished the elections at the extremes in Table 5? In most cases it was the degree of existing competition. The Alpha elections were intensely fought, with great expenditures of time, energy and money. As a result, Alpha citizens had a good opportunity to develop an image of the various candidates. In Gamma, votes were pursued somewhat less assiduously as measured by the expenditure of money and the amount of organizational effort. And in Beta, candidates did almost nothing to inform the voters about themselves or their intentions. Candidates with few exceptions refused to take positions on local issues. The mayoralty candidates did some campaigning, but councilmanic candidates did little or none.

This explanation of the differences in angle of slope can be further checked by looking at the variations within Alpha and Gamma. In spite of a paucity of incidents in Gamma, two examples do support the competition hypothesis. In the 1956 Gamma election the "prevailing slate" ran three candidates for the three positions to be filled. The most prominent opponent of the slate, an excouncilman and labor leader, withdrew on the eve of the election because of poor health. This greatly reduced voter choice of a competitive alternative is associated with both the lower correlation and the slope, as compared with 1950. In Alpha, the 1949 election found a full "opposition slate" in the field and the resulting competitive situation is shown by the extremely steep slope (.94).

An analysis of the city-wide mayoralty races in Beta and Delta gives further supporting evidence to the competition hypothesis. The mayor is not popularly elected in Alpha and Gamma. In these races, again, the choices are simple and clear, and the honors of the office are enough to invite a contest between the candidates. Table 6, Columns 1 and 3, shows the coefficients of correlation between the vote for the successful candidates and the partisan vote for the Republican candidate for governor in the corresponding election. Columns 2 and 4 indicate the slope of the least-squares line. The resulting correlations are significant and the slopes generally range from .5 to .8. Thus, the competitive mayor's race in Beta stands in sharp contrast to the phlegmatic councilmanic races of that city.

Table 6. Beta and Delta: Correlation of Percentage of Vote Between Winning Mayoralty Candidate and Republican Vote for Governor, and The Resulting Slope of the Least-Squares Line

Year	Beta			Delta		
	No. of Precincts	1 Pearsonian r	2 Slope	No. of wards	3 Pearsonian r	4 Slope
1949	20	.858	.70	9	.887	.73
1951	20	.891	.53	9	.803	.70
1953	20	.947	.83	9	.840	.80
1955	20	.912	.75	9	.699	.45
1957	24	.977	.75	9	.862	.50

So far the analysis has shown a significant correlation between votes for nonpartisan slates and party votes, even though at times the nonpartisan vote is more a dim reflection than an actual picture of the partisan voting pattern. However, there appear to be definite causative factors producing the relationship between the votes in the two political arenas. The more assiduously *issues* in the nonpartisan elections were pursued, the more the resulting vote conformed to the partisan pattern. The issues in these elections will be described in the chapters below. Of course, competition over issues would in theory also serve to *decrease* the relationship. We found one such instance: in Alpha in 1953 a full "opposition slate" comprised of conservative businessmen appeared on the ballot. The issue was the one concerning municipal ownership of an electric power plant and the two sides were represented by opposing slates of businessmen. In the ensuing election, the vote had a lower correlation with partisan voting than usual, though it was still significant. (Note the .769 correlation and the .52 slope in Table 5). This was the one exception we found. In all other contests, the more issue-oriented the campaign, the higher the correlation between nonpartisan and partisan voting patterns.

THE POLITICS OF NONVOTING

Up to this point we have concentrated on demonstrating that patterns of voting exist in nonpartisan elections. Attention to voter turnout figures can aid in analyzing the implications of these patterns for electoral dominance.

From other studies we know that nonvoting in national elections is related to lower educational levels among citizens, to urban workers and hence, in most areas, to potentially Democratic voters. Little is known of municipal nonvoting patterns, but we might infer from the partisan election evidence that Democrats, as compared to Republicans, would have a poor voting record in nonpartisan elections. The fact that the bread and butter issues of the laboring man are frequently a function of state and national, rather than local, partisan politics might further deter Democrats from voting in municipal elections.

Table 7 shows the rank order correlations by precinct in Alpha, Beta, and Gamma and by ward in Delta between local voting and Republican strength.[4] Local voter participation is measured by taking the total municipal vote in each precinct or ward as a percentage of the total vote for governor in the corresponding partisan election. Republican strength refers to the percentage received by the Republican candidate for governor. The resulting correlations show that only in Alpha and Gamma is our hypothesis about Democrats as local nonvoters borne out. However, even in these two cities the effect of the apathetic Democrats upon the outcome of municipal elections is probably not the same.

Just as Table 1 showed a correlation of support of the "prevailing slate" with Republican votes in Alpha and Gamma, so here we see a correlation between voter turnout and Republican strength. Consequently, the voting-nonvoting distribution appears to favor the slates. In strongly Republican Alpha this nonvoting pattern probably does not affect the outcome of elections, but in a competitive city (in partisan politics) such as Gamma the implications are more important. If the Democrats in Gamma who failed to vote in the city elections had cast their ballots in the same manner as the Democrats who did vote, the outcome of the elections would have differed considerably. As it was, predominantly Republican precincts gained their preference among city candidates much more frequently than did the Democratic precincts.[5]

Table 7. Alpha, Beta, Gamma, Delta: Rank Order Correlation of Precincts Between Republican Strength and Local Voter Participation*

Year†	1 Alpha		2 Beta		3 Gamma (City primary)		4 Gamma (City general)		5 Delta	
		n		n		n		n		n
1949	.541	32	.315	19	.700	16	.708	16	−.506	9
1951	.614	32	.677	20	‡		.670	18	−.67	9
1953	.762	32	.159	20	.731	20	.682	20	.103	9
1955	.731	32	.123	20	.754	20	.757	20	−.584	9
1957	.687	31	.473	23	.807	21	.797	21	−.450	9

	Critical Values	
N	5%	1%
9	.600	.783
16	.425	.601
18	.399	.564
20	.377	.534
22	.359	.508
30	.306	.432
32	.295	.417

* Local participation totals are not exactly comparable between cities. Alpha is based on actual total ballots cast, Beta and Delta on total vote for mayoral candidates, and Gamma on average vote for councilman races.

† 1948, 1950, 1952, 1956, in Gamma.

‡ Data not comparable because of precinct boundary changes.

Gamma elects three and four councilmen in alternating elections every two years. Totaling the results of five consecutive elections, Republican precincts (measured by the vote for governor on the same day) saw their top three choices elected thirty times, while only fourteen Democratic precincts were equally successful. Twenty-two Democratic precincts had one or none of their choices elected, while no Republican precinct was so unfortunate. During this same period, the Democratic candidate for governor won 51 precincts while the Republican candidate won only 43. Much of the failure of the precincts oriented toward the Democratic party to gain their choice must be attributed to nonvoting. The extent to which the nonpartisan ballot contributes to this nonvoting pattern cannot be conclusively established by the present data. However, the inference is strong that more local votes would have been forthcoming from Democratic precincts if these offices had been tied to the party ballot. Local voting participation as a percentage of partisan voting was 1.6 times greater in the top quartile of Republican precincts than it was in the top quartile of Democratic precincts in the five elections.

While Table 7 does not show Beta substantiating the hypotheses concerning association of Democratic and local nonvoting patterns, one modification in the analysis brings this city into line with Alpha and Gamma. When the four strongest Polish precincts are omitted, the correlations jump from .1227 to .710 in 1955 and from .4729 to .744 in 1957.[6] Ethnicity in this city stands as a qualification to our hypothesis. But it must be remembered that Beta's elections were not intensely competitive, issues were rarely exploited, and the dependence upon name identification might thereby have been maximized. The status strivings of a reasonably compact ethnic group and its desire for representation on the council might be articulated to a greater extent in the absence of other types of divisive forces in the electoral process.

Delta poses the most serious difficulty for the hypothesis in question. Its Democratic precincts had a superior voting record as compared with the Republican. The Delta council was elected by wards and an active city employees' union strongly influenced the elections. The union concentrated its efforts in the Democratic wards where, indeed, the crucial elections for control of the council always took place. By contrast the councilmen from the Republican wards had long tenure and there were few interest-provoking contests. Even when there was no contest in the Democratic wards, there was a relatively high turnout. Perhaps this indicated a habituation to participation in local affairs. Labor unions have long claimed that ward politics and ward elections stimulate greater political interest among their members than do city-wide elections. The Delta situation gives supporting evidence to their claims.

Our hypothesis that Democrats would be least inclined to participate in local nonpartisan elections, while having some general validity in the four cities, must stand as a qualified generalization at best. Voter turnout seems to be related to ethnicity, whether councilmen are elected by wards or at large, to the degree to which voters regard themselves as having a meaningful stake in the election, and probably to other factors. The narrowness of our sample suggests that we should report or findings only as case studies. Nonvoting at the local level seems to be a matter requiring multivariate analysis.

THE POLITICS OF CONSENSUS

Thus far electoral dominance has been analyzed in terms of slate-party correlations and patterns of nonvoting. The data admit of one other analytical approach. In city-wide elections, where the voters choose from a large field of candidates, consensus within a group should increase its political power in comparison with other groups, which scatter their support. The question then is whether the Democratic or Republican precincts displayed greater agreement in selecting candidates. As Beta and Delta nominated by wards, this analysis had to be confined to Alpha and Gamma.

The top quartile of Democratic and Republican precincts, as determined by gubernatorial votes, was analyzed for consensus in choosing nonpartisan city candidates.

Table 8. Alpha, Gamma: Degree of Agreement in Ranking Candidates Between Top Quartiles of Democratic and Republican Precincts*

Election	Alpha variance ratio (F)	Critical value 1%	Gamma variance ratio (F)	Critical value 1%	Critical value 5%
1	2.709	1.59	−1.433	4.16	2.69
2	1.163	1.74	2.386	2.52	1.91
3	4.620	1.59	3.124	3.29	2.29
4	5.366	1.60	1.107	2.52	1.91
5	2.995	1.60	3.545	3.56	2.43

* Analysis of variance of ranked data.

The statistical tool employed was an *analysis of variance of ranked data* (see Table 8) . According to this measure, a larger positive variance ratio (Columns 1 and 3) indicates greater agreement displayed by Republicans in comparison to Democrats. A negative figure indicates the reverse. The critical value columns indicate that the distribution at the per cent level could result from chance only once in 100 times.

While the relationships were not uniform, there was a greater tendency for the Republicans to have consensus in candidate selection. Just why this should be true is an interesting matter for speculation. It may be that the lines of communications through such community organizations as the service clubs, chest drives, chambers of commerce and business associations enable the Republicans to reach informal agreements not possible for the bulk of Democratic voters. Certainly, Democratic industrial workers have fewer functionally equivalent institutions through which to develop such consensus. It is also possible that consensus is partially a function of awareness of interests at stake on the part of groups in the community.

Perhaps the more provocative information in Table 8, however, concerns the difference between the two cities. Two facts might explain the relatively greater Republican consensus in Alpha: (1) Slating was more continuous and established in Alpha. (2) Gamma had a primary election and Alpha did not. In Alpha, sometimes twenty or more candidates ran for seven positions. In Gamma a primary limited the general election to twice as many candidates as there were positions. This often meant in fact three incumbents against three challengers. The alternatives were at least simple in a numerical sense. The Alpha

Democratic precincts seemed to scatter their votes badly.
Despite the presence of some appealing candidates, their
votes often were spent on ethnic names and neighborhood
favorites. This suggests that the communications net of
a middle-size city may be such as to affect differentially
the political power of various groups in an election involving a large field of candidates.

SUMMARY

Let us now relate the insulation theory of nonpartisanship to our findings. Local and party organizations were
structurally separate. Candidates were recruited from separate pools of leadership. In voting the slate support was
analogous to but not the same as that for the political
party candidates. The affinity between the two voting
patterns increased as issues were more sharply drawn, thus
the inference was made that local issues were not completely distinct from those engaging the principal political
parties. Of course, these were the sentiments Charles A.
Beard expressed to the National Municipal League in
1917 in his celebrated address on the subject of nonpartisanship.[7] However, his speech predated the New Deal
and the other intervening events that have nationalized
the policies Beard singled out as essentially partisan. He
argued that as long as the cities were dwelling places of
the needy, no one could depoliticize city politics.

Our findings indicate that even the docile brand of
urban politics practiced today continues to produce citizen responses that simulate the Republican-Democratic
division. In brief, while nonpartisanship has introduced
a politics without reference to party, it is not without
reference to policy. Furthermore, nonpartisan elections

have a policy effect of their own. Our data indicate that, in these four northern middle-sized industrial cities, non-partisanship strengthened the influence of those persons who traditionally vote Republican. Or perhaps more ac-curately, nonpartisanship is a structural device that favors the values held by those on the upper end of the socio-economic continuum.

There were exceptions, however. As the case of Delta showed, organization remains a potent political weapon, which can be successfully exploited. Secondly, commu-nities characterized by ethnic-group conflicts may develop subsystems of political behavior that are at variance with the general norms.

NOTES

[1] This chapter was first published in slightly different form as "The Insulation of Local Politics Under the Nonpartisan Ballot," *American Political Science Review*, Vol. 53 (December, 1959), 1052-1063. Used by permission.

[2] Cf. Charles R. Adrian, "Some General Characteristics of Nonpartisan Elections," *American Political Science Review*, Vol. 46 (September, 1952), 766-776 and Eugene Lee, *The Politics of Nonpartisanship: A Study of California City Elections* (Berkeley: University of California Press, 1960).

[3] The fact that the slopes are all below one indicates that the distribu-tion of precincts is in every case dispersed over a wider range when measured by percentage of party support than when measured by per-centage of slate support. This calculation may be influenced by the fact that we are comparing an individual election on one side to the average of a group of elections on the other.

[4] In the previous analysis a simple coefficient of correlations was com-puted because of the necessity of determining the slope. In addition, the hypothesis implied a straight linear relationship. In this case the easier-to-compute rank-order correlation, with its curvilinear assumptions, is adequate to indicate higher and lower orders of relationship.

[5] These calculations are based upon precinct data. Conceivably it might be the Republican voters in predominantly Democratic precincts who constitute a large percentage of the nonvoters, but this is unlikely. Our analysis is subject to a second qualification. The correlation figures could be affected by "plunking," i.e., the practice of voting for less than the

maximum allowable number of candidates. If plunking were more characteristic of Democratic precincts, the correlations would be reduced. But plunking is a technique of minorities, or shows a voter's lack of knowledge about candidates. In either case it is a functional equivalent of nonvoting. It shows a disassociation from local politics by large numbers of Democratic voters.

6 A precinct boundary map was unavailable for the earlier elections, forcing a restriction of this analysis to the two years. The coefficients of correlation are significant at the 1 per cent level.

7 Charles A. Beard, "Politics and City Government," *National Municipal Review*, Vol. 6 (March, 1917), 201-205.

Chapter V

Referendums

The home rule charters of four cities were written so that voters could retain a tight rein on the city councils. All general obligation bonds had to be approved at the polls and in three of the cities (Gamma being the exception) a three-fifths favorable vote was necessary. Because the powers of the councils were narrowly defined, most innovations required a popularly approved amendment to the charter. Finally, the petition provisions which enabled citizens to place ordinances on the ballot were sufficiently liberal to permit well-organized minorities to appeal their causes to the general public. As initiatives and referendums by petition constituted a source of embarrassment to councilmen, they frequently would place controversial matters on the ballot to avoid this possibility.

There were great variations in the voters' responses to issues placed on the ballots in the four cities. The citizens of Alpha and Gamma generally supported bond issues and those in Beta and Delta turned them down. The same general pattern of response pertained to nontax proposals of the city councils. A more detailed statement of these various responses will be made in Part III where the subject of municipal differences will be the central concern. In this chapter, the object is to determine what general patterns of voting behavior emerged. Is it possible to identify specific groups common to all the cities that were consistent in their attitudes toward the issues presented?

While there was a great variety of issues presented to the voters, most of them were in fact requests by the council to approve a certain course of action, which the legislative body had selected. This was the case whether the proposal was for a bond issue to build a sewage-disposal plant or a charter amendment authorizing the creation of an independent hospital board. To be sure the council's proposal was often itself a compromise measure, but this is irrelevant. Generally councils placed on the ballot only those issues which were designed to solve a pressing problem and did so in a fashion that was designed to satisfy the pressures to which they were being directly subjected. By eliminating those referendums in which the council was neutral or no clear council majority was favorable, we can ask: Who supported the city council?

The factors which motivated individual citizens to vote as they did were undoubtedly varied. Some probably opposed issues simply because they did not want to pay higher taxes. Some negative votes may have been based on a knowledgeable disagreement with the solution posed, and others probably voted "no" out of distrust of the incumbent councilmen. This list could be made much longer. Through a composite analysis of all the issues, we may be able to isolate certain groups within the citizenry which generally favored the solving of problems, and others which preferred no solutions. In the language of the typology, we can isolate the persons who favored caretaker government.

WHO SUPPORTS THE COUNCIL?

The most obvious grouping of the electorate for this question is along socioeconomic lines. Unfortunately, census tracts, even when available, did not coincide with the election precincts. Consequently, the precincts were first identified by the traditional party allegiance in an effort to establish a rough socioeconomic index. Through inspection and interviews it was determined that such a scale was approximately accurate, especially at the two extremes of wealthier, high-status areas and poorer, low-status areas.

The most consistent support for the referendums came from the more wealthy areas in each city. The people who would pay the most taxes (but perhaps who were also more able to pay) were the most willing to pay. This pattern was consistent regardless of the city or who the incumbent councilmen were at the time. Even in Delta, where the city council was controlled by the Democratic working-class areas and the individual councilmen were not of a type to breed confidence in a typical businessman, the middle-class Republican wards continued to be the most dependable sources of councilmanic support on referendums.

At the other extreme the strongest opposition to tax increases or any innovations usually came from the lower socioeconomic areas. However, the turnout was often light in these areas, minimizing the effectiveness of these voters. In the groups lying between these extremes there were strikingly different patterns of behavior from election to election and city to city.

These general assertions require demonstration and partial qualification; consequently, a city by city analysis of referendums will be undertaken here. In Table 9, a rank-

order correlation is given between Republican votes for
governor and pro-council votes in the referendums. The
computations are based upon precinct totals. The Alpha
council favored every measure that called for increased
revenues whether from tax increases or, in the one case,
from parking-meters.

Table 9. Alpha: Rank-Order Correlation Between Republican Vote for Governor and Precinct Support of
Council-Approved Issues in Referendums (Selected
sample)*

Issue	Correlation	Adopted	N
1. Provide off-street parking	.731	Yes	32
2. Install parking meters	.816	Yes	32
3. Alternate one-way street plan (initiative)	.659†	No†	32
4. Annexation proposal	.873	Yes	32
5. Raise council salaries	.684	Yes	32
6. Bond; construction of sewage plant	.428	Yes	32
7. Bond; storm sewers	.741	Yes	32

* Critical values: 1%-.417; 5%-.296.
† Council advocated a "No" vote; correlation is between Republican
strength and "No" vote.

The rank-order correlations show relative support but
do not indicate the degree of opposition. There were
seven precincts among the thirty-two in Alpha that were
Democratic. All these precincts opposed installation of

parking meters (No. 2) and the issuance of storm-sewer bonds (No. 7). On the other hand, two issues carried in every precinct: annexation (No. 4) and the sewage-plant bond issue (No. 6). The Democratic precincts formed the core of the opposition to the salary increases for councilmen and to the one-way street plan. In these two votes as well as in the parking-meter and storm-sewer bond vote, two other blocs of precincts should be bracketed with the Democratic precincts. One was a transitional area where some Negroes were moving in, displacing a white population that included many elderly people. The second area was an industrial working-class area. Both of these were normally Republican by small margins, but they tended to side with the Democratic (lower socioeconomic) precincts in city referendums.

At the other extreme, the wealthiest precincts, which were also the most Republican, showed a most steadfast support for tax increases and other council proposals. The following figures show the degree of their support:

Table 10. Support of Council Proposals by Wealthiest Precincts

Issues		1	2	3	4	5	6	7
Pre. 1	%	77	80	80	92	75	95	75
Pre. 2	%	79	76	72	89	71	92	74
Pre. 3	%	76	69	74	85	68	99	73

The pattern in Beta resembled the one in Alpha, as revealed by the correlations in Table 11. However, while most of the measures passed in Alpha, they failed in Beta. Nevertheless the strongest support for the council's position in Beta also came from the strong Republican precincts. Six Beta precincts voted 70 per cent or more Republican in each of the gubernatorial races used in computing partisan allegiance. On the four storm-sewer referendums, the "yes" vote never fell below 59 per cent and ranged as high as 90 per cent in these precincts. Across town in the most Democratic districts (which were also working-class residential areas), support fell as low as 14 per cent. Taking the composite vote on the four storm-sewer issues, Democratic precincts voted on the

Table 11. Beta: Rank-Order Correlation Between Republican Vote for Governor and Precinct Support of Council-Favored Referendums*

Issue	Correlation	Adopted	N
1. Set charter tax limit	.952	No	20
2. Set charter tax limit	.902	Yes	20
3. Parking bond issue (initiative)	.830	No	20
4. Storm-sewer bond	.926	No	20
5. Storm-sewer bond	.879	No	20
6. Millage for police and fire pension	.916	No	24
7. Lift rent control†	.687	Yes	20

* *Critical values*:
   N-20 1%-.534; 5%-.371
   N-24 1%-.485: 5%-.343
   † No official council position on issue. Correlation is with "yes" vote.

matter 32 times and on only three occasions was the "yes" vote in the majority. Only on the parking meter revenue bond issue did the staunch Republican areas fail to return majorities; even then their "yes" votes were invariably a higher percentage than in any other areas of the city.

A close look at the "no" vote on the two referendums dealing with a charter tax limit indicates that the opposition of the Democratic area was not simply an economic response. For technical reasons, the effect of the first vote setting a tax limit in the charter was to permit the raising of taxes, and the effect of the second issue was to set a tax ceiling. Straight economic motivation would lead to an opposite vote on the two questions. On both occasions there was a high correlation with the party vote. Because the second vote actually placed a tax ceiling in the charter (thus limiting councilmanic power to raise taxes), the rational vote for the tax-sensitive individual would also have been "yes." But the precincts that voted heavily in opposition to all tax increases also voted "no" on this question. It is true that the issue was somewhat complicated and not given great publicity. The less well educated, who might be assumed to be more numerous in the lower income parts of town, may simply have reacted negatively because they did not understand. The noneconomic factor may have been ignorance or it may have been lack of confidence in the council and city government generally.[1]

Delta had a pattern similar to Beta's. Not only were the outcomes of the elections generally similar, but so were the correlations with partisan votes. Republican voters generally supported to a greater extent than did Democrats increased powers for the city council, expanded service levels, construction of capital improvements and increases in remuneration for city employees and officials. The correlations are shown in Table 12. When efforts were made to curtail the discretion of the council, as was the case with Issues 1 and 2 in Table 9, the Republican voters were more opposed to the restrictions.[2]

Table 12. Delta: Rank-Order Correlation Between Republican Vote for Governor and Ward Support for Proposal. Selected City Referendum Issues*

Issue	Correlation	Adopted	N
1. Lower charter tax limit†	−.833	No	9
2. Create segregated funds for each major city function	−.683	No	9
3. Increase local improvement bond limit	.984	No	9
4. Authorize council to issue bonds "for any purpose"	.884	No	9
5. Water system improvement bonds	.700	No	9
6. Housing authority ordinance	−.616	Yes	9
7. Create independent board for city hospital	.950	Yes	9
8. Designate 20 per cent of hospital for use of osteopaths	−.816	No	9
9. Liberalize retirement system for police and firemen	.817	Yes	9
10. Change election of council to at-large	.967	No	9
11. Salary raise for council	.650	No	9

* *Critical values*:
1% .783; 5% .600.
† Council advocated "no" vote.

The two issues on which there was a negative correlation between the Republican vote and councilmanic support involved one with ideological overtones, and a second related to general socioeconomic class preferences. The first, No. 6, was an advisory vote on public housing and the second, No. 8, would have authorized osteopaths to practice in the municipal hospital. (The clients of this group of physicians usually center among the lower socioeconomic groups.) The atypical subject matter of these two referendums underlies the reversal in normal voting pattern of Republican support of councilmanic proposals.

The rank-order correlations only indicate voting tendencies and do not show the extent of commitment by the various blocs of voters. On seven of the measures, the vote was relatively close, falling within the 40 to 60 per cent zone. (Items 2, 3, 5, 6, 7, 8, and 9.) The other four were very one-sided contests. The effort to lower the tax ceiling (No. 1) lost in every ward, but by a larger margin in the Republican ones. The No. 4 item proposing increased bonding power for the council passed in only one ward, and it was predominantly Republican. Similarly, the effort to raise council salaries (No. 11) and to elect councilmen at large (No. 10) passed only in the three Republican wards.[3]

THE FRAILTY OF PRECINCT DATA

The correlations that emerged in the first three cities virtually disappeared in Gamma, as can be seen by scanning Table 13. Several factors were probably active in causing the difference. The demographic makeup of this city was peculiar in several ways: (1) Both economic extremes of the community lived beyond the city limits.

Not only were there two incorporated "executive-villes," but there was another suburb where large numbers of production employees lived. (2) The income levels within the city itself were distributed rather evenly throughout the living areas. The city was divided topographically by water bodies and natural barriers. Historically, the community had developed around rather distinct neighborhoods, which gradually grew together. In each of these areas, there was to be found a mixture of old and new

Table 13. Gamma: Rank-Order Correlation Between Republican Vote for Governor and Precinct Vote in Favor of Selected Referendums*

Issue	Correlation	Adopted	N
1. Storm-drain bonds	.229	Yes	18
2. Additional storm drain bonds	−.211	Yes	20
3. Ordinance to authorize issue of parking bonds	.104	Yes	20
4. Provide health and accident insurance for city employees	−.604	Yes	20
5. Reduce working hours of firemen†	−.785	Yes	18
6. Increase salary for municipal judge	.114	Yes	20

* *Critical values*:
  N = 18   1% = .564
           5% = .399
  N = 20   1% = .534
           5% = .377

† Formal council approval only, a majority of councilman and the manager actually opposed the proposal.

housing. This somewhat unusual pattern was very clearly seen in the voting records. While Alpha and Beta each had a number of precincts that habitually voted between 80 and 90 per cent Republican, a return of 70 per cent in Gamma was extremely rare. There were a few heavily Democratic precincts, but most of the areas fell within the 40 to 60 per cent range.

The mixed character of the Gamma precincts was dramatized when descriptive data were sought on the various areas from a local newspaper reporter. As a long-time resident steeped in local history, he would begin discussing each neighborhood by relating its distinctive reputation. However, under cross examination he always revealed that these distinctive qualities were characteristic of the city in 1910 or 1920. Invariably he concluded that the neighborhoods had since lost their identity and were now something of a hodgepodge.

In brief, this more homogeneous city did not lend itself to the rank-order correlation instrument. There were too many precincts hovering around the midpoint and shifting back and forth. However, these shifts, when carefully studied, suggested factors at work that influenced the correlations. Some neighborhoods, with distinctive features, shifted their referendum votes from election to election in a manner not found in other cities. Their voting records were traced and the results indicated some real limitations in the use of partisanship as a socio-economic index.

Three neighborhoods will be singled out for some attention. We must speak of neighborhoods rather than precincts, for the precinct lines were redrawn four times during the ten-year period. However, by segmenting the city into larger blocs, the precinct records could still be

used for limited analysis. The three areas were (1) a
working-class district, (2) an area that was developing with
new, modest homes, many of which were being purchased
by production workers, and (3) an area formerly an ethnic
neighborhood, but now containing a large number of
older persons, not necessarily identifiable ethnically.

Taking them in reverse order, let us first consider the
old ethnic neighborhood. This was a Republican area,
but it was also the outpost of intransigent opposition to
council proposals. In the six referendums listed in Table
13, this area was responsible for a total of 22 out of a total
of 116 precincts voting. If we segment the precinct returns
in each election by quartiles, 15 of the 22 were in the
lowest quartile of "yes" votes and 4 were in the second
lowest quartile. Thus on only three occasions was a precinct in this area above the city-wide average in its predisposition toward favoring a proposal.

This would suggest that among the most important
proponents of a caretaker type of government are the
retired citizens on modest fixed incomes. Such persons
were predominantly Republican in Gamma, but because
of their ethnic makeup Democratic in Beta and Delta.
This pattern therefore gave support to the correlations
between a Democratic vote and a negative vote on referendums in the latter two cities.

What of the voting behavior in the second neighborhood, the new development of modest homes? Two of the
three precincts in this area were Democratic and one was
usually Republican. All three supported the storm-sewer
bonds by the highest margin of any area in the city. The
reason was obvious: This was one of the areas that needed
the facility badly. On the parking-bond ordinance, all
three precincts shifted to the opposition. On the issues
regarding city employees, the precincts divided along

party lines with the Democratic precincts favoring the improved benefits and the Republican precincts opposing them. This was obviously an area where property taxes bore heavily on the mortgage holders, and so the result was rather unexpected. In the other two cities where similar issues were on the ballot, the Democratic precincts usually opposed increased benefits for city employees.

If the factor distinguishing the Democratic from the Republican precincts in this newly developed area was union membership, this may also have explained their behavior in referendum voting. The unions were better organized on local issues in this city than was the case in the others. City elections coincided with national elections and it was easier to get working-class citizens to the polls. The AFL-CIO council supported the city employees' claims for fringe benefits. Their demands carried in the working-class district (the third area specified above), and may have influenced the outcome in the new development area. The union also favored the parking plan, and it, too, carried in the working-class district. But, as we have seen, it lost in the Democratic precincts of the new development. Thus, even if labor was the factor, the unions certainly could not deliver the vote at will. The working-class area was also lowest in support of the sewer-bond issues, behavior that was more typical of the pattern in the other cities. In short, while working-class areas were generally the outposts of caretaker government in Alpha, Beta and Delta, there was some deviation in strongly unionized Gamma.

DIRECT DEMOCRACY AND THE POWER STRUCTURE

The material presented in this chapter points to a locus of power that has probably been underestimated in many of the studies undertaken during the vogue for community "power structure" analyses. No realistic assessment of the active or potential "power structure" of the community can be made without recognizing the enormous veto power that the electoral majority of a community holds as a result of the peculiarly American emphasis upon the referendum. In a great many cases involving the nonroutine expenditure of money, the American city council *must* go to the people for a direct vote, especially where capital outlays are concerned. In home-rule states, the same general procedure is used for changes—often very small changes—in the substantive powers of the council through the process of charter amendment. Because much legislation is written directly into charters, many policies that in other nations would be matters for the decision of the council or the executive are voted on directly in the United States.

It is one thing for a power elite, if it exists, to make vital decisions in the secrecy of someone's sumptuous recreation room (as Hunter saw things in Regional City), quite another for that group to convince a majority of voters to permit the elite to rule. Well-established tradition often makes it impossible for the leadership to circumvent the legal rules of the game—rules that require direct voting on major (and many minor) issues. In order to dominate, then, it is necessary for the leaders to engage in the time consuming and uncertain business of propagandizing the general citizenry in order to sell their program.

In our study, the leadership in Alpha was able to secure popular approval of its position each time it went to the polls. The Gamma council's proposals were nearly always adopted during our study period, but the pattern of support was so erratic that it would be difficult for a policy leader to know how or where to pitch his appeal. The council had much less success in the other two cities, however. The Delta council, knowing it had a low-tax constituency, nonetheless felt compelled to ask the voters for additional money from time to time, and nearly always lost. In Beta, the realtors had the voters with them more often than did the council majority. Yet, the former could not be called members of the apex of a power pyramid by any existing definition of a "power elite" known to the authors. The realtors' basic program was to oppose all decision for action. In other words, there appeared to be well established and prevailing community values that placed definite limits on the discretion of the leadership.

SUMMARY

The findings of this chapter may be stated briefly. Major support for measures referred to the people by the councils—measures involving innovations, increased financial burdens, or questions of general support for the council as a legislative body—came from the higher socio-economic sectors of the cities. Opposition to these measures was greater in working-class districts, and when these areas also constituted ethnic neighborhoods, opposition was probably reinforced. Finally, there was some indication that caretaker preferences were held by retired citizens who were living on modest, fixed incomes.

Because a portion of the analysis relied upon party voting patterns, an additional observation is indicated. The Republican party has traditionally opposed centralization of policy-making and consequently has favored strong local government institutions. While this outlook can be rationalized in terms of economic class interests, it may be that the principles of local self-government attract persons to the Republican ranks who do not fit the economic stereotype. Thus the high correlations between Republicanism and support of the council may be less a function of economic interests than of shared values. It may be that if our tools were refined and comparisons were made between income and support for the council, the correlations would be lower.

NOTES

1 This may also have been an example of "political alienation," described by Wayne E. Thompson and John E. Horton, "Political Alienation as a Force in Political Action," *Social Forces,* Vol. 38 (March, 1960), 190-195. Thompson and Horton point out that the referendum is the only opportunity for those who feel politically powerless to have a clear chance to participate in a policy decision. Their findings indicate that those who feel "alienated" have a greater tendency to vote "no" on referendums than the rest of the population. For further discussion of political alienation see Melvin Seeman, "On the Meaning of Political Alienation," *American Sociological Review,* Vol. 35 (December, 1959), 783-791. Murray B. Levin and others, *The Alienated Voter: Politics in Boston* (New York: Holt, Rinehart and Winston, 1960); Elmo Roper, "New York Elects O'Dwyer," *Public Opinion Quarterly,* Vol. 10 (Spring, 1946), 53-56; Arthur Kornhauser and others, *When Labor Votes* (New York, University Books, Inc., 1956) .

2 The first of the issues involved the lowering of the council's discretionary tax limit, while the second would have created a number of segregated funds, thereby removing much flexibility from the budget-making process.

3 In addition to these eleven referendums where significant correlations developed, five others were tested in which no significant pattern emerged. These issues were (1) authorization of payment of all black-topping from the general fund; (2) establishment of an electric-utility sinking fund; (3) authorization of issuance of water improvement bonds; (4) authorization of the leasing of the hospital to a private nonprofit association (5) liberalization of the fire and police pension system (first vote). The last of these issues failed the first time and passed a second time only with stronger support from the Republican wards. While the authorization for water-improvement bonds passed with uniform support, the actual vote on the bonds found the more Democratic districts voting "no." The correlation appears on Item 5 in Table 12.

Chapter VI

The Main-Street Merchants

Robert and Helen Lynd's Middletown (Muncie, Indiana) studies[1] and Kenneth Underwood's investigation of Paper City (Holyoke, Massachusetts),[2] were not centrally concerned with the decisions of local government. But both went sufficiently into the matter to conclude that political systems had developed that systematically excluded the possibility of local solutions for pressing social and political problems. These two studies may furnish a point of departure for the next three chapters, which are concerned with the efforts of the four cities to meet their problems.

The Lynds contrasted the symbols of politics that lauded the virtues of local, close-to-the-people government with the facts as they interpreted them. They saw an essentially corrupt government whose officials were concerned with personal patronage and gain and who were uninterested in problems of public policy. The issues that the community faced in 1925 remained unsolved in 1935. The polluted river wending its fetid way through the city, becoming more vile and stinking with each passing summer, was the symbol of civic ineptitude. In the crowning debacle, the city could not even extricate itself from its own sewage when the Federal government offered to build and pay for the needed treatment plant. It could not even mobilize consensus to accept money. This massive impassiveness was encouraged and supported by an upper economic stratum, which exercised just enough control over the confusion of local politics to prevent any harm to business interests.[3] An effective local government might have been a threat to this elite dominance of welfare and labor policy. Consequently, the system rewarded a mayor of personal integrity with threats of jail, and made an ex-convict his successor.

Underwood found the same economic class presiding over a similar type of government in Paper City. At least this was true in the period contemporary with that of the Lynd study. Patronage and low taxes were the grist of local politics. The economic elite tolerated patronage politics as long as it did not result in taxes that pressed upon profits. This type of activity diverted the local politicians, who might otherwise become concerned with issues, a preoccupation that might result in even greater tax increases.

In many respects these are the shortcomings of city government in America, which have been decried from the time of Lord Bryce. The findings of contemporary research in local government usually modify, but sometimes confirm, this picture. The prewar studies identifying pyramidal community elites—as in the works of Lynd and Warner—reached a postwar peak in the assertions of Floyd Hunter, but the power structure model is currently undergoing extensive criticism, as was noted in Chapter I. The criticism of simplistic power structures may reflect less on the accuracy of the earlier studies than on the changes in the urban milieu, foremost of which have been: the professionalization in the administration of welfare and labor programs and their establishment on an intergovernmental basis; the nationalization of corporations, which has diminished the number of locally rooted economic elites;[4] the erosion of politically identifiable ethnic blocs; and the growing political sophistication and economic security of rural-to-urban migrants. Thus the interests and bases of the earlier economic elites, which were frequently of industrial origin, have passed from the scene. The content of urban politics has largely shifted from considerations of welfare and labor conflict to problems emanating from changing technology, national housing policy, a rising standard of living, and a rapid rate of increase in urban population.

In this new urban politics of land-use controls, transportation management, urban renewal, and the provision of a variety of consumer services, the stakes of the economic-producer class may still be significant, but they are relegated to a lower level of importance. In the chapter on leadership recruitment above, it was pointed out that the examples of egress into public office from every class in the community occured in one city or another. In addition, it was stressed that representatives of lower-status groups were not necessarily recruited as pawns of "elites." However, the process of leadership recruitment was not considered in the context of concrete policy decisions. One of our purposes in the next three chapter will be to trace the implications of the recruitment patterns already described.

Although the ruling elite of Middletown tradition may have passed from the scene in most cities, the Lynds' statement about the disparity between symbol and reality in local politics has not necessarily also disappeared. While this series of chapters might be titled "the politics of innovation," the phrase would contain an overtone of irony when applied to certain situations. The property tax still acts as a brake impeding municipal actions. This restraint is no longer applied from above by a powerful economic elite so much as it is from below, as the hard-pressed householder of modest income rebels at the costs of modern urban life. Perhaps the main factor that prevents the picture from being similar to that in Middletown is the aid that the cities receive from state and Federal governments.

In addition to elaborating the content of policy, we will consider the problems facing major sectors of the community in mobilizing support for their objectives. The principal groups to be discussed include the downtown merchants, neighborhood residential groups, industrial interests, and organized labor. These groups will be described as they interact with the local political institutions.

From the data on the recruitment of elective officials it is possible to distinguish between Alpha and Delta on the one hand and Beta and Gamma on the other with reference to the structure of politics. In Alpha and Delta, formal organizations successfully assumed the responsibility for recruiting and electing a majority of the city council. The councilmen elected by the Alpha Citizens' Committee and the Delta union organization did not always vote as a bloc, but they strongly influenced the general value orientation of their respective councils. While there was some organized recruitment of candidates in Beta and Gamma, there was no continuing organization of equal influence. These two patterns will be henceforth referred to as structured and unstructured.

One objective in describing the content of politics will

be to relate the importance of persons and institutions in policy development to the presence or absence of political structure. Does the role of the council, the mayor, the manager, the planning director and the interest groups vary between cities with structured or unstructured politics? Role will be differentiated according to initiatory leadership, continuing support, and the exercising of a veto. Initiatory leadership will refer to the introduction of a proposed policy or program related to a matter of public concern, continuing support to the mobilization of sentiment in furthering a resolution of conflict over an issue, and the veto function to the withholding of support so as to prevent the adoption of a proposal.

COMPETITOR-PARTNERS IN THE CENTRAL BUSINESS DISTRICT

As is the case among states, all cities are in many ways competitors: they compete for customers, industries, increases in the tax base, and prestige. While local patriotism may be a nearly universal trait, the concept of the desirability of growth as a prime ingredient of local pride is particularly common to American cities. Why a city needs to grow in order to be a better place in which to live is not entirely clear. Perhaps there is some psychic reward in knowing that others elect to live in the community in which one lives. Perhaps it is a survival of the frontier spirit, when growth symbolized the creation of civilization out of the wilderness. To some city dwellers, however, the rewards of growth are much more tangible. It is with this group that we are now concerned.

For the downtown merchant, the question is not just one of growth, but of assuring that the central business district will benefit from any growth. Thus competition operates on three levels. There is competition for industry with more remote cities, with the surrounding fringe for commercial development and control of the physical environment and tax base, and among the merchants in the CBD itself. One of the main responses to the threat from the fringe has been a re-examination of the downtown area. If the traditional core commercial area is to compete with fringe development, revitalization measures are necessary. Revitalization spelled out means improved traffic flow, additional parking, and physical rebuilding. All four cities made some efforts in the first two directions. The battle of the parking meters had been fought and won in all the cities by 1950. The establishment of off-street parking and one-way streets took place during the study period. Someone in all the cities at least dreamed of a revitalized commercial core. These grander plans were in a varied state of realization when the study period closed. Generally the earlier period was characterized by superficial palliatives in response to the postwar auto congestion. In the later phases of the development of downtown policies, more and more complex solutions seemed to be needed. As the dimension of the problem became more apparent, the public generally or, at least, the city governments became more directly implicated.

It will be necessary to treat each city separately, as the pattern of responses to "the downtown crisis" were quite different. However, several generalizations are in order about the interests involved. In the first place, the downtown interests were not a unified group. In one sense every store and every owner of a separate parcel of land is a discrete interest when it comes to the actual application and administration of a downtown policy. Traffic patterns, parking lots, and condemnation proceedings have such diverse effects that each proposal exposes the stresses and strains among those concerned. However, general declines in retail sales volumes prove very effective in pointing out the existence of a common interest.

Of the four cities Alpha went through the most complete cycle in downtown programs, from parking meters to a $13,000,000 redevelopment plan calling for recasting the physical environment of most of the downtown area. The parking-meter stage caused little controversy, but the initiation of one-way streets brought a spirited debate. When it became apparent that traffic congestion was a problem, but one to which there was no solution agreeable to all downtown merchants, the council proceeded to develop a policy and to find ways to secure its acceptance. An outside engineering firm was called in to make a traffic study. Although its representatives devised a plan that nearly duplicated the one already designed by the city engineers, the outside concern gave the weight of the "independent expert" to the council decision.

The opposition was able to delay implementation, however, and eventually the dissident merchants placed an alternative plan on the ballot by initiative. The controversy was prolonged largely as the result of an enterprising lawyer who welded the opponents into a dues-paying organization for which he acted as attorney. The general role of both the council and the city administration in this controversy appeared to be one of siding with the larger downtown faction. Their position was eventually vindicated at the polls.

Municipal parking lots began to appear in the other

cities once the downtown merchants were able to develop an organization to coordinate their demands upon city hall. Alpha was blessed with a fair private parking system. But the need was still substantial. The initiative for remedial action did not come from the merchants. Instead, the merchants of Alpha were often pulled by council leadership, which had grander plans than they for the commercial core.

The three principal sets of actors in the drama of Alpha's downtown redevelopment plan were a mayor, the principal property owners, and the merchants. The merchants' association was a typical one, thinking in terms of circus gimmicks, like prize weeks and merchandising stunts, to attract customers downtown. But the mayor and the major property owners were not typical.

The mayors of Alpha were nearer to being policy leaders than were their counterparts in the other cities. This was true despite an unpromising mode of election. The candidate receiving the highest vote for city council became mayor, which made it difficult for a person to run specifically for the office. As elections in Alpha were often issue-oriented, the mayor was likely to be the person who could draw support from several shades of opinion. Of course, his high vote in combination with a campaign involving issues enabled the mayor to act with a mandate.

The downtown property ownership was highly concentrated in Alpha. A family group, the Brinton-Lowes, controlled between 65 and 75 per cent of the downtown property. The Brinton-Lowe clan was financially prominent in every segment of the community's economic structure including real estate, banking, industry, and retailing.

About midway in our study period an attorney, John

Wells, became mayor. His father had been a substantial business man in the community. However, neither Mr. Wells nor his father was associated with the Citizens' Committee. This group did not endorse him in his initial campaign. His organizational support stemmed primarily from university faculty members. According to one man active in his campaign, Mr. Wells and his associates in developing their campaign asked the question, "What does Alpha need most?" As they surveyed the possibilities including education, cultural institutions, human relations, capital improvements, and the industrial base, it was decided that the central business district was in most need of attention. The selection was not guided primarily by an interest in gaining the support of merchants, according to the respondent. Rather it was felt that the community deserved a better central shopping area, higher quality stores, better restaurants: in brief, the orientation was toward a central business district that would "better serve the city" rather than simply raise sales for existing merchants.

According to a member of the Citizens' Committee, Mayor Wells did not initially have the confidence of many businessmen. Perhaps this explains why the Brinton-Lowe group, which also decided to pay some attention to the downtown, did not immediately work through the mayor. The group instead hired a consultant for $50,000, using its own resources plus small contributions from other downtown interests, to make a study of the central business district. However, the mayor in consultation with university personnel was able to persuade the Brinton-Lowe representatives to hire a firm that could be counted on to draft a comprehensive and bold plan. This may have been a crucial act of leadership on the mayor's part, for instead of a conventional parking and circulation study, the planning firm developed a radical, long-term plan that involved completely rebuilding the downtown area, creating a pedestrian island at the center, a traffic ring, and large parking areas: a striking departure from the existing physical arrangement.

When The Plan was first published it received negative reactions from the newspaper and most of the merchants. The Brinton-Lowe group and other sponsors made no attempt publicly to defend The Plan. Leadership in its defense fell to Mayor Wells, who supported it before any group willing to listen to him. The immediate result was to activate the merchants, who formed an organization, the Merchants' Association, to study alternative courses of action. A board of directors was appointed, one member of which was also a city commissioner and a supporter of The Plan. Few of the other board members held the same conviction.

The Merchants' Association undertook two courses of action. Members visited other cities actively working on downtown plans, and they brought in a series of consultants. The cities chosen for visits included a number in which radical remedial programs were being followed, and these examples gave implicit support for The Plan already suggested for Alpha. In addition, the university reference group guided the selection of consultants so that some of them would express ideas consistent with The Plan. Lastly, the merchants hired as executive secretary a person from a local university who had been among the original Wells supporters. The Mayor himself suggested this appointment. As a result of these events, the Merchants' Association Board of Directors arrived at the conclusion that some major redevelopment action should be undertaken, though not necessarily The Plan.

Once this commitment was made, The Plan was well on the way toward adoption, because there were no real alternatives. When the Board of Directors asked for a recommendation from its executive secretary, he was able to suggest The Plan as the only comprehensive study which provided details on how to proceed, and he could point out in addition that The Plan had the support of the major property owners and the city government. The merchants adopted this recommendation and at the same time broadened their organization to include all parties interested in the CBD. The first step of The Plan was instituted when a pedestrian island in the center of the city was created. The city bore half the cost and the adjacent property owners paid the other half through special assessment. This action represented a symbolic commitment of the downtown interests to The Plan. Tearing up the Main Street pavement probably meant that no turning back was possible.

As envisioned the completed plan would cost between ten and twelve million dollars over a ten- or fifteen-year period. The property owners were expected to bear two thirds to three quarters of the cost and state and Federal funds some of the remainder. Nevertheless, some sizable expenditures from the city's general fund were to be involved. While there would undoubtedly be political controversies over this matter in the future, the very initiation of The Plan indicated the feeling that it would continue to have the support of the majority of the city council.

The downtown redevelopment politics of Alpha contained several factors deserving special note for comparison with the experiences of the other cities. (1) The formal leaders (the mayor and at least one councilman) were actual leaders supplying key actions in introducing, coordinating and promoting the development plan. (2) The city council had a capital of public confidence enabling it to operate without the continual expectation of unfavorble public reaction. Earlier a local opinion poll had indicated public confidence in the council's ability to handle parking policy. While the statistical validity of the poll cannot be ascertained, it was accepted as valid by councilmen and strengthened them in their policy of taking on major decisions. In addition, there was the long tradition of local support for the council, of which the one-way street vote was but one illustration. (3) The property owners were united by the simple fact of virtual monopoly in ownership. This enabled the plan to be financed by special assessment if the private assent of the Brinton-Lowe group was obtained. (4) The downtown merchant group was the one that had to be convinced to support the project before redevelopment was possible.

BETA

Some councilmen assume the existence of a unity of objectives for the city and feel their election indicates the community has accepted the candidates' assessment of these objectives. They believe they have a mandate to vote their convictions. Other councilmen have a more pluralistic conception and look upon themselves as the vehicles for the expression of diverse interests. Behaviorally, they invite the public to work through them as delegates toward the achievement of a great variety of objectives. The concerns of "the people," rather than the solutions of problems, are the guides to action. For example, the solution to downtown traffic congestion through maximizing flow may be subordinated to consideration of the impact of such a policy upon individual merchants. The result of this attitude is often dilatory action and inconsistent policy.

In Alpha there were never more than two councilmen who regularly acted upon "delegate" assumptions. In Beta, this outlook characterized the majority. For every council decision to create a one-way street downtown, there was a subsequent one to reconsider the decision, sometimes resulting in a return to two-way traffic. In Alpha, adversely affected businessmen could win only two converts in the traffic-pattern controversy, and thus continuity of policy was preserved. In Beta nearly every councilman was a possible recruit for the aggrieved, even after the policy had been initially decided. While a one-way grid system was finally superimposed upon the downtown area, it came only after many false starts.

Efforts by the city council to provide off-street parking led to similar experiences. With each proposal for a lot location, objections were raised and the council retreated. A citizens' committee to study the matter was proposed by a leading merchant and the comittee plan was instituted over the objections of the private parking lot operators. An engineering firm was hired and subsequently a parking authority was formed to devise a rather ambitious $1,200,000 revenue bond program to be supported by meter revenues. This course of action was backed by the Chamber of Commerce, the newspaper, and the merchants, but was immediately attacked by the Low Tax League, an organization actively supported by many realtors and real-property interests. It objected to the removal of downtown property from the tax rolls, opposed the mortgaging of on-street parking revenues, and asserted that the total meter revenues might not be sufficient, thus jeopardizing general revenues. In addition, there was insinuations that the whole enterprise smacked of socialism. The Low Tax League challenged the authority of the city council in the court and forced the issue onto the ballot by petition. While the courts upheld the council, the voters did not.

Some councilmen interpreted their referendum defeat as a rejection of the means and not the end; consequently, parking continued to be a subject for governmental consideration. Initiative passed back to a group of downtown merchants. This group offered to buy parking-lot sites and clear them with their own funds, then sell the lots at purchase cost to the city. The private group could purchase without publicity and therefore acquire land more cheaply than the city could through condemnation procedure. This proposal received a scant council majority and the city proceeded to buy a few lots from current meter revenues. After several years the city built up its parking lots gradually and four years following the referendum defeat, the council again voted a revenue bond issue of a half-million dollars to accelerate acquisitions. The Low Tax League split on this issue. Some property changes had shifted the interests of the previous League leaders, the new bond issue was more modest, and with the gradual build-up of lots it would be supported by more meters. As a result, the prospective interest rate on this second venture was much lower than on the first one. The League effort to place the matter on the ballot for referendum failed. But the realtors who supported the League's efforts claimed subsequently, with substantial basis in fact, that they had saved the city money by opposing the first parking venture. The collapse of the second opposition effort indicated that much of its strength was based upon tax considerations rather than upon direct opposition to downtown interests or to the ideological implications of a municipal parking operation. But to a minority of this bloc, the principle of municipal lot operation remained an anathema.

In summary, downtown policies in Beta were initiated and promulgated by the merchants in an association. The principal difference from the situation in Alpha was the absence of any dependable leadership from the elected officials. Even the question of lot site selection was controlled by the merchants through their purchase proceedings. The council acted as a review board, but merchant recommendations were normally adopted. At the same time the council was not simply a rubber stamping group. The merchants never had more than a tenuous one-vote majority throughout the purchase program. The minority was a shifting group which objected to specific locations, opposed all lot installations, or harked back to the adverse public opinion exhibited by the referendum. But property tax considerations were the most constant element in all arguments of the opposition. Lastly, redevelopment of downtown Beta did not progress beyond parking and one-way streets. At the close of the study period, consideration was being given to the construction of a new access route into the downtown area. The biggest CBD deficiency, a major railroad crossing on the main street, continued to create massive traffic tie-ups.

It should be pointed out that the downtown policies of Beta were bogged down so long as the council exercised major jurisdiction. The parking program really got under way when the merchants' association pre-empted the leadership. To be sure, council consent was obtained, but the real bargaining of price, location, and priorities took place largely outside the governmental structure. As we turn to Gamma we can see an entirely different course of action. Gamma benefited neither from a downtown propertly ownership monopoly and upper-class controlled council, as was the case in Alpha, nor from a merchant group capable of concerted leadership as in Beta.

GAMMA

Gamma was similar to Alpha in the ambitiousness of its long-range plans (reflecting the comparable quality of its professional planning staff) and similar to Beta in the difficulties experienced in implementing them (reflecting a similar tenor of public opinion and council leadership). The physical layout of Gamma played a large role in downtown politics. The city, located on a lake, was a terminal point for transportation routes. Consequently, state highways could be planned from the core of the city outward, rather than only about its periphery. These made promising commuter and customer thoroughfares. The problem was what to do with the automobiles once they had arrived in CBD. The one-way grid system proved politically feasible, but developing consensus on a parking program offered a real challenge to the political system.

The first traffic survey took place in 1946 under the aegis of the planning commission. It revealed that there was a need for 700 additional parking spaces. In 1949, a plan to provide these cleared the planning commission and in 1951 it achieved city council approval, but first another survey was felt to be in order because of the time elapsed. The new report indicated the deficiency had become 1,050 spaces. Subsequently, an $800,000 revenue-bond issue was voted by the city council in order to provide for 550 spaces, which was less than the 1946 "minimum need." This proposal was accepted by the voters and the lots were completed in late 1955.

When the planning commission originally recommended the $800,000 parking meter revenue bond issue, it immediately encountered opposition. The downtown merchants objected to the lot locations and the priority system. But unlike in Beta, the proposal was kept under the jurisdiction of a public body, rather than a merchants' group, so the issue had to be settled in the public arena. The affected property owners objected, fearing they would not get a satisfactory price. The realtors objected fearing loss of commissions on sales to the city, and the private parking lot operators objected for obvious reasons. Opposition coalesced around the latter group, which formed an organization that successfully petitioned for a referendum. This group soon included not only the lot owners, but also persons whose property would be taken for lots, and others who felt the project might lead to a burden on the general taxpayer. Subsequently, this latter fear was proved to be unfounded.

A revised proposal received not only the support of the downtown interests, but also of the newspaper (informally) and of organized labor. This latter endorsement was achieved by a labor representative on the council. (Interviews with labor leaders revealed that many rank-and-file members felt the merchants should pay for their own lots and not ask their customers to do so.) In a comparatively light turnout, the voters approved the entrance of city government into the parking business by a 5-4 margin.

Until after the parking referendum, the downtown

business interests were not well organized. The city administration (though not the council) had furnished the leadership in favor, and the merchants rallied to support as individuals when the parking plan came under attack. As the lot program began, it became evident to some that the city plan was not going to move quickly enough to bring the kind of resurgence in business some merchants and owners desired. Consequently, an organization was set up on the impetus of some property owners. (The ownership pattern in the downtown area was more widely dispersed in Gamma than in Alpha and 60 per cent or more of the property on several key blocks was held by a number of absentee owners.) As originally conceived, the downtown association was to bring owners and merchants together to promote a common cause. The membership of the merchants' group grew rapidly at first, for sales were declining as the result of local economic difficulties. The association moved slowly, but gradually evolved a plan to augment city efforts through a parking plan based on special assessments of downtown properties. While a definite plan was evolved envisioning a half-million-dollar matching contribution from special assessments, it became apparent at the hearings that the merchants, and not the property owners, were behind the scheme. As a consequence, the city did not proceed with an election.

The city administration worked out a revised plan in which the definition of the downtown was altered to include properties whose owners were more receptive to the use of special assessments. The new area plan modified the earlier city parking lot scheme by shifting the projected lots closer to the core of the CBD. The threat by a major chain to pull its store out of the downtown, the change in the position of the banks, and increased interest of a few property owners (vacant stores were increasing in number) helped bring the matter to a head. Even so, the special assessment election that followed resulted in defeat for the proposal.

Because a special assessment election does not utilize a secret ballot, it is possible to draw some conclusions from the vote. The opponents fell into three classes, as analyzed by city officials. (1) The absentee owners who were living on estate incomes. They presumably were unwilling to reduce present income in favor of the possibility of increased income in the future. Their position differed markedly from the local-resident owners in Alpha. (2) The grantors of long-term leases. Some owners had their property tied up for long terms and it was impossible for them to renegotiate their leases in order to recoup some of the costs of the special assessment. (3) The ideological conservatives, who favored private development of parking on principle.

At the end of the study period, Gamma had an even smaller parking program than Beta, but it had financed some major traffic improvements. These were not designed solely for the central business district, but in the long run they provided the basis for revitalizing it.

DELTA

The account of downtown activities in Delta can be brief, for little was accomplished in that city. The ward system of Delta produced a council that was not particularly concerned with downtown problems. Some effort was undertaken in the matter of traffic flow with the development of a one-way grid system in the downtown area and the construction of a bridge, which provided a new access route across a river that bisected the city. (The latter was accomplished primarily with Federal and state funds.) Perhaps the prevailing concerns of the council can be conveyed by two small illustrations. In the traffic system, a no-left-hand-turn ordinance was passed for the terminal intersection at the end of a bridge. An ex-councilman then asked for and was granted permission for special turning privileges allowing him to enter his business without having to circle several blocks. (This was later withdrawn when protests developed.) When the bridge was completed, the council entered into spirited correspondence with the state highway department over maintenance rights. The object of the city was not to have the state maintain the bridge, but the opposite. The city council wanted the patronage jobs at issue. (The state would pay the cost.)

Of the four cities, Delta expended the least effort in developing municipal off-street parking. Even so, the result was the provision of public off-street spaces equal in number to those in Alpha and Gamma. This was accomplished by the simple expedient of carving up a portion of a downtown park. (Such action the amenities-oriented councilmen of Alpha would undoubtedly have considered an outrage.) In the over-all parking picture Delta had its problems, however. There was no effort to finance additional facilities, with the exception of one small lot that was purchased on an installment plan. The council was not friendly toward municipal parking and as a result a number of merchants provided their own customer parking facilities. At the end of our study period, merchants organized to press for municipal parking, but at their first meeting, members of the city council were not encouraging. The general attitude seemed to be that parking was a merchant, not a taxpayer, responsibility.

SUMMARY

The central business district is a community resource. Policies concerning the physical organization and arrangement of CBD may serve a variety of ends. They may serve the convenience of customers through providing adequate parking, freely flowing traffic and an adequate variety of commercial outlets to satisfy a maximum variety of shopping needs in one centralized place. Policies may also be designed to insure maximum tax return from the CBD. The objective may be to maximize the profits of merchants. There are undoubtedly other values that may be served. Conceivably a design could be developed to satisfy nearly all these values. If such an objective is to be realized, policy must be made by the local government, for there is no other reliable mechanism for reconciling the inherent conflicts. The central business district can be developed as a community resource only by a council with sufficient power to reconcile and compromise competing claims, and one which is backed by a planning staff competent to furnish technical direction.

The difficulty with this analysis is that broadly representative councils are not likely to have the power to act. The experience of the four cities indicates that the city councils which were generally representative of many elements in the community (as in Beta and Gamma) were placed in just this difficult position. Councils in cities with more structured politics (as in Alpha and Delta) possessed the power to act but were also less broadly representative. However, representatives on any given issue may not be exclusively a function of the manner in which councilmen are elected.

The persons most immediately concerned with CBD policies were those with immediate pecuniary stakes. Consequently, it was not surprising to find the major initiative for action coming from the merchants and the CBD property owners. In all cities except Delta, continuing support for CBD programs developed among some public officials. The only significant response in Delta was the robbing of a city park for parking space. The role of the public officials in the other three cities differed one from the other and in each case this meant additional values were interjected to complicate the picture. In Alpha the mayor was not interested simply in serving the merchants and property owners. He also wanted to develop the CBD as a community resource. A similar set of values was interjected in policy development in Gamma through the professionally strong city planning office. In Beta the councilmen as individuals interjected low-tax considerations.

Stated in terms of the roles of the political actors, where politics was unstructured, groups outside the elected officials could and often did exercise a veto on proposed CBD policies. The property owners in Gamma and the Low Tax League in Beta did so. In Alpha and Delta no nonofficial group exercised such a veto.

It may be argued that this analysis is too formal. The "real power" did in fact lie with the Brinton-Lowe family in Alpha and the union organization in Delta. Even conceding this fact, the essential point of the foregoing analysis remains. Under structured politics the formal legislative body, whether the souls of its members were possessed by other groups or not, did assume responsibility for a policy that was actually carried out. In the unstructured cities either they could not agree on a policy or could not carry through once agreement was reached, and the effective arena of political action shifted outside the. legally constituted legislative forum.

NOTES

1 Robert S. and Helen M. Lynd, *Middletown in Transition* (New York: Harcourt, Brace and Company, 1937).

2 Kenneth Underwood, *Protestant and Catholic* (Boston: Beacon Press, 1957).

3 Lynd and Lynd, *op. cit.*, p. 321, and Chapter IX, generally.

4 C. Wright Mills, *The Power Elite* (New York: Oxford University Press, 1956); Norton E. Long, "The Corporation, Its Satellites, and the Local Community," in E. E. Mason (ed.), *The Corporation in Modern Society* (Cambridge: Harvard University Press, 1960, pp. 202-217); R. O. Schulze, "The Role of Economic Dominants in Community Power Structure," *American Sociological Review*, Vol. 23 (February, 1958), 3-9; William H. Whyte, Jr., *The Organization Man* (New York: Doubleday Anchor Books, 1956).

Chapter VII

The Local Interests of Labor

Local government has ceased, in most cases, to be the battleground for the competing claims of labor and management. The New Deal, World War II, and succeeding events have consigned welfare policies and the regulation of labor-management relations to the state and national governments.[1] Consequently, the local political activities of both labor and industry have become marginal. But given the general low key of politics in such cities as our four, even these marginal intrests may have significance.

Since the "big" issues for labor are handled outside the local community, it might be assumed that local labor leadership would be left free to take care of those interests which do remain locally controlled. Our study, however, did not bear out such an assumption. Labor as a local interest group operated under a severe set of handicaps. The union officials did not have the time, fiscal resources, or skill to develop a forceful action program. The full-time staff was largely committed to the maintenance of the organization and to carrying out activities that aided the national or state labor programs. Local activities had to come out of the spare time of labor leadership. This created the anomalous situation in which trade unions were scoring paper victories in Washington in the form of housing and urban-renewal legislation while failing at the local level, where these same policies were ultimately implemented.

Although the state or Federal government controlled most welfare policies, local jurisdiction over some welfare decisions remained in two places. First, the local administrative units for direct welfare were the counties, which dispensed funds and surplus commodities provided by the state and Federal governments. The county welfare board was chosen by the county board of supervisors which, in turn, consisted of representatives from the cities and townships. Thus the unions had to operate through city government in order to reach the county welfare board.

The second locally controlled welfare area was under the jurisdiction of quasi-public groups. These operations, financed through community chest and the hospital drives, were maintained in lieu of governmental action. Medical welfare was of particular concern to labor, and concerted efforts were made to gain access to the policy-making boards. Labor exerted more energy toward influencing decisions of these private welfare agencies than it did toward those made by city and county government. In each of the four cities the local labor council had a staff member who devoted a substantial amount of his time to working with the social agencies. Despite the importance of these activities, they had to be declared *ultra vires* to this study for practical reasons.

Because of their restricted resources in local politics, it is not surprising that most labor leaders were antagonistic to such reform measures as council-manager government, nonpartisanship, and at-large representation. The latter device was especially objectionable, for only a political system which is rooted in working-class neighborhoods can overcome labor's local organizational failings. A ward aldermanic system is more congenial to the aspirations of laboring-class persons than is one based on at-large elections for several reasons. It overcomes the handicap of habitual nonvoting among lower-income groups. Under the ward system, it makes little difference whether 10 per cent or 90 per cent of the electorate turns out, but under the at-large system, low-voting neighborhoods are placed at a disadvantage. Secondly, ward-election campaigns are cheaper and within the resources of working-class candidates. A personal effort may be all that is necessary in cities up to and beyond 50,000. Thirdly, because members of the laboring classes are numerous, the neighborhood representatives will also be numerous if the wards are drawn roughly according to population. Lastly, and perhaps most importantly, ward elections assure each neighborhood a spokesman and representative who is easily accessible to all. Considerations of access were also reflected by labor respondents in their objections to the manager plan. The professionalism of the manager often stood as a barrier to the objectives of labor. The manager was the person to whom the councilmen could often pass the buck, much to the annoyance of the citizen whose demands remained unfulfilled.

WAGES, UNIONIZATION, AND INDUSTRIAL OWNERSHIP PATTERNS

Before taking up the local political activities of organized labor, some descriptive material on the industrial complex and wages in the four cities is in order. The fluctuations in employment have already been set forth above. Alpha had the most stable growth pattern and least unemployment, while the other three cities experienced sporadic periods of high unemployment. However, there was little relationship between employment and real wages for production and manufacturing employees (see Table 14). Beta consistently had the highest wages for production workers, while Alpha and Delta were low, except for 1939 when Gamma was lowest. Wages of manufacturing employees generally were similar among the four cities, although Gamma tended to be lower in 1939 and Delta in 1947 and 1954.

Table 14. Real Wages for Production and Manufacturing Employees, 1939, 1947, 1954.*

	1939		1947		1954	
	Production workers	Manufacturing employees	Production workers	Manufacturing employees	Production workers	Manufacturing employees
Alpha	$2,189	$2,492	$2,956	$3,259	$3,500	$3,906
Beta	2,387	2,696	3,140	3,378	3,937	4,027
Gamma	2,006	2,230	3,193	3,354	3,694	3,985
Delta	2,139	2,417	2,996	2,889	3,501	3,789

* U.S. Census of Manufacturers.

The wage and salary scales bear no direct relationship to unionization in the four cities, at least when we use the percentage of large industries unionized as a measure of unionization. The unionization data, however, can be made more meaningful by first classifying firms by size

Table 15. Distribution of Manufacturing Labor Force Between Home- and Absentee-Owned Industries, Employing over 100, by Size of Firm

Size of Firm‡	Alpha*		Beta†		Gamma		Delta	
	Locally owned	Absentee owned	Locally owned	Absentee owned	Locally owned	Absentee owned	Locally owned	Absentee owned
100—250	11	6	10	3	10	2	8	4
251—500	3	3	7	2	3	0	3	0
501—1000	3	4	0	2	1	3	3	2
1001-3000	1	1	0	3	3	4	0	3
3000+	2	0	0	0	0	2	0	0
Total employees	14,300	6,050	4,020	8,230	7,450	16,900	4,190	6,730
Percentage§	70	30	33	67	31	69	38	62

* Data missing on one known firm.
† Data missing on three known firms.
‡ Self-reported figures appearing in a directory of manufacturers plus supplementary sources.
§ Percentage of total employees in home-owned and absentee-owned industries, employing over 100 persons.

and type of ownership. Data were collected on all industrial firms in the cities employing over 100 employees in the years 1956-57. The employment figures were all self-reported by the firm either to a state directory of manufacturers or to the local chamber of commerce. On the basis of these reports firms were classified by size. Each firm was also classified on the basis of home or absentee ownership. An industry was defined as home-owned if a majority of the board of directors lived in the metropolitan area. This information was gathered from the annual reports of corporations filed with a state agency.

The results of both classifications are reported in Table 15.

At the base of this table, percentages are given for the proportion of total employees in the surveyed firms employed in home-owned and absentee-owned firms. Alpha was different again. Approximately two thirds of the employees were in home-owned industries, while the ratio was reversed for the other three cities. The largest industries in Alpha were home-owned while the opposite was generally true in the other three.

This survey was undertaken in a year of high employment. A spot check of 1950 (for which data were more sketchy) indicated a similar pattern. The one exception was in Delta, where one home-owned firm had a very large employment in that particular year, which would have made the total employment in the two categories about equal.

Changes in ownership between 1950 and 1956 were also checked. It was found that some locally owned firms in Alpha, Beta, and Gamma were sold to outside interests. The trend was especially pronounced in Beta and Gamma; Delta had stability of ownership. New firms employing over 100 employees appeared during this period in all the cities but Delta. The number of industrial firms in the latter appeared to be fixed.

The firms were surveyed to determine whether they were unionized. In Delta, all but one company had a union. In Beta, six of the 13 firms in the 100-250 and one in the 251-500 class were nonunion. In Gamma four from the 100-250 and one from the 251-500 class were not organized. In addition, one large firm was characterized by the AFL-CIO officers as having a "company union." In Alpha seven small firms in the 100-250 range, one in the 251-500, one in the 500-1000 and one in the 3000 plus category were nonunion. Thus Delta had the highest percentage of plants unionized and Alpha the lowest.

With four exceptions (and these were small plants) all the nonunion shops in the four cities were home-owned. The nonunion shops in Alpha not only tended to be large ones, but also included several industries that had existed in local families for several generations. These industries were strongly identified with the community. Without exception, the larger absentee firms were unionized in all the cities. The old antiunion attitudes of owner-managers lingered on in our cities.

The final distinction pertaining to unionization in the four cities is that Alpha industries tended to be organized by old AFL unions and industries in the other three cities by CIO unions. While the pattern was not uniform, generally the United Automobile Workers and the Steelworkers were more active politically than the other unions.

ORGANIZED POLITICAL ACTIVITIES

Alpha, the least unionized of the four cities, was also heavily Republican. Labor political activity was slight, but one attempt, though unsuccessful, to gain representation on the city council was made in 1948. A slate of five candidates received labor endorsement and one of these individuals was a labor-union official. The unions taxed their treasury for two thousand dollars, nearly depleting their resources. The venture produced poor results, however, with the labor official coming in tenth in an election where the first seven were elected. One union-slate member was Geoffrey Post, who was re-elected. The other three choices finished at the bottom of the list.

No subsequent attempt was made to run labor-recruited candidates for the city council or to expend funds for local elections. One labor leader, who had been active in city affairs, told us that labor's ranks did not include individuals who could do as good a job as the incumbent councilmen. The council had pursued a policy of granting labor representation on most citizen committees and this appeared to satisfy the union leadership. The role of these union representatives was to guard the interests of specific labor groups. For example, during negotiation for the transfer of a bus franchise from one company to another, a union representative spoke for the bus drivers. Other typical union interests were a request that the city use union-made sewer pipe and that contractors pay union-scale wages. The union goals of Alpha did not include a distinct set of welfare objectives.

While organized labor in Beta was much stronger in the shop, local political aspirations of the group were nearly absent. Union leaders who were interviewed displayed nearly total ignorance of local electoral politics. The head of the labor council was not sure which city candidates, if any, had ever received union endorsement. Several officials were unaware that the elections involved use of a nonpartisan ballot. Although the city representatives to county government were directly elected by wards, no attempt was made to run candidates with the aim of influencing county welfare policies.

On substantive issues, the union council usually did take an official stand. Union officials felt that past reluctance of the council and voters to invest in capital improvements was making the city unattractive to new industry. They therefore supported every planned improvement, including school operating-millage increases, school construction bonds, downtown parking, a new city hall, urban renewal, storm-sewer bonds, and a public-health program in the county. However, the voting record of the city wards, in which large numbers of union members resided, indicates that the rank and file and leadership did not see eye to eye (Chapter V). The leaders apparently saw capital outlays as avenues for more jobs in the long run; the workers viewed them as tax increases. Here, then, we had a division within labor: the leadership leaning gently toward boosterism, the workers themselves toward the caretaker philosophy.

Labor activities in Gamma stood in distinct contrast to that in Alpha and Beta. While both the latter cities were heavily Republican, the two parties were evenly matched in Gamma. This may have encouraged local political activity. Most shops were unionized. Gamma had a large wartime influx of Southerners, which may also help explain the strength of the Democrats in that city. While both Beta and Delta shared in unemployment problems, only in Gamma was a concerted attempt made by labor to control county welfare policies in order to aid the plight of the unemployed. The union always endorsed and sometimes ran candidates for city council.

The unions were nearly always successful in having at least one candidate from their own ranks on the city council. Frequently, several others were elected with their endorsement. It is difficult to judge the impact of labor support. Many union-endorsed and supported candidates fared poorly, indicating that a candidate had to have more than labor backing.

While the Beta union leadership advocated municipal capital improvements, its recommendations were not backed by the bulk of the membership. In Gamma, the leadership was much more aware of the attitudes of the rank and file members. Retired and unemployed workers expressed their objections to tax increases directly to the labor council. Although the leaders desired to join in supporting civic projects, they were constrained from doing so by membership objections. Labor council members, besieged by cross pressures, frequently responded by taking no action. This was the case, for example, in an urban renewal project. Many of the residents of the proposed urban renewal area were union members who were retired or nearing retirement. While the union leadership initially favored the idea of blight eradication, it also felt a responsibility toward its senior union members. As a consequence, it took no stand on renewal. The silence of the Gamma union leadership on many city policies was not a function of disinterest or ignorance, but of its inability to find consensus among its constituents.

In discussing labor politics in Delta, a distinction must be made between the activities of the city employees' union and those of the general labor council. The city employees' union was the nucleus of the political organization. Because it drew its principal political support from lower-income groups, its policies were generally compatible with views of members in unions affiliated with the labor council. This situation made it less necessary for the latter group to devote its energies and resources to municipal politics. There was, however, no formal connection between the two groups.

The employees' union organization was primarily interested in the wages, hours, and working conditions of city employees, but it also followed a low-tax policy. Its two objectives were, of course, contradictory. At times this led to severe internal dissension within the employees' political organization.

Policy concerning the administration of a city hospital offered an example. Use of the hospital for a patronage outlet had made its operation so costly that a tax subsidy at one point seemed the only way toward fiscal solvency. (This issue is discussed at length in Chapter XII.) The patronage-caretaker ambivalence also developed in Delta in connection with employment in the streets, fire, and police departments. There was a tendency to overstaff for patronage purposes on the one hand and to economize on salaries for top supervisory personnel in an effort to redress the balance.

Ostensibly, there should be no reason for unions to object to the professionalization of city management. As taxpayers, union members have reason to be as interested as anyone in efficiency and economy. Unions have long objected to the patronage system, where it has existed in the shops. To the extent that professionalization is accompanied by provisions for job security and regular pay increments, unions, as such, have reason to support profesional standards for city employment. Yet in fact this was not the case. Patronage may well be the only cementing agent available to labor that can be used to put together a political organization. The civic organizations of the upper-income groups have an advantage here. They have a greater supply of organizational talent, and in addition, the talent is often subsidized. Civic participation is part of the cost of doing business for some firms. Labor unions have little spare talent; they only have the votes. Patronage apparently is the most reliable way to mobilize an organization to bring these votes to the polls. The great nineteenth-century bosses found this to be so, and despite vast changes in our economic and welfare systems, patronage still seems to be very effective under some conditions.

PUBLIC HOUSING

Public housing was the one welfare area in which labor took a strong position regardless of cost implications. Immediately following World War II and extending through the Korean conflict, there was a pronounced shortage of low-cost housing in all four cities. In each of them, the issue of public housing was raised and organized labor was active in bringing the matter before the citizens.

Shortly after World War II, Alpha acquired 100 emergency dwelling units from the Federal government. A citizens' study committee was appointed in 1948. It reported that there was dire need for 300 to 500 additional housing units for families that could not afford to buy housing at existing prices. The chairman of the committee stated that some kind of industrial or philanthropic subsidy was needed. The city council took no action. The following year the possibility of urban redevelopment with newly provided Federal aid was explored. The study committee advised against this course of action, because clearance of slums would have necessitated public housing for the displaced. A minority on the committee urged further exploration of public housing possibilities, but the city council adopted the majority report and continued consistently to support this decision. It rejected a petition submitted to it the following year urging a comprehensive survey of housing. It abolished rent control without waiting for action by a study committee, which eventually issued a *post factum* report advising retention of control. A majority of the Alpha city council was ideologically opposed to Federal control or subsidy of housing. Demonstration of need was considered irrelevant. Labor was represented on these various study commissions, but its role was never prominent. Principal opposition to the council majority was furnished, not by union leaders, but by citizens and groups interested in welfare.

The Beta city council never articulated the hostility to rent control and public housing that Alpha's did. Instead, it displayed its usual tendency to vacillate under the cross-pressures of various groups. At the same time, there was never a clear council majority that favored either public housing or rent control. The question of public housing was first raised by a prominent Republican who later became an important local figure in the 1952 Eisenhower campaign. He was responsible, with union support, for having a study commission created. The commission was composed of several teachers, a physician, a minister, and a number of businessmen, some of whom were known for their liberal views. Few of the members were prominent in community affairs. Their report to the planning commission recommended a 200-unit project. The planning commission received the report with something less than enthusiasm and passed it on to the city council without recommendation.

While the prominent Republican who initiated the study continued to give it public support, the other major favorable support came from the unions. The newspaper was cool; the realty group, opposed. The latter announced it would petition for a referendum if the council approved the project. After several months of delay, the council announced that it would put the question on the ballot. It never did do so, however, and the issue was soon forgotten and never even accorded the dignity of a formal burial.

Labor's quiescence on the referendum issue is probably

explained by its experience with rent control. At the end of 1950, the Federal rent-control law shifted the burden of decision to local governments, leaving to them the question of whether or not to continue controls. The Beta city council first delayed action and then, following re-peated petitions from labor, put the issue on the ballot. Rent control was decisively defeated. Thus, on both issues the city council escaped the necessity of a decision. While labor could accuse the council of killing the issues by passing the buck, the individual councilmen could reply that the voters, not they, had decided.

The Gamma city council could never completely avoid the housing issue because labor always had at least one representative on that body. Prior to the Korean conflict, a labor councilman initiated a housing study. An in-genious device was formulated by the council: it had the realtors and the unions conduct a joint survey. The re-sulting report, understandably perhaps, was indecisive. Nevertheless, the labor councilman introduced a proposed ordinance to establish a housing authority. The measure was never brought to a vote by the council.

Some wartime housing had been inherited by the city and shortly after the public housing issue was raised, a Federal agency moved Negro families into what had been an all-white Federal housing unit. The reactions in the neighborhood were immediate. Although the city admin-istration had no authority in the matter, city officials were bombarded with telephone calls. One councilman reported that he had had seventy calls a day for a week. Because most Negroes in the metropolitan area lived outside the core city, public housing became identified with the entrance of more Negroes into the city.

Subsequently, the Chamber of Commerce undertook a

survey of low-cost housing. While this survey bore no
immediate fruit, the various groups concerned with housing conditions eventually coalesced in support of the
urban renewal project described below. The project did
not include public housing. Despite the relative strength
of labor in Gamma, the question of Negro living areas
and one decision by a Federal official probably foreclosed
the possibility of public housing in the city.

Delta was the only city in which a majority of the
city council favored public housing. As in the other four
cities, the issue had the support of organized labor.
Indeed, this was the one important issue on which the
Delta central labor council actively entered into municipal politics. The authorization for a housing authority
was submitted to a public referendum as was required by
law. It received a favorable response from the voters by
an eight to seven majority. The Delta city council then
adopted the measure by a five-four vote, which was apparently a fairly accurate numerical reflection of community sentiment.

Even though the housing authority measure was approved by the council and the voters, it was effectively
blocked by a mayoralty veto. As the voting analysis in an
earlier chapter revealed, Delta's mayor had a constituency
different from the combined councilmen. The candidate
most favored by the Republican and upper-middle-class
areas invariably won this post, for the employees' union
made no serious effort to control the office. (This was one
of the very few issues in the decade where the mayor
played a major policy role.) The inflationary nature of
public housing during wartime was the reason given for
the veto. The unions spent $2,000 to bring in a staff
member from the Federal Reserve Board to contradict

the mayor's reasoning. The mayor countered with his own expert, held fast, and carried the day. His action may have been influenced by middle-class citizens who feared invasion from a nearby city with a much larger Negro population. With the acceleration of private housing following the Korean war, the housing shortage was eased and there was no further attempt to build a public housing project.

URBAN RENEWAL

The Federal Housing Act, which sets forth the national policy on urban renewal, embraces a variety of goals. Despite the diversity of purposes, urban renewal legally incorporates objectives that might be characterized as welfare aims. Organized labor has been one of its many supporters at the national level.

At the local level in these four cities, organized labor was not prominent in initiating or promoting urban renewal and rehabilitation projects; indeed, on several occasions it was in active opposition. Since the projects, regardless of sponsorship, affected the lives of union members and usually involved the union leadership at some stage, it seems fitting to consider the subject of urban renewal as one of the local interests of labor.

In surveying the interest groups in the four cities it was difficult to find any that were concerned about these projects, yet three of the four cities were well on the way to completing a renewal or rehabilitation program as our study was completed. The building industry was in favor of construction of any kind; the banks gained some opportunity for investments. But this about exhausted the list of those deriving direct pecuniary benefits. In these four cities there were no individuals of the Zeckendorf type who profit through supplying the skill, knowledge, and driving force in renewal efforts. If one were to single out any group primarily responsible for initiating projects it would be the professionals on the city payroll.

The urban renewal projects are the fulfillment of the administrator's dreams. To the city manager and the planning director, they offer an opportunity to become identified with a major city project in which administrative magic may be performed through showing the city council how a local blemish can be removed for very little local money. By crediting normal city expenditures to the local contribution for a renewal project, the professional can often convince tax-sensitive officials that urban renewal offers a prime opportunity for making a start on something that is generally popular: the elimination of slums.

The second group that came to the aid of the projects once begun were the professional welfare workers. Frequently, these persons were either on state or quasi-public organization payrolls, but because their lobbying for urban renewal was often seen as a nonpolitical, professionally sanctioned activity, they were permitted to rally to the support of the projects without retribution by opponents or civil service commissions.

There was, however, no private interest group that provided the natural basis for public support. The deficiency was, in each case, formally remedied through appointed advisory committees, but their role was usually passive. Certainly the citizens in the blighted areas did not provide organized support. In the first place, the low-status, inarticulate persons in the affected neighborhoods are usually not equipped to organize their interests effect-tively. Secondly, urban renewal affects redevelopment-area dwellers differently. Many fear economic loss rather than gain by the projects. There are social objections as well. Neighboring patterns are threatened with disruption. Residents fear rent increases and possible relocation in neighborhoods with life styles different from their own.

Again, the four cities responded differently to the idea of urban renewal. During the study period, Alpha and Gamma received approval from the Federal agency for urban rehabilitation or renewal projects. Beta was initiating such a project at the close of the study period. Delta had made no effort. However, this variation in pattern did not reflect differences in the physical conditions in the cities, as these could be detected by inspection or general inquiry. No comparable data exist other than the 1950 housing census, which is not very satisfactory, since its figures pertain to entire cities and do not indicate the degree of concentration of blighted dwellings. (Of course, even when blight is scattered, Federal renewal funds may be used to combat the condition.)

Table 16 shows that the number of substandard dwellings was roughly comparable in the dilapidated category and in the total units not dilapidated and with hot water and toilets. Beta had the largest number of congested units and Alpha the least. Gamma and Delta had the greatest quantity of wartime and immediate postwar construction, and Gamma had the lowest number of units constructed prior to 1920. From these admittedly superficial data, the slight statistical variations gave no indication that housing conditions existed that would make renewal or rehabilitation less desirable in Delta than in the other cities.

Table 16. Selected Housing Characteristics: Four Cities*

	Alpha	Beta	Gamma	Delta
Total dwelling units reported	17,000	16,200	15,300	15,500
Percentage with hot water, toilet, and not dilapidated	75	76	78	78
Percentage dilapidated	4	6	5	5
Percentage of units with more than 1.01 persons per room	6.6	10.3	8.9	8.7
Percentage of units built 1940 and later	4.8	4.1	12.2	11.6
Percentage of units built prior to 1920	75	75	60	74

* Source: United States Census of Housing, 1950.

In Gamma, the initiative for an urban renewal project came from an administrator in the city government. The planning staff selected the area to be used and computed the manner in which the city contribution could be handled in terms of school, street, and other improvements—improvements that were scheduled to be undertaken in any event. City officials, especially members of the planning staff, were active in soliciting support for the project from any group that would listen to them. The major negative reaction came from the people residing in the proposed project area where indigenous opposition leadership developed. These leaders specialized in highly emotional appeals, demonstrated poor knowledge of the actual operation of the plan, and often rallied support by assertions that had litttle or no relationship to the project itself. The city administrators were baffled by their inability to discuss the plans in specific terms. In their offices and at public meetings, they were often met with loaded questions that would have given Solomon uneasy moments: Isn't this the way they do things in Russia? Isn't local government dead if all the important decisions are made in Washington? Do you believe in the American Way? What did you do while I was fighting for our country during the war?

The people who were asking these questions were from an all-white neighborhood consisting of families of various ethnic backgrounds. There were previously no social organizations common to this particular geographic area. The organization that formed to oppose the renewal project apparently offered the first experience in organized political activity to many of those who participated. Perhaps some of the random characteristics of their questions reflected a lack of experience in organizational techniques. Aside from the generalized criticisms of the project, there were also more specific objections. Most residents resented the use of the term "slum," which appeared on one of the Federal forms. Local officials tried to dissociate themselves from this term, but without great success. A portion of the residences were owner-occupied. These residents had specific objections. The elderly persons did not want to make a major neighborhood change late in life, and, in addition, to many, relocation meant resumption of mortgage payments on higher priced homes. Many of these retired persons probably believed that owning even a shack outright was preferable to making monthly payments on a project "pillbox." Generally, those persons who owned or were buying homes had chosen the project area for the very reason that it furnished cheap shelter. The fact that it was substandard in the eyes of the community was of less importance to them than the fact that it offered the least expensive available housing.

The city officials were prepared to address themselves to the concrete economic problems. But instead of questions involving dollars and cents, they were invited to discuss communism and war records. This kind of appeal, from the specific to the highly general, occurs with such frequency in municipal politics that it needs additional attention. For example, there was a striking similarity between the activities of renewal opponents and the efforts of those opposed to the manager form of government as reported in other studies. Perhaps this was another expression of "political alienation": people who generally feel politically impotent lashing out in opposition to proposals that seem to threaten to remove decision-making even further from them and making their stand from emotional, nonrational bases. These persons sometimes seem to organize protest movements as an emotional catharsis for themselves, or to "teach a lesson" to those who are presumably in power. The theory of alienation implies that the local political community contains festering sores of dissatisfaction, blocs of local citizens waiting for an opportunity to discharge the pent-up venom of their discontent.

Floro and Stene, in their study of manager abandonments, found that when the opponents to manager government were successful in abolishing the plan through a referendum, they tended to lose all interest in city politics. The successful protest appeared to satiate their political appetites. Actual control of city government was never sought.[2] Thus, in Gamma, the opponents of urban renewal carried the issue into a city election campaign for the council posts. They generally vilified all incumbent councilmen. Radio time was purchased and invectives were hurled in a fashion previously unheard of in Gamma election campaigns. The result was the defeat of three incumbents and the election of a leader of the project area protesters. Yet when the question of continuing the project came up for vote after the new council had convened, the renewal program received unanimous endorsement, even by the new councilman. Oddly, this vote was not followed by a new wave of agitation in the renewal area. The renewal opponents apparently felt satisfied by their election victory. The fact that they failed to affect renewal policy appeared to be less important than the fact that they had proved their political strength in a vote.

Throughout these developments the local labor council pursued a policy of neutrality. This neutrality was neither a function of disinterest nor of lack of identity with the project. The council was simply caught between opposing forces. A number of labor leaders favored renewal. It was a local source of jobs; it was designed generally to upgrade working peoples' residences; and it would make the city generally more attractive, a value prominently held by labor leaders in this area of chronic unemployment. However, the project area residents were mostly union members. The council could not ignore their protests. The result was that the labor council took no official position.

Urban renewal in Beta followed a pattern similar to that in Gamma, although the cycle began a little later.

Again, it was the professionals who initiated the idea.
The advisory committee was a favorably disposed, but
largely inactive group. The Beta experience did, however, differ in several respects from that in Gamma. In
the first place, the redevelopment area was inhabited
mostly by Negroes. As a self-conscious and easily indentifiable minority, it was a group in a poor position to
organize a protest.[3] Secondly, the income level of some
of the residents of the area was so low that relocation
presented special problems. Public housing was not a
possibility, for the real estate group announced it would
seek to defeat the whole project if that were made a part
of the proposal. Considering the impressive record of
political success of the real estate group, alternative plans
had to be discovered. Thirdly, the opposition that did
develop stemmed from nonresident property interests in
the area. One financial institution held nearly 150 mort-
gages on property in the area and there was some evidence
that it was exploiting home buyers. One respondent, at
least, reported that many "buyers" were permitted to
pay off little of the capital and were, in essence, making
nothing but interest payments on an almost undiminish-
ing mortgage.

The relocation problem was very difficult and was
solved in a novel way. Because there was community
resistance to geographic dispersion of Negroes, it was
considered necessary to relocate the families within the
redevelopment area. In several areas where total clearance
was planned, there were about 70 houses sound enough
to warrant preservation and removal to other sites within
the area. They served as the key to the relocation plan
worked out jointly by a citizens' committee and the city
administration. A financial pool was developed by local

banks and savings and loan associations on a nonprofit basis. Its funds were used to buy vacant lots in the rehabilitation area (there was considerable vacant land) and to move the seventy good houses onto new foundations. The buildings were supplied free by the city. This enabled the financial pooling organization to sell homes to the families in the area for a very low sum, including only the cost of the lot, moving, and foundation. This often meant a figure of around $4,000. With FHA mortgages, the monthly payments could be so low that even families on welfare could afford to buy them. Realtors who had promised to fight Federal public housing without giving quarter were willing to accept this local subsidy plan. Ostensibly the difference between the two was that the persons would now be buying their homes and therefore would have a stake in their maintenance. The basic realty interest in housing, of course, relates to commissions on ownership turnover or rental brokerage, commissions which are nonexistent in public housing.

Except for the solution of the relocation problem, the entire project was very much an activity of the professionals. The elected officials played a minor role. Several councilmen who were interviewed about the project had little knowledge of it. One councilman, for example, did not know whether the cleared land was to be used for residential or industrial purposes.

In Alpha the elected officials played a more prominent role. With a city council having a tradition of leadership and participation in policy-making, the administrator had much less freedom. As pointed out above, the council held a firm grip on public-housing and rent-control policies. Initially urban renewal was tied to the relocation of transportation routes and to industrial as well

as residential reuses of land. However, the Federal agency
vetoed any continuation of adjacent residential and industrial uses in the project area. This dampened the ardor
of some council proponents of renewal. The renewal area
residents in Alpha also reacted negatively to the first
announcement of the plan, the objecting groups bearing
a marked affinity to those in Gamma. In the face of continued resistance in the area, the project was gradually
scaled down from renewal to rehabilitation and the area
involved was diminished.[4]

Delta alone among the four cities never undertook an
urban renewal or rehabilitation project. We do not know
whether this lack of activity was a product of the type
of representation on the council or of the absence of
professionals in the public service at the top managerial
level. Of course, these factors are not independent variables, for the absence of a professional group in Delta
is related to the particular political demands that were
elevated to greatest importance in that city. Still, it can
be pointed out that Beta was in many ways similar to
Delta in policy orientation; both were guided by low-tax
policies. However, professionals had maintained a continuous if somewhat tenuous claim to employment in
Beta. They had aimed a consistent pressure for an increased capital improvement program and had had occasional successes. Urban renewal offered one of their best
opportunities for expression. The city employees of Delta
—almost all recruited from among the residents of the
city—were largely persons without aspirations for advance-
ment in the hierarchy of their professions, whether they
were city managers or engineers assigned to planning.
Consequently, they were more a docile group having no
real personal motives for pressing the city commission
into action.

Thus the story of urban renewal politics at the local level can be told virtually without mentioning organized labor as a supporting force. While labor accorded renewal its official approval in Alpha and Beta, this was more ritual than reality. There is no indication that the course of urban renewal would have been changed one whit had the unions remained completely silent. Only in Gamma were the unions seriously involved. And here, after initial support of the idea, the local labor council became neutralized through the objections of union member residents of the renewal area.

SUMMARY

Our earlier observations about cities with structured and unstructured political traditions hold valid for the policies discussed in this chapter as well. In urban renewal the vacuum of leadership under the unstructured conditions was not filled by the interest groups, as was the case in CBD policies. Rather it was the professionals in the manager's office and in the planning department who stepped into the breach. In both Gamma and Beta the professionals were largely left on their own initiative as long as they could demonstrate that the taxpayers would not be given a large bill. These administrators negotiated with the opposition groups, mobilized support, devised plans to remove obstacles and generally set the tempo of renewal policy. In Alpha and Delta this was not the case. Without a professional bureaucracy, Delta had no renewal policy. Alpha had the professionals, but the renewal project was continually cut back by the elected officials who were not warm to the basic philosophy involved, and who were preoccupied with other matters —primarily reconstruction of the central business district.

Similarly, with regard to public housing the councils of Alpha and Delta developed positions. In Beta and Gamma the councils ducked, dodged, or buried the issue and tried to avoid commitments. Probably the overwhelming majority of the councilmen in both of these cities were opposed to public housing, though a clear statement to this effect could not be expected of them. The institutional pattern that had developed in both cities was to avoid taking a stand on all matters, whether there was agreement or not. There is no necessity for councilmen to take positions if they have no joint stake in presenting a common image to the public.

NOTES

[1] There are, of course, exceptions. Medical welfare and direct relief are important in large cities, and police may be used to curb unions in smaller towns, especially in the South.

[2] Edward O Stene and George K. Floro, *Abandonment of the Manager Plan* (Lawrence, Kansas: Government Research Center, University of Kansas, 1953), Government Research Series No. 9.

[3] As this manuscript was being completed, a protest group was organized nonetheless, though the specific content of its objections was not ascertained.

[4] Renewal generally involves the clearing of land and removal of most structures, while rehabilitation stresses the improvement of existing structure and the removal of only those hopelessly deteriorated.

Chapter VIII

The Neighborhoods

A city of 50,000 people appears to be too large a political unit for the democratic processes to operate according to the grass-roots model of local government. This model, typified by the New England town meeting and incorporated into the mainstream of American democratic thought by the Jeffersonians, stresses the necessity of preserving primary relationships in the process of making local political decisions. Urbanization has rung down the curtain on that chapter of our history and has relegated this view of urban government to a romantic memory. Even though the urban neighborhood was looked upon by some as the vehicle for preserving this tradition, contemporary experience has not proved encouraging.[1] The research of sociologists has documented graphically the fact that geographic subdivisions rarely become viable social-political units in the modern urban setting, except in ghettoized areas. With this knowledge in mind, we did not expect to find spontaneous socio-political organizations arising in the neighborhoods of our four cities.

On occasion the neighborhood was the basis of organized political activity. For instance, in the previous chapter it was seen that the renewal neighborhoods did organize politically in opposition to threats to the *status quo*. But this is because they were the *affected areas,* not because they were homogeneous political-action units, and this was the typical pattern. While neighborhoods were not natural political units, geographic proximity did define a shared interest for specific policies, and this was usually the only occasion for neighborhood-oriented interest-group activity.

There were two partial exceptions to this. The neighborhoods of Delta came the closest to providing a general basis for socio-political institutions, though from every indication the legal system was more responsible for this survival than was the distinctive character of the neighborhoods. Thirty years before our study, when the ward lines were redrawn (after a brief trial with at-large elections), the boundaries of the ward unit were largely defined by ethnic lines. Three minority groups—Poles, Germans, and French-Canadians—lived within particular areas of the city. The at-large elections threatened the influence of their leaders and they combined to regain neighborhood representation. In the familiar pattern, the nationality groups also had their separate churches. Thus the old Delta ward neighborhoods represented a union of religious, social, and political institutions. Even in some native Protestant areas of the city, a particular church dominated the religious life of a ward. During our study, in at least one Protestant neighborhood, the councilman always was a member of a prestigeful Presbyterian church in that ward. In fact, the church lay organizations of Delta served as the principal hunting grounds of candidates seeking volunteer help during campaigns. In many respects, religious solidarity had outlived ethnic solidarity. For example, the French-Canadians no longer dominated their old ward and a man with a German name represented a "Polish" ward. (See Appendix for ethnic data.)

The other exception was in Gamma, where several neighborhood improvement associations existed in wealthier sections of the community. One of these neighborhoods was interested in maintaining certain physical characteristics, modeled after some of the plushy suburban areas. Located near a park, the neighborhood maintained a parklike character in its physical make-up by eliminating sidewalks and curbs. A formal organization existed to represent its interests at city hall.

Generally speaking, however, the politics of the neighborhood was only a function of crisis. When the neighborhood was threatened, group activity emerged. These efforts were often highly effective in forestalling the actions of the city.

MAINTENANCE OF THE STATUS QUO

Threats to the *status quo* in a neighborhood usually came in three forms of proposals: (1) traffic routing changes, (2) zoning changes, and (3) urban renewal projects. Regarding the first, no solution except a bypass of the entire city will satisfy every neighborhood—any other policy pits one neighborhood against another. Decisions on traffic routing are usually made by engineers, without reference to any guiding set of community values. Two generalizations are apparent. The older parts of the city, which are usually built on a rectilinear pattern, make the alternative choices nearly infinite. Only the more recently built areas, with their curvilinear and dead-end streets, are immune to the threat of conversion to arterial streets. The engineer's preference is for the shortest and fastest route, which often means a pair of one-way streets. This may be politically unattractive to city councils, for it doubles the number of potentially outraged citizens.

While the glacial creep of zoning changes can transform a neighborhood over a period of years, the variances rarely provide an occasion for an entire neighborhood to become alarmed. But even when the proposed changes affect but few, the advantage in almost any given case is with the proponents of the *status quo*. In all four cities, the council rarely objected on the basis of planning principles to a zoning recommendation by the planning commission. But in every city, the council was the last best resort of the aggrieved party. In both Alpha and Gamma the council gave great weight to planning commission recommendations. The zoning ordinances were of recent origin, the staffs were highly professional, and the members of the planning commission relied heavily on professional advice. But even here, the strongly expressed views of a small group of householders who saw their neighborhood adversely affected by a change could often win maintenance of the *status quo*. The only distinction between the two cities in this respect was in the use of personal lobbying. In the case of Gamma, it was a common and frequently successful practice. In Alpha, there was nearly total reliance on the public forum for hearing protests. The Beta planning commission operated with a small professional staff and what professionals in the field considered a rather outdated plan. While the planning commission had considerable prestige, the council showed a ready willingness to reject its recommendations if serious protests arose. However, our interviewees in Beta were not willing to say categorically that the advantage lay with the *status quo*. In Delta, the planning commission members were not of high status and the professional staff was nonexistent. Zoning details were controlled by the individual councilman, and proposed changes had to be cleared first through the appropriate representative.

In Gamma, an upper-middle-class residential neighborhood successfully resisted the placement of an industrial location in their area. The combined wishes of the chamber of commerce, the board of realtors, the newspaper editor, and the mayor could not overcome neighborhood opposition. The impact of a hundred irate housewives, who directed a barrage of phone calls to councilmen and packed council meetings, proved a greater political force than the arguments concerning the need to attract industry during a time of local economic distress. What Beta or Delta, the other economically pressed cities, would have done in a similar situation cannot be said. Thy were not troubled by such a choice during the study period.

Except for those particular situations where city policy affects a specific neighborhood, there is little reason to expect neighborhoods to be political-action units. While physical proximity may be the necessary condition for grass-roots politics, it was not a sufficient basis for political action on most subjects in these cities. A decentralized form of politics in juxtaposition to centralized services appears unrealistic. Consequently, the neighborhood was an unimportant unit both for administration of city policy and for political interaction among the citizens.

THE SUBURBAN NEIGHBORHOODS

The neighborhoods usually in the greatest need of self-conscious political organization and activity are those in the poorest position to act. These are the new neighborhoods being created on the fringes of every urban community. Not only are the people strangers to one another, but there may be no organized local government to which they can appeal.

The four cities in this study were all core cities in standard metropolitan areas. They were all experiencing "urban sprawl" and many new dwellings were being built beyond the jurisdiction of the core city. The surrounding county in each case circumscribed the urban complex. In 1950, the percentage of the county population living in the core cities was approximately as follows: 45 per cent in Alpha, 47 per cent in Beta, 40 per cent in Gamma, and 59 per cent in Delta. While there was some variation in the percentages, the situation was essentially the same.

Gamma had a few incorporated satellites, but most of the fringe residential areas were growing without city services. These unincorporated areas were engaging in practices and establishing land-use patterns that promised to set the character of the neighborhoods for generations. Often this was taking place with little forethought about future implications. The consequences of unplanned urban growth, deficient services, low building standards, and piecemeal utility and transportation development have been given great attention in other places, and we need not review the subject here. There was a variety in the degrees of self-consciousness among these new residential neighborhoods concerning their needs and problems. The question often facing them was whether or not to annex to the core city. Similarly, the core city had to decide whether to accept them. Each community had a different reaction to this situation.

Under the state law, fringe areas could be annexed

only with the consent of the area to be annexed and a majority vote of the citizens in the combined "affected" areas. "Affected areas" refer to the city and the balance of the township from which the area was to be withdrawn. The crucial vote was usually in the area to be annexed. Voters here had to weigh the advantages of gaining core-city services against the increases in taxation, which this usually implied, and the putative disadvantage of being "swallowed" by the larger unit. Initiation for a vote was by a petition from the area desiring annexation. Although there were discussions about annexation in all four cities, only Alpha actually held elections on proposals.

The value of annexation to the residents in the core city was not always clear. Many of the supposed advantages, such as land-use planning controls, were intangible, and their specific consequences difficult to demonstrate. While annexation of an industry or of industrial sites brought at least the prospect of increases in the tax base, the annexation of residential areas usually offered no tax advantage and, perhaps, even a disadvantage to the core city.

Because of this diffusion of interest in fringe policies, coherent or well-organized groups favoring or opposing annexation are rarely found in the core city. The city administration and the elected officials who are brought face to face with suburban service problems as a result of their duties often act on behalf of the city with little public support. The professional leadership in such organizations as the chamber of commerce, manufacturers' association, industrial recruitment association, or occasionally, a bank, also had interests causing them to see advantages in comprehensive plans for the area. In brief, the persons whose orientation came not from the interests of a specific piece of property or of a business, but from some broader identification, were the promoters of alternative fringe policy proposals. Of course, there is always a small group of citizens with specific interests in some type of solution to a particular fringe problem. Citizens owning property outside the city may want services to enhance its value. Lawyers and realtors may front for fringe residents who want city services. Some downtown merchants see the extension of city zoning as a means of controlling peripheral commercial developments. Chamber of Commerce managers see new annexations on the fringe as a form of rejuvenation—as a hedge against the aging of the established areas of the city.

Interests combined in a variety of fashions in the different cities to achieve differing patterns of success. In Alpha, the city administration and the council throughout the period favored annexation of the fringe. But they were also in agreement that any overt move on their part might raise suspicion in the fringe areas that could defeat their aim. One manager studiously avoided the subject of annexation and refused to make public comments about it. Leadership for annexation eventually originated in the fringe area. A prominent bank official, who resided outside the city, promoted annexation in various fringe areas. Only when citizens of a fringe community invited the city officials to confer with them did the manager relate the advantages and expectations that could be derived from annexation. This strategy, which stressed fringe-area initiative, resulted in a series of annexations over a period of four or five years that substantially increased the physical size of the city.

In Beta, no fringe areas applied for annexation during the ten-year period. On several occasions owners of land on which no persons resided applied for annexation. In these cases, no vote was needed; only the consent of city and township officials was necessary. These areas were accepted by the city, but the necessary township-government approval was withheld. Frequently, fringe areas requested extension of urban services, usually water and sewerage. The city council followed an erratic line of alternately approving and rejecting these requests. A highly vocal minority on the city council wanted to stop all extension of services as an attempt to force annexation. On some occasions this view would win a majority, but when an area subsequently applied for services, permission to extend city water or sewers was granted if property owners agreed to pay a higher rate for service than that charged city residents. The pro-extension faction argued that this procedure would promote friendly relations with the township governments and residents, though how it would lead to annexation was not made clear. Ultimately, one township formed a water authority to which the city sold water at a rate calculated to cover full costs and perhaps to yield a profit. The result of the failure of the Beta city council to agree on a policy toward fringe areas appeared to be an intensification of hostilities between city and township officials.

This hostility deserves additional comment. Many cases of friction were reported in the city newspaper. There were frequent news stories quoting either township officials or city councilmen making harsh statements about the motives or the alleged lack of civic responsibility on the part of the other group. None of the newspapers in our other three cities reported similar outbursts. The authors had the distinct impression that it was the policy of the Beta newspaper to give prominent coverage to such conflicts simply to sell more newspapers. The images prominently reported by the newspaper, in turn, may have had reciprocal effects on attitudes toward fringe policy. This city-township friction had serious results. For a number of years the Chamber of Commerce and its allies attempted to create an industrial park adjoining the city on a plot which lay in two adjacent townships. Annexation was desired to assure control over land use and the offering of a full range of services for the potential purchasers. While the annexation was achieved after the close of our study period, negotiations between the city and the townships repeatedly broke down and it took nearly six years to consummate the agreement.

In Gamma, the situation differed from that in the other three cities because a number of small satellite cities had been incorporated around its fringe prior to the time of our study period. Several of these had purchased utility services from Gamma for a number of years. Although some unincorporated urban areas remained around the border of Gamma, annexation did not offer itself as a final "solution" to the core city's fringe problems. Under state law, peripheral cities could not—realistically speaking—be annexed.

A citizen study committee, involving all the units of government, was formed about midway through our study period. While the initiative came from a number of Gamma residents, it was arranged for the opening statement to be made by one of the fringe-area members. The study committee reported in favor of area-wide consolidation. This policy had the backing of the Chamber of Commerce, the newspaper, and the city council in Gamma. No opposition was expressed by groups within the core city. The most active promoters of the study and the projected consolidation were industrialists who found dealing with seven separate local units of government a nuisance. The argument was also made that no effective recruitment of new industry was possible until an area-wide government was formed to furnish the necessary utilities and other services, including port development. At the close of the study period, legal difficulties were delaying a vote on consolidation.

One of our industrialist informants stated that in their business life, industrial executives strongly supported consolidation. The petty frustrations stemming from fractionalized local government was viewed by many of them as an inefficient arrangement. At the same time, the informant stated that the consolidation issue would probably lose in the satellite cities where the bulk of the executives lived. He felt that the wives, especially, did not share the sentiments of their husbands—if the proposal came to a vote, the residents would probably retain their small independent city suburbs and their custom-tailored amenities.

In Delta, the city council was consistently unsympathetic toward an annexation policy. One ex-member of the city council stated that most councilmen were not interested in annexing new areas to their own wards. Such changes would mean more people to represent—in this case people who might bring with them costly service demands. Furthermore, a change in ward boundaries, whether the result of annexation or some other action, always posed a threat to the balance of forces within a ward, a balance that had permitted the incumbent councilman to be elected. Because the city council of Delta did not exercise leadership in area-wide problems, matters such as planning and industrial recruitment had been taken over by the county officials.

The interests of professional public employees are

important in relation to fringe area matters. In the three cities where professionalization had gone furthest, city hall remained a repository of sentiment in favor of expanding city boundaries. By training and professional values, this group was most aware of the issues of integration, area-wide planning, and the presumed difficulties of being hemmed in by an urban ring over which the core city had no control. In each city, the officials were vocal in informing both officials and citizen groups about these factors. One city manager of Beta, reflecting on the course of events, surmised that he may have been too active along these lines, because the outspoken councilmen he had encouraged may have unnecessarily raised suburban fears.

The one group in all the cities (except for Delta) which was most frequently identified with fringe problems was the Chamber of Commerce. The chambers had area-wide memberships and were embued with a philosophy of community growth. In the area of industrial recruitment, the Beta and Gamma chambers (and the manufacturers' association in the latter city) were acutely aware of the problems of intergovernmental friction. For example, the Beta plan for the development of an industrial park was frustrated by intergovernmental friction. The professionals in the chamber and manufacturers' groups of Gamma continually faced problems related to intermunicipal cooperation and friction.

The problems of industrial growth did not touch the fringe area residents. As any new industries would have to build outside the city limits, the fringe areas would reap the tax advantage. It was only when fringe residents had insoluble service problems that the city offered advantages. Annexation was possible only when it appealed to the consumer-service interests of these people. Therefore, it is perhaps not surprising that only Alpha was able to annex successfully. The Alpha government enjoyed a high reputation. It was controlled by the upper-middle-class groups, which had overlapping memberships with residents in some of the areas annexed. The self-conscious faction that controlled the Alpha council enabled that body to maintain a consistent strategy diminishing the possibility of alienating the suburbs.

But Alpha may have had successful annexations because of fortuitous circumstances. If this were true, some doubt would be cast on our consumer theory. The city comprised a large area in the center of the township. This meant that the township, if it attempted to develop its own services, would be faced with administering an awkward doughnut-shaped territory. The other cities were on the edges of townships, making it easier for unincorporated areas to develop services for a more compact urban area.

SUMMARY

The institutions of core-city politics provide poor mechanisms through which the interests of the many urban fringe groups could be channeled. Legal factors often made annexation an unrealistic policy in any event. But in our study other alternatives, such as joint planning commissions, could not rely upon any significant interest group for support, except for city officials and the Chamber of Commerce. The elected officials were guided mainly by short-term tax considerations and the latter group by desires for industrial expansion. This inevitably placed a complex policy question in a rather narrow context.

This excursion through neighborhood politics has led

us to view disparate policy areas. The consideration of politics of neighborhoods within the core cities led to the assertion that geographic neighborhoods rarely furnished the natural basis for a link between the citizens and the city government. Exceptions to this occur when the city is engaged in specific area improvements such as street repaving, construction of a park, urban renewal, or zoning changes. Zoning was explored as an example of neighborhood politics. Our previous division between structured and unstructured politics is of relatively little use in distinguishing between cities on zoning policies. Permissiveness regarding amendments to the zoning ordinance were more a function of the attitudes of the planning staff and the vociferousness of individual protesters. In a policy area that was not amenable to a comprehensive resolution, as was the case with the CBD, public housing, urban renewal and rent control, structured politics produced no continuous official policy.

With regard to annexation policies, all the cities except Beta had a consistent position. However, only Alpha and Delta, the two cities with a structured politics, were able to attain their objectives. It is of interest that the Alpha council was able successfully to adhere to an annexation policy requiring delicacy and an agreed-upon strategy. It is doubtful if such a course of action could ever have taken place in Beta, and probably not in Gamma.

NOTES

[1] This is not meant to imply that urbanism has produced an anonymous mass of citizens, totally devoid of significant primary relationships. The authors are aware of the writings of Morris Janowitz, *The Community Press in an Urban Setting* (Glencoe: The Free Press, 1952), and Joel Smith, William Form, and Gregory Stone, "Local Intimacy in a Middle-Sized City," *American Journal of Sociology*, Vol. 60 (November, 1954), 276-284, who have qualified earlier sociological accounts stressing a totality of secondary relations in the city.

Part III

A Typology of Civic Policies

Chapter IX

Type One: Promoting Economic Growth

In the next four chapters each of the policy types is applied to the four cities. The intention is to compare the four cities in terms of conformity to the criteria for the types set forth in Chapter I. Some new data will be developed and some already presented will be briefly recapitulated.

First several questions must be raised: Whose values are being assessed? City councilmen's? The general public's? The city administration's? The interest groups'? Do we classify a city according to values held or feats accomplished? By answering the second question the first can also be answered. The cities are classified according to performance: Which city through official action has launched the farthest-reaching policies for economic growth? Which has provided the highest levels of amenities? Which has most steadfastly opposed new functions? Clearly, the rating that a city receives according to a single type may be a product of a variety of factors. Initially we are only asking to what values the total political process has been most responsive in its official actions. The judgments about policy preferences may reflect general community value preferences, but official actions may also reflect particular circumstances. However, a development, such as economic growth, that takes place in a city without reference to any municipal government activity has no relevance to an assessment of policy orientation. Only developments that flow from or are related to political activity are relevant to the typology.

Of the four types of policy orientation, the promotion of economic growth is the most familiar. The booster spirit is the civic incarnation of the ethos of American capitalism. Throughout the nineteenth century competitive growth was one of the major preoccupations of our cities' leaders. City bonds were floated to attract canals and railroads. Taxes were kept low and union organizers were chased out of town in order to "maintain a favorable climate for business." Cities competed with one another to become the "biggest city" in the United States, west of the Appalachians, west of the Mississippi, south of the Mason-Dixon line, or in Apple Valley. In brief, the speculator and the speculative spirit were strong forces in civic policy.

It is probably accurate to say that most cities still want to grow. At least, there are many persons who identify their interests with a growing city. This fact was certainly documented by the rash of protests coming from the core cities when the 1960 census reported a drop in populations. (Population-based state grants and shared taxes had something to do with these protests, of course.) However, it is less clear today than it was in the last century just how a city proceeds toward the goal of economic growth. Most core cities in metropolitan areas cannot grow in population unless they expand their boundaries, a process often found to be politically difficult. In reference to a policy for economic growth in the entire metropolitan area, the alternatives have little clarity. Cities can adopt few specific measures in order to entice new industries. This may explain the tax moratorium offers made by some Southern cities. Short of such a radical procedure, the avenues are often quite indirect. But economic realism and community folklore are two different things. Consequently, there are those in every city who insist that something be done to make the city more attractive to new industry. This may result only in civic breastbeating at the luncheon clubs, but it may also affect city policy in a number of ways.

Before considering some of the options open to city government, it is necessary to identify more specifically the interests involved. One thing is clear: while all businesses are interested in their own economic growth, they are not all interested in economic growth for the community.

Heretofore, we have referred to producer interests as opposed to consumer interests. In doing so we stressed the differences between policies related to the consumption as opposed to the income phase of economic life. At this point we need to refine further what we have termed producer interests. A distinction needs to be made between the interests of industries and industrial-related firms and consumer-sales organizations, whether merchants or purveyors of services. Many industries care not at all whether the community in which their plant is located grows. Indeed, many are opposed to growth. Growth may mean more competition for the labor force, greater congestion, rising real estate values, and changed land usages, which may inhibit corporate expansion plans. Furthermore, existing industries may find themselves helping to pay for capital improvements, which are

needed only to serve new firms. Industries are more likely
to be interested only in specialized types of growth:
specifically, new customers or suppliers. Thus the rational
interests of an industrial firm are very complex and a
favorable attitude toward community growth depends a
great deal on the particular type of firm involved and
the character of growth anticipated.

Not only are many industries uninterested in community economic growth, but frequently they are equally
uninterested in city government. This is especially true
for some larger industries that are not dependent on the
city for utilities and services. Some modern large industries supply their own water, waste-disposal facilities, and
even police and fire protection. Although technology has
contributed to the independence of the industrial firm
from city services, most industries use some. In case of
dissatisfactions, firms are in a strong position to black-
mail the city into providing improvements by threaten-
ing withdrawal from the community. In our observations,
city officials appeared to welcome the opportunity of
granting special privileges, for they otherwise rarely had
a chance to demonstrate their willingness to cooperate
with industry.

In addition to services, industries depend on the city
for some matters relating to their employees. A public
transit system is a convenience. A plant may want to
keep the beer taverns away from its door to cut down on
noon-hour drinking, but again modern firms depend on
local government only in a minor way to maintain the
social decorum of the rank and file employees. Top management people, of course, may live in the community
or its suburbs. The environment of the community may
well be a matter of interest to them, but this expresses

itself only in consumer demands. If the plant is owned by an absentee corporation, the managers are more likely to look upon their stay in the community as a temporary sojourn and the general amenities are matters of relative indifference.[1] They are corporation- rather than community-oriented.

Industries are the source of new jobs, which means new customers and increased income for the purveyors of goods and services. But the merchant bride often has very little dowry with which to attract the industrial groom. Plant locations are largely determined by industrial-cost factors unrelated to local policy: such factors as location of markets, supplies, and raw materials, transportation costs, and labor costs. Consequently, the local boosters operate in an "everything else being equal" situation. If everything else is equal, a plant may be located where the taxes and utility rates are lowest, space for original construction and expansion is most convenient, and living arrangements are pleasant.

Consequently, it is not fully accurate to say that there is nothing that can be done by a local community to attract new industry. As a minimum, the boosters may make potential plant builders aware of their city's existence. Utilities, especially water and sewage facilities, must have sufficient capacities to handle any additional load. Land must be made available. This usually means that cooperative efforts must be undertaken between core city and the fringe area. Zoning, utility extensions, and street arrangements must be planned in accordance with potential industrial use. Last, nothing should be done by officials which indicates the city is hostile to business, or is corrupt, hopelessly inefficient, or difficult to deal with. Most research into the factors of plant location do mention attitudes of the community leaders as one factor among many.[2]

Despite the marginal influence that city policy may have on economic growth, the rhetoric of boosterism takes up a disproportionate part of the discussions concerning city policies. The "attracting industry" and "favorable climate for business" arguments are introduced at nearly every juncture and in connection with every decision, no matter how far-fetched the connection. Most communities appear to have distorted collective egos prompting many to view every civic act as a performance before a vast audience, which takes appropriate notice. Consequently, if we should take the utterances in civic debates as an index of commitment to promotion of economic growth, this type would dwarf all other policy considerations. Obviously, we must look elsewhere for a standard.

The use of the actual growth of the communities would be equally unsatisfactory, however. As we have just related, city policy is only one of many factors underlying industrial location. Certainly, actual growth in the cities studied was not related to the specific effort expended. Alpha had the greatest growth while giving industrial recruitment less overt attention than was the case in either Beta or Gamma. But as has been indicated, economic growth expresses itself as a policy in subtle ways as well as in the more obvious. Perhaps in this area, the most appropriate standard for our purpose is the actual political attention given to the welfare of business enterprises. In applying it we must spin a web of circumstantial evidence, rather than apply any rigorous checklist of accomplishments.

Using this approach, Delta was obviously different from

the three other cities. Not only did the Delta council show little concern for industrial recruitment, but it was generally unsympathetic to business aims. It was the only city council without imperialistic designs on the suburbs. Indeed, annexation was opposed by the council majority, The merchants were given an unsympathetic ear in regard to CBD policies. A running battle was conducted against the power company supplying electricity, which the city distributed. The council was generally recalcitrant on utility expansion; the city voters defeated water bonds proposals. Even the city Chamber of Commerce appeared to reflect the general spirit of accepting the *status quo*. The council considered industrial recruitment the job of the Chamber of Commerce, but the Chamber secretary, a long-time incumbent who was not highly esteemed even by businessmen, was disinclined to expend much energy in this activity. Those business interests active in industrial development by-passed the city government and worked nearly exclusively with the county. Delta County was the only county government more favorably disposed toward taking on new functions than was the government in the core city.

It is more difficult to distinguish among the activities in the other three cities. In each case the central responsibility for industrial recruitment was in a private organization, sometimes the Chamber of Commerce and sometimes a larger organization in which the Chamber played a prominent role. Perhaps this function was too important an assignment to entrust to local politicians. It was often a private preserve as viewed by the Chamber bureaucracy. When a Beta mayor appointed his own industrial recruitment committee, it was disbanded after a brief period. According to the newspaper, disbandment occurred because the mayor's committee duplicated the function of the Chamber of Commerce. The Gamma industrial recruitment activities were the most aggressive. The city had a long history of economic difficulties and an equally long tradition of aggressive industrial recruitment programs, which had usually managed to bail the community out of difficulties. The private industrial recruitment group in Gamma had established a fund for financing new industries, which was responsible for a number of successes. Despite these achievements, however, the community continued to fight an uphill battle to recoup the industrial losses of the previous decade. The city council played a part, though probably an unimportant one, in industrial recruitment generally. The council was brought in on negotiations with firms considering Gamma for plant locations. According to one informant this was done to encourage the council to identify more closely with local business interests. Some of the councilmen were undoubtedly flattered by this experience.

A positive action, which clearly distinguished Alpha, Beta, and Gamma from Delta, was in the area of metropolitan matters. All the cities were facing a diminishing supply of potential industrial sites within their boundaries at the beginning of the period. One policy that could be undertaken to encourage plant locations was bringing core-city services to the vacant, available land in the hinterland. All the cities were willing to extend services on a contractual basis to peripheral industries, but often this was not enough. Capacities of city utilities had to be expanded to anticipate those industries which might want these city services. Agreements had to be worked out with suburban areas in conjunction with land development.

Some concerted planning efforts were considered advisable.

All the cities except Delta moved in this direction. They were not all equally successful, but development on the periphery remained the official policy of each city. Alpha annexed large areas of the surrounding township. These annexations not only brought many residential areas into the city, but also gave the city industrial "growing room." Thus the city could potentially exercise control over fringe-area commercial development, enrichment of the industrial tax base could be anticipated and the commercial interests could see themselves in a favorable position to reap the benefits which growth might bring.

While Beta was willing to extend services to new industries beyond municipal boundaries, actual performance was handicapped by a history of friction between the core city and the suburban township areas. The vagaries of municipal politics caused township-city relations to operate in an uncertain environment. City officials, over-zealous in safeguarding the city's tax dollar, frequently appeared to desire to drive a hard bargain in utility sales to township governments. Thus, when the successful development of a large industrial park was contingent upon annexation of the area to Beta, the negotiations became long and difficult. It seems most likely that negotiations would have been expedited had there not been a history of mutual recriminations. Under the duress of difficult economic conditions in the years following the study period, some area-wide cooperation for economic development began to emerge.

Annexation or extension of services was not the answer to the growth ambitions of Gamma. Ringed by other small incorporated cities and natural barriers, there was little the city could do unilaterally. Accordingly, the city officials were active in an effort to achieve metropolitan consolidation, but success in this would require enormous effort—an effort that business and government leaders eventually decided had less likelihood of payoff than did more conventional industrial-recruitment activities. Failure here was hardly an indication that Gamma lacked dedication to a policy of economic growth.

Regarding central business district policies, the cities acted in a more comparable environment of conditions than was the case in fringe-area policies or industrial recruitment. In reviewing the actions in this area, it should be reasserted that policies which merely favored one business as opposed to another within the core city are not relevant to the present discussion. We are only concerned with policies calculated to aid the competitive advantage of core-city businesses generally. In making the central business district more attractive for shopping, the cities did discriminate against neighborhood merchants, but this was incidental to the primary objective in the four cities. The major motivations came from the specter of peripheral shopping centers and the declining tax return from central city properties.

In Alpha, Beta, and Gamma the services of the city council and the administration were at the disposal of CBD interests on two minimum conditions. First, the CBD interests had to settle their internal differences and secondly, they had to formulate a plan that was not a burden on the general tax levy. The Delta council did not go this far, asserting essentially that CBD improvements were not the city's responsibility. Alpha and Gamma went somewhat beyond the minimum conditions. Their governmental resources were used to design and

promote a plan that would achieve the goal of revitalizing the core business area. The goal was substantially
achieved in Alpha, while in actual performance Gamma
was less successful than Beta in parking-lot development,
though superior in developing highway access to the CBD.

The performance of the four cities in promoting economic growth, in summary, showed clearly that this value
received a high priority in Alpha and a low one in Delta.
The other two cities are more difficult to categorize, but
even in them, community growth was a value toward
which the officials were responsive. However, there were
competing values which held back over-all performance.
In Beta and Gamma, neither the interested groups, nor
the public generally was sufficiently motivated or organized to achieve a full program for economic growth. Consequently, on the scale of performance, they must be
paired somewhat below the high rating of Alpha.

NOTES

[1] R. O. Schulze, "The Role of Economic Dominants in Community
Power Structure," *American Sociological Review*, (Vol. 23 February, 1958),
3-9.

[2] For a brief summary of literature of plant location, as well as comments on community folklore, see W. Paul Strassmann, "Rigor and
Ritual in Plant Location," *Business Topics*, Vol. 8, No. 1 (Winter, 1960),
66-74.

Chapter X

Type Two: Providing Life's Amenities

A large portion of the traditional job of local government is to provide a bundle of services to its citizens. An analogy is frequently made between municipal and private corporations because of the similarity between the city's activity of furnishing services to its citizens and the private firm supplying goods and services to its customers. The deficiencies of this analogy need not concern us now. The point is that cities are engaged in an allocation of consumption items among the members of its public. Cities differ in the kinds of consumers favored in this distribution process and consequently certain distinctions must be made among the beneficiaries.

The first two categories of the typology distinguish between producer-oriented and consumer-oriented policies. Producer-oriented policies affect the income levels; consumer-oriented policies affect the pattern of expenditures. The former are directed toward the conditions of employment; the latter, toward the conditions of the place of residence. The two are related in that tax-supported amenities represent a reduction of disposable income for other purposes. However, it would be a gross oversimplification to say that all opposition to increased amenities is made in the name of promoting producer interests. Opposition may stem from values expressed by the other two policy types. Furthermore, to summarize the politics of these cities as a struggle between producer-oriented and consumer-oriented interests would be misleading. It revives an image that may have been close to describing city politics at a previous time in history, but is inappropriate today.

Many of the earlier community studies portrayed city politics as a struggle between business—and especially industrial interests that tried to keep the local tax rate as low as possible—and the broad citizenry who wanted to improve living conditions. While it would be inaccurate to say that the business and industrial leaders were oblivious to local taxes in the four cities, these groups did not represent any monolithic low-tax bloc. Indeed, business and industrial leaders were frequently the most vocal in favoring increases in tax-supported amenities.

The first problem in gauging the comparative receptivity of the four cities toward policies expanding amenities is one of definition. Amenities has been defined to include the pleasantries and necessities of life, as opposed to merely the latter. However, the term "pleasantries" is not a very precise one. To one person the dismantling of old cars in the back yard may be one of the supreme joys of life, while to his neighbor this practice may render the neighborhood odious and unpleasant for residential purposes. For most a flush toilet is a necessity, but a few may want to forego the cost of this accommodation in order to buy more whisky. In brief, amenities cannot be standardized, because the pleasantries of life are defined differently by various individuals and cultural subgroups and are, in any case, essentially subjective in character.

But while the variety of choices is unlimited, the agreement on their character is also substantial. Indeed the whole professionalization of the service occupations has been predicated upon this consensus. Cleanliness is preferable to filth. Protection from theft is better than exposure to it. Malicious property damage cannot be afforded by most. Soft water is better than hard water. In brief, if one of the cities appeared to give the consumer more service than another it was rated as more inclined toward the amenities type. In some particular cases, a quantitative measure was hardly appropriate. Expenditure patterns are only indicative, for they ignore comparative efficiencies of operation and differing satisfactions provided. It is possible for one city to perform a service more satisfactorily than another for less money. For a qualitative measure of standards we turned to the professional. We interviewed experts in various specialties, persons who were not only recognized authorities, but also were intimately acquainted with the four cities. They were simply asked to rate the communities in terms of their own professional standards. It was our assumption that professionals would advocate greater public stress on their particular service area and would rate the cities highest which came closest to fulfilling their expectations.

The whole process of rating was fraught with difficulties for a variety of reasons: (1) The conditions varied sufficiently so that some cities operate under a severe handicap, making it difficult to distinguish effort from performance. (2) When not all cities provided the same services comparison was not possible. (3) Sometimes it was impossible to secure information on all four cities. (4) On occasion, reliable information was available only for a few of the ten years. (5) Service levels were sometimes a function of the life span of a department head. Poor leadership was sometimes retained for reasons of personnel morale, and it was difficult to judge the merits of such retentions in terms of their effects on services.

Despite these infirmities the survey did give us some general impressions that appeared to be valid. A numerical rating was not attempted in every category. Sometimes we relied on general description. We shall treat the major categories separately.

GENERAL ADMINISTRATION AND PERSONNEL

While administration is not a service area, it was assumed that the quality of municipal services in some respects was a reflection of the quality of general administration and personnel. In Table 17, the comparative salaries are listed for selected municipal positions. The cities are ranked from 1 through 4, with Number 1 the city paying the highest salary or wage. In this table there is the further assumption that there is a correlation between quality of personnel and the pay scales, and that a better paid municipal staff will do a better job of providing services.[1]

The positions included in the table were chosen primarily because of the comparability of data. This means the table was weighted toward the traditional jobs in city government. Many of the supervisory positions in the more technical services were grouped differently from city to city or changed over time. The over-all summary indicates that Alpha generally paid the highest salaries, Beta and Gamma were tied for second, and Delta paid the lowest. The positions are divided into three groupings, corresponding to manual labor, technical supervisory positions, and top administrative posts. The primary variation in the over-all pattern appears in the first of these categories. Delta ranks second here, while last in the other categories. This seems to reflect the activities of the union political organization. Delta tended to stress higher wages for the lower positions at the expense of supervisory and administrative salaries.

The wage scales appeared to be a function of city policy rather than of prevailing community wages. Alpha had the lowest general wage scale of the four cities yet paid its municipal labor wages virtually comparable to Beta and Gamma. (In rank order it was last.) Beta, with the highest wage scale, paid the firemen and policemen the least.

Table 17.

City Ranks by Salary Scales for Selected Positions*

	Alpha	Beta	Gamma	Delta
Common labor	4†	2†	3†	1
Foreman	1	3	4	2
Fireman	1†	4	3†	2†
Patrolman	1	4†	3†	2†
Water superintendent (1 year only)	3	2	4	1
Pumping station supt. (2 years)	1	3	2	4
Electrical inspector	1†	3	2†	4
Supt. of streets	1	3	2	4
Purchasing agent	1	4	3†	2†
Parks and recreation director	1‡	2	3	4§

Chief engineer or dir. pub. works	1	2	4	§§
City planner	1	3	2	4
City manager	1	3	2	4
City assessor	1	2	3	4**
City attorney	1	3††	2††	4††
City clerk	2	1	4	3
Police chief	1	3	2	4
Fire chief	1	3	2	4
Personnel director	1	2	3	4‡‡
Average rank	1.31	2.73	2.78	3.16

* Ranks based upon an average of even years (1948-1956) unless otherwise indicated.

† Wages or salaries practically identical, ranks based upon slight differences (see Appendix B).

‡ Positions separate, each with high salaries.

§ Parks and Cemeteries.

** Also acted as personnel director

†† Part-time.

‡‡ No position, therefore ranked last.

While recruitment practices of some of the particular departments will be considered later, it is important here to state that the city managers in Alpha, Beta and Gamma were professionally trained for their positions and had prior experiences as managers. Delta never had success with professional managers. The incumbent was an ex-city councilman. With respect to professional salaries, there was a wide gap between those paid in Alpha and Gamma and those in Beta and Delta (see Appendix B).

Planning, like admistration, is only indirectly related to services consumed by the public. However, a well developed planning staff may abet the amenities of a city through controls that are manifested in the preservation of the character of neighborhoods, the prevention of industrial and commercial encroachment on residential areas, freer and safer circulation of traffic, more equitable distribution of such facilities as parks and playgrounds and, perhaps, a city more attractive physically. Of course, the talents of the planning department as well as those of general administration may also be dedicated to a variety of ends, none of which may benefit the citizen-consumer. Several techniques were applied to assess the quality of the planning operations in the four cities, including the number of staff members, size of budgets, and the evaluations of a panel.

By the close of our period of study, all four cities had functioning departments. The departments recorded the following patterns of growth (the first of the two figures refers to professionally trained planners and the second to other employees):

Table 18. Growth Patterns of Planning Departments.

	Alpha	Beta	Gamma	Delta
1948	4–0	0–0	0–0	0–2
1950	4–0	1–0	0–0	2–0
1952	2–1	0–1	5–0	0–0
1954	3–0	1–1	5–2	2–0
1956	5–3	2–1	6–4	2–1

With respect to the salaries of the planning director, the rank was Alpha, Gamma, Beta, Delta in that order (see Table 17).

Two professional specialists were consulted to evaluate the planning activities in the four cities. They agreed that the programs and achievements in Alpha and Gamma were vastly superior to those in Beta and Delta, but they disagreed on the specific order within these two pairs. Both Alpha and Gamma were rated superior because of the quality of their personnel and the established practice within both of these city governments of using planning as an integral part of the city operations. Councils in both cities had been willing to back the planning staffs with ample funds.

Neither Beta nor Delta had a full-time, professionally trained planning director at any time during the study period. Subsequent to 1957, Beta hired a planner for a metropolitan-area project, and a new land-use study for the area was begun. Prior to this time, the zoning ordinance and the decisions of the planning commission were ostensibly based upon a quickly formulated 1920 plan supplied by a consulting firm. Throughout the study period the person acting as planning director was a part-time employee without any professional training. He was given scant budgetary support for the collection of relevant data. His energies were largely devoted to the concerns of businessmen.

Delta never had a professional planning department. The planning function was carried on by engineers or landscape architects. On occasion, the city hired persons having just received undergraduate degrees in planning, who were not yet prepared for the responsibilities assigned them. Even these persons were given nonplanning and routine jobs such as measuring building frontages and checking the location of street lights. The lay planning commission was made up of persons of relatively low prestige in the community. The major source of leader-

ship from the planning professionals in the Delta area
came from the county government.

For certain services, such as police and fire protection,
it is impossible to distinguish between the benefits that
accrue to householders as opposed to businesses. On the
other hand, services such as inspection, rubbish removal,
and parks are oriented chiefly to the citizen as a resident.
However, with respect to all services, no precise book-
keeping of benefits between producer interests and consumer interests is possible. The assumption is made that
citizens as consumers are much more dependent on the
socialized character of city services and, consequently,
higher service levels really cater to citizens as consumers.
Business enterprises are much more independent of these
services in general and higher service levels generally
represent an increase in business costs, which may or
may not return equivalent benefits. Higher service levels,
in brief, frequently represent a subsidy of the citizen as
consumer by the citizen as producer.

Police Protection and Traffic Control. In police, as in
many of the other service areas, Alpha rated high according to most of the rating measures, while Delta rated low.
Gamma and Beta followed a more erratic pattern between
these extremes. According to the financial statistics Alpha
not only paid the highest salaries, but also had the highest
per capita expenditure and the highest ratio of police
employees to total population (see Table 19). Thus
Alpha rated high in quantity and quality as reflected in
pay scales. The pattern among the other three cities was
less clear. Beta and Delta had a similar statistical profile

of patrolmen salaries and size of force in relationship to the population, but Beta paid its chief more and Delta had a larger over-all police expenditure per capita. Gamma paid its chief well, but economized on salaries in the lower ranks and by maintaining a small force.

Table 19. Comparative Statistics on Police

City	Chief salaries*	Patrolmen salaries†	Per capita expenditures‡	Population per employee§
Alpha	$7,800	$3,960	$7.30	610
Beta	$6,200	$3,860	$6.70	630
Gamma	$6,700	$3,770	$6.70	650
Delta	$5,700	$3,810	$7.15	630

* Average 1948, 1950, 1952, 1954, 1956.
† Median of medians, 1950, 1952, 1956, 1958.
‡ Average for 1948, 1950, 1952, 1954, 1956. Population estimates computed separately for each year.
§ Years and population estimates same as in (3).

While the statistics do not show great differences among the cities, the panelist suggested that there were actually distinctions to be made among the departments. He used as his criteria training programs for the personnel, quality of top personnel, and cooperation between the department and the city council. According to his rating, Alpha had the best trained personnel and leadership and used the "most contemporary concepts in organization and administration." Furthermore, he stressed that the city council gave the police administrator strong and sympathetic support. Gamma was rated second and it was stated that its department was also very good and was making strong efforts to improve the training of police personnel. Delta was rated third largely on the basis of a superior police chief who had served for a long period in that city. However, the panelist downgraded the city because the chief was undercut by local "politics," presumably by considerations of patronage and favoritism. Beta was rated last. This was not to imply it had a poor department, but in relationship to the others, it did not have any outstanding personnel.

Thus in respect to general performance of the police departments Alpha appeared to be superior by all measures. The panelist indicated that despite the lower expenditure figures for Gamma, the quality of its department remained high.

Table 20. Traffic Safety Ratings

	Alpha	Beta	Gamma	Delta
1954 Total program	76.4	82.4	65.9	63.2
Total program and accident record	54.8	56.4	45.4	43.3
1955 Total program	84.5	72.9	71.6	63.5
Total program and accident record*	82.1	64.9	75.1	64.0
1956 Total program	86.0	75.0	72.0	66.0
Total program and accident record	76.0	68.0	64.0	62.0
Safety index*	70.7	63.1	61.5	56.4

* Arithmetic mean of the "Total program and accident record" figures for the three years.

Traffic problems were singled out for separate treatment. Here consideration was divided into safety and traffic engineering. The police force is more involved in the first of these than in the second.

For our safety ratings, we relied upon the records of the National Safety Council in its *Annual Inventory of Traffic Safety Activities.* This rating system is based upon eight factors: the death and injury record, accident record, traffic engineering, police traffic supervision, traffic court, traffic safety education, public safety education, and safety organization. Table 20 records the composite ratings for a three-year period in the four cities. Scores range from zero to 100 with the greater safety indicated by the higher score. A summary of these rankings places Alpha first in safety, followed by Beta, Gamma, and Delta. Again the pattern of the extremes is a familiar one.

While traffic engineering was a component of the safety-rating system, it was also singled out for special attention. Traffic engineering standards related not only to safety but also to general circulation. For instance, the proper designation of major streets reduces congestion and assures greater convenience for motorists. During this period, the state routes through each of these cities were reconsidered. Changes in the state highway system and urban growth had rendered the prewar arterial routes in the cities obsolete. The state highway department, under the law, was involved in the designation of major streets and of arterial routes. The designations were usually a matter of negotiation between city and state officials. As a result of this state work, two traffic engineers could be located who had worked in the four cities and consequently were qualified to judge in terms of prevailing engineering standards. A further precaution was taken: *former* state highway personnel were interviewed.

The first panelist rated the cities for cooperation with the state agency and for city traffic management in terms of state recommendations. Unfortunately, this person had not worked with Alpha, but he rated Gamma, Beta, and Delta in that order. He asserted that Gamma had the best record of achievement with the least well-trained staff. On the other hand Beta had the best traffic engineers, but they experienced interference by "small interest groups" who objected to the application of engineering standards. He felt that Delta had done little to solve its traffic problems.

The second panelist (who had worked with all four cities) offered similar comments with regard to the acceptance of state suggestions regarding major street designations and city routes for state highways. He reported that the state had the greatest difficulties with Delta. In his words "that city council would close its ears and not even listen to what you were saying." (However, it did eventually accept the state policies after extended negotiations.) In Beta, the newspaper was the major source of difficulty. The editor took exception to the state route designations and rallied local political opposition. Both Alpha and Gamma accepted the state recommendations without reported incidents.

These two reports do give some insights into the politics of the cities. The state designations are made through engineering techniques including traffic counts, timing, and distances of alternative routes. State engineers were interested only in which route would move the traffic most quickly and cheaply. This also is generally the view of the motorist, the consumer of the traffic engineers' product. But to those who dwell or, especially, have businesses along the wayside, other considerations are more important. The service station or motel operator wants to be on the state route and resists changes which, he fears, may eliminate his profit margin. The retailers dislike being on state routes, because curb parking restrictions are often enforced along its entire length. Residents dislike being on heavily traveled streets. In Beta and Delta, the individuals who were aggrieved could penetrate the council and win political support to dispute the engineering standards. In Alpha and Gamma, apparently the governmental system operated to give the technicians political protection in implementing their suggestions. On this particular matter, it is safe to conclude that the engineers were on the side of the interests of the motoring consumer in most instances.

Fire Protection. The statistical data on the four fire departments parallels closely that of the police departments (see Table 21). The salaries for the chiefs reflect the

Table 21. Comparative Data on Fire Departments

	Salary of Chief*	Salarie of Firemen†	Per Capita Expenditures‡	Population Per Employee‡
Alpha	$6,950	$3,930	$7.60	650
Beta	$6,500	$3,850	$7.30	590
Gamma	$6,660	$3,770	$6.80	650
Delta	$5,730	$3,830	$9.00	470

* Average for 1948, 1950, 1952, 1954, 1956.
† Median of medians, 1950, 1952, 1954, 1956, 1958.
‡ Average for 1948, 1950, 1952, 1954, 1956. Population estimates by year based on 1950 United States Census and preliminary report of 1960 Census.

pattern of salaries in the cities generally, with Alpha first, Gamma and Beta in a tie for second, and Delta lowest. However, if we glance at the third and fourth columns of Table 20, differences occur. Delta had a much larger per capita expenditure for fire protection than any of the others. This may be explained by its having the largest force in relationship to its population. However, this larger expenditure did not result in greater protection, according to the insurance companies. By their standards, Alpha had a rating of three and the other cities a less desirable rating of four.

Of course, from the viewpoint of most consumers, insurance costs are the most important consideration in evaluating a city fire department. The few individuals who may have their life or property saved by firemen may be eternally grateful for fire protection, but they do not loom large in the general public. The professional fire-department expert is not just interested in ratings. He knows they are not always accurate indexes of the standards he feels to be important. For one thing, fire-insurance ratings often are not re-examined for decades. In the second place, water-supply facilities figure heavily in the considerations given.

To a professional fireman, the prevention of big fires is the most important test. It is also poor work in big, destructive fires that gives a department a bad reputation, which may eventually be reflected in pay scales. As all firemen, including our panelist, have a certain *esprit de corps*, salaries and working conditions are stressed as important. At the same time, however, the incidence of big fires in a city is not a good test, especially over a short period of time, because fortuitous circumstances may influence these statistics. Our one panelist knew all four of the fire departments during the study period. He judged them on the basis of training programs, competence of the chief, and morale. This particular individual felt morale was very important for a team organization that performed its most valuable service during the first five minutes at the scene of a fire. The following were his judgments:

The Delta department rated highest. It had a good chief, high morale, public support, and a well-trained organization. The only deficiency was a retirement age of sixty-five, which is generally considered too old for firemen. The department operated on a straight appointive system. The chief made all personnel decisions. All other cities had some form of civil service.

Gamma rated second. The quality of the department varied considerably over the period as the city had a number of different fire chiefs. Morale, training, and supervisory personnel fluctuated from high to acceptable under the various chiefs. (The last chief stressed home inspections, which is probably a consumer service, though one which is frequently not appreciated by the home owners, who may be forced to make costly improvements.)

Alpha rated third, largely on the basis of low morale, a weak administrator as chief, and the absence of an adequate training program. The turnover in the Alpha department was reported to be one of the highest in the state. At the same time the department was considered acceptable and adequately supervised.

Beta was judged as one of the poorest departments in the state for a city of its size. The panelist reported that during the 1948-57 decade morale was low, supervisory personnel were relatively weak, and the department had little public support. (Public support was a euphemism for a combination of newspaper backing, and pay and working conditions accorded through council or referendum decisions.) The department was faction ridden and some members allegedly did not confine their love for alcoholic stimulants to off-duty hours. (Subsequent to the study period, a new fire chief was appointed and many policy changes were made.)

In summary, three of the cities had departments of high repute. Alpha had the lowest insurance rating, Gamma had a good over-all department most of the time, and Delta had a generally outstanding department, according to our panelist. Beta obviously had the poorest fire organization.

Sewage Treatment. Sewage treatment is an item of cost either to the city producing the sewage or to the next one downstream. City dwellers may be recreation users of a stream and hence have an interest in requiring the city to treat effluence adequately. However, the principal incentive to provide adequate sewerage facilities is found in state and administrative procedures. If a city refuses to treat its own waste, under the state law a bond issue can be forced upon it and a treatment plant built as a result of court order. There are real advantages to the use of this recourse so far as local office-holders are concerned. It relieves them of the unpleasant responsibility of having to ask for a large bond issue and forces this upon the anonymous state bureaucracy. In addition, the bonds sold under court order have a lower interest rate than they would otherwise. On the other hand, long-range planning may involve some economies. The fiscal reputation of the city is not enhanced by the forced bond sales. Perhaps, as much as anything, there is a certain health risk involved for the residents of the city in letting conditions get bad enough for the state to have to take action. Lastly, there may be a factor of civic pride involved in being known as the city that does not pollute rivers, takes care of its own waste, and is not chastised by the state. In any event, most cities keep a jump ahead of the state enforcement agency. But as stream pollution is very common, the state agency has to pursue a somewhat selective policy and act only in extremely serious situations.

The city sewage-service ratings were largely based upon conformity with state standards. However, it should be added at the outset that the cost for meeting these standards varied considerably from city to city. The sewage of a city on a small stream must be treated much more fully than a city located on a large stream. The following ratings do not take into consideration cost, as such, and promptness of compliance is often a function of cost.

Gamma ranked highest, having no record of state warnings. The city, situated on a large body of water, had an advantage and it had kept its treatment plant abreast of its needs.

Alpha ranked second. Situated on a fairly small stream, the cost for this city was much greater than for Gamma or Delta. While Alpha never had been a serious violator, on at least one occasion the city fell behind the schedule of capital improvements recommended by the state agency. However, the main problems in Alpha were not derived from the city system, but from the industries not using municipal sewage facilities. The city can be held partially responsible for their failure, however, for greater local pressure for compliance could have been applied.

Beta was third in conformance to standards, but it was also in the poorest location, in cost terms, for handling disposal problems. Located on a small stream, the summertime water volume available for diluting the sewage was at times very low. During the 1930's the city received considerable Federal aid to help relieve this problem. In the 1950's, it again sought outside aid. On numerous occasions the state had to bring matters to the city's attention, complaining of such things as the condition of sanitary sewers, the existence of poisonous waste in sewage, and clogged major interceptor lines.

Though situated favorably on a large body of water, Delta resisted modernization of its disposal facilities. It consistently refused to take any action in response to state agency warnings and was eventually taken to court. As a result of this stalling, the city paid a lower rate of interest on the court-ordered bonds that financed a new treatment plant.

Two other factors should be mentioned in this appraisal. While Beta and Delta had combined sanitary and storm sewers, Alpha and Gamma had separate systems. The latter arrangement permits a more satisfactory control of treatment and discharge and is therefore preferred by engineers. Storm sewers are, from one point of view, a more important service item for city residents than is sewage treatment. During the period of this study, three of the cities developed drainage problems. Delta was favorably located for easy drainage. In Alpha and Gamma, bond issues were successfully sold before flood threats became serious. In Beta, as related above, storm sewer bond proposals were defeated on three occasions before a seven-year pay-as-you-go plan was passed. The three bond issues were defeated despite widespread basement flooding and a serious health threat that followed each rain.

In summary, these various facts indicate that Alpha and Gamma were more willing or able to pay for maintaining a higher level of service in the area of sewage treatment than were the other two cities.

Water. A water system for a modern city involves a wide complex of considerations. The technician is concerned with alternative sources, distribution systems, and processes for treatment. The chemical content of the water may affect its usefulness for a variety of industrial purposes. The residential consumer is interested in relatively few things. He wants plenty of water whenever he turns the tap, even in the middle of August when he competes with his neighbor in an effort to keep the bluegrass from turning into a coarse brown matting. He wants the water to be tasteless, odorless, and colorless, preferably soft, and cool in the summertime. All four cities did a reasonably good job of meeting these demands and consequently most residents in the four cities were probably unaware that the supply had resulted from consciously developed city policies.

Again a technician was requested to interpret the water situation in the four communities. The major water problems for a city begin with the source of supply. Alpha and Beta depended upon ground water and Gamma and Delta used lake water. Only Alpha was not blessed with unlimited supplies. However, the technician stated that this city had done a "phenomenal" job of locating supplies so that the best water sources were located and tapped. In terms of distribution, all four cities possessed systems that were adequate and there was no water rationing during the summer months of our study period.

Gamma had the softest water at the source, while the ground water of Alpha and Beta was noticeably hard, that is, it contained significant amounts of insoluble calcium compounds. Delta, which tapped a source of intermediate hardness, was the only city that softened its water. This was the one case where Delta provided a consumer service not found in other cities. Many homes in Alpha and Beta had home water softeners, representing substantial investments. One report stated that some industries opposed the softening of water in Beta. All four cities flouridated the water and Beta added phosphate to control iron.

Streets. Under a state law passed in the early 1950's all urban streets were required to be inventoried annually and then classified according to their adequacy. Adequacy is defined in engineering terms by the state highway department and the inventory is administered locally by the city engineer in charge of streets. While there may be some variations in local administration, there is no incentive for intentional bias. However, some gross year-to-year discrepancies appeared in reports occasionally, usually indicating a change in local personnel. After the program had been in effect several years, the reporting became more accurate, or at least showed fewer fluctuations, as local as well as state officials began to see the usefulness of the information in scheduling their future programs. The results for 1954 and 1957 were used as sample years (Table 22).

It was here that Delta excelled. Its government had initiated a policy whereby the city paid for blacktopping of streets out of the general fund. On the other hand, Gamma had a rather stringent set of provisions requiring street improvements to be paid largely from special assessments unless they were part of the state system. The results were obviously visible to the most casual visitor.

The principal part of the cost of local street improvement was paid from state funds. However, this state aid always needed some local supplementation. Variations in the conditions of the streets depended upon the size of the state payments, the special assessment provisions of each city regarding payment for the initial paving of streets, and the general efficiency and technical skill shown in exploiting the funds available. Many of the deficiencies in Gamma street conditions were a legacy of the fiscal straitjacket imposed by the tax limits existing prior to 1948. This tax ceiling, described above in Chapter XI, applied to Beta also, but not to Alpha and Delta. When this limitation was removed in Gamma, the city faced a backlog of needed improvements. While street conditions were a major need, remedial action in a number of areas had to await storm sewer renovation. Toward the end of the study period substantial amounts (over $1 million) were being paid for street improvement. A large portion of this sum was spent for streets in the central business district area and for major streets. The authors were in no position to evaluate this allocation, but arterial streets that were classified as "too narrow" rather than residential streets were the major beneficiaries.

Table 22. Adequacy of City Street Systems

	Alpha		Beta		Gamma		Delta	
	1954	1957	1954	1957	1954	1957	1954	1957
Adequate primary	41.1%	50.1%	35.1%	52.1%	24.6%	43.1%	57.1%	58.5%
Adequate local	62.4	49.5	27.8	34.2	20.6	35.0	63.0	64.8
Total adequate*	54.6	49.7	30.2	40.5	21.8	37.5	61.5	62.5

* Based upon total mileage, not on an average of first two lines.

Recreation. When the rating question was posed to a professional in the recreation field, the immediate reply was "Alpha, Gamma, Beta, and Delta in that order, with the gap separating the cities increasing as you go down the list." Upon probing a little further it became apparent that the specialist was thinking of the total recreational facilities and activities of each community and not simply the contribution of the city government. Most recreation programs were a cooperative venture of the schools and the city governments, but the ranking was not changed as a result of isolated city government activities.

Recreational programs are sufficiently cooperative affairs that isolation of city government was to a certain extent artificial. The schools have the physical facilities that make a recreation program possible. City governments often supply the funds, though in some cities a substantial item in the school budget is also earmarked for recreation programs.

Alpha was the first of the four cities to initiate a substantial cooperative program between the city and the schools. It had been a going concern for some years and was one of the most outstanding in the state. Similar joint programs were developed in Gama and Beta, especially in the former. Delta had very little in the way of a recreational program.

Alpha had a separate director for parks and for recreation. Beta and Gamma joined these two positions. Delta had no recreation director, and the park director was also in charge of cemeteries. Of the four cities, Delta had the least developed park system, though it benefited from an adjacent state park. Gamma enjoyed this advantage, yet it had a substantial city park system as well. Beta had a large total acreage in parks, but it was concentrated in one section of the city, which, incidentally, was also the wealthiest section and least dependent on public recreational space. The one large park was a gift to the city made many years ago. While the city had a good total acreage of parks in relation to the population, not only was the location skewed, but there was a shortage of play areas. A projected renewal program in progress at this writing would make a modest correction for this situation. Alpha had a better distribution of recreational areas. It, too, was in the process of building a park in a low-income area of the city.

Miscellaneous. In addition to the above functions, the citizen as consumer received preferential treatment in a variety of minor matters. Gamma and Delta provided municipal rubbish removal service; Alpha and Beta did not. Higher standards did not necessarily exist under city service. For example, backyard pickup was required in Alpha and Gamma, no provision existed in Beta, and relatively inexpensive curb pickup was practiced in Delta. Delta residents received only one pickup every two weeks, while Gamma received weekly service and the private contractors in Alpha were required to make pickups three times every two weeks. In Beta, the matter was an uncontrolled contractual arrangement between customer and scavenger.

A research study (not a part of this one) surveyed the four cities on the question of snow and ice removal practices. No reply was received from Gamma, but the other three cities responded to the following question: How many hours does it take to remove snow following a four-inch accumulation? Alpha replied it cleared business and through streets within four hours and residential areas within 16 hours; Beta that it took three hours on business streets, eight on through streets, and twenty-four in residential areas. Delta said five, five, and ten hours for the three categories.

The pattern was similar with regard to ice control. In the year of the two surveys (1957), Alpha spent three times as much as the other two cities on its snow and ice operations. Alpha was a larger city than the others, but not by very much. The questionnaire also turned up the fact that only Alpha swept up the abrasives in the spring, a practice befitting a city settled by the Dutch. Beta was most solicitous of street conditions in the business areas, while Delta was most concerned with residential streets. Alpha was roughly the mean of these extremes.

Budgetary figures suggest a few additional measures. Alpha and Gamma spent the most per capita on the non-food inspection services (building, plumbing, electrical, mechanical, and weights), followed by Beta and Delta. Virtually the same budgetary pattern applied to judicial expenditures and to the salaries of the municipal judges.

SUMMARY

Is it possible to add all these evaluations and come to some meaningful generalization? If we should impose a numerical rating on the cities for each category and then averages made, a kind of *consumer index* could be produced indicating how favorably consumer claims were weighed in each city. This was precisely the intent of this chapter, but the nature of the data would make any use of a concrete figure deceptive and artificial.

We propose, however, to do descriptively what we shy away from doing quantitatively. The most obvious conclusion is that Alpha was ranked first, and was viewed favorably by the professionals or received commendations for performances in most of the service categories studied.

Gamma ranked as an uneven second. In a few areas it stood first, but its deviations were more likely to be toward a lower rank, usually exchanging positions with Beta. The panelists rated Gamma second in police, fire, planning (one ranked it first), and recreation. It was appraised high in its handling of traffic engineering, water and sewage facilities, and second in the minor services such as rubbish removal and inspection. It was a scant third in its over-all salary schedule, while at the same time it paid the second highest salaries to its manager, planning director, police and fire chiefs. It ranked below Beta in safety performance and last with respect to street conditions.

In Beta, but more especially in Delta, low ratings by the professionals often centered about complaints of the incursion of "politics" as disruptive of the professional's standards. Outside specialists who had to deal with the Delta city council shook their heads in dismay over the attitudes exhibited by that body. The police panelists spoke of "political interference" with the department. The traffic engineers related difficulty in getting their ideas accepted or even listened to. The recreation panelist dismissed the council as not interested in his work. The sewage disposal technician cited the lack of cooperation in meeting state standards. The National Safety Council found the city wanting in developing a safety program.

From what has already been seen of the politics in Delta, it can hardly be said that the interests of the consumer-citizen were subordinated to the producer-citizen. There was little evidence that business interests, whether industrial or retail, had much influence over the city

council. On the other hand Alpha, the city rated highest
on our consumer-service index, numbered among its civic
leaders many persons who had attained community prominence for activities associated with their activities as
producers: industrial executives and leading businessmen.

Why did Delta, the city least subject to business
influences, have the lowest standards of consumer services?
The most obvious answer lies in the differences in consumer preferences of economic classes. The upper-middle
class that controlled Alpha not only preferred a fuller
range of amenities supplied by the city government, but
also realized that the professionals were natural allies in
achieving these goals. While the laboring groups that
controlled Delta may have desired some of these same
things, they were unwilling to pay for them, were not
sufficiently aware of the alternatives available, were more
interested in neighborhood conveniences than in broader
considerations, and in addition, perhaps, may have been
more suspicious of the professionals, from whom they
were often separated by language and education. However, it is interesting to note the amenities that the Delta
political organization did choose to emphasize. Concentration was placed on the service most visible to every citizen.
The Delta ward alderman made sure that the service that
symbolized his stewardship to constituents lay in sight
just beyond every voter's front window: in the condition
of the street, the prompt removal of ice and snow, and
the fire equipment that sped past occasionally, advertising
its service on every run.

The upper-middle-class orientation of Alpha civic
policies not only expressed itself in the levels of city
services, but also in a variety of other quasi-public facilities. In terms of libraries, museums, auditoriums, sym-
phonies, and civic-player groups, Alpha had superior

offerings, while these same programs were poor or non-existent in Delta. These cultural manifestations were often a product of philanthropy, at least in the first instance. Perhaps it was not a coincidence that Gamma was the other city that most closely approximated Alpha in obtaining these fruits of private donations. It was the only other city where the wealthy assumed a considerable role in the city's political life.

The value pattern extended to the city regulatory functions as well. Alpha and Gamma prohibited carnivals and street shows, and Alpha also prohibited circuses, amusement parks, drive-in theaters, merry-go-rounds, and commercial ice rinks. These same facilities could be licensed in both Beta and Delta. While Alpha was solicitous of the recreational needs of the people of lesser incomes by providing playgrounds and directed "creative" activities, it apparently looked askance at the more vulgar forms of commercial entertainment. One is reminded of the paternalistic plans of the early Fabians when they dreamed of replacing the workingman's favorite recreation—pub crawling—with something more "constructive."

The consumer-service pattern in Beta and Gamma appeared to be a product of political systems that often lacked well-defined purposes. These two cities excelled in few consumer services but rarely neglected any particular area completely.

NOTES

[1] The data used in this table, as with several other tables, were developed under conditions less than ideal. Anyone who has endeavored to work with municipal statistics should appreciate this fact. Municipal records are often poor and are rarely kept in uniform fashion. Central recording services including the *Compendium of Municipal Finances* of the United States Bureau of Census, state and private agencies, are not completely reliable. In the face of these odds the researchers can only report that they did the best they could.

Chapter XI

Type Three: Maintenance of Traditional Services

A policy of maintaining only traditional services, which we have for the sake of brevity dubbed caretaker government, essentially denotes a preference for private as opposed to public allocation of resources. Those who hold to this commitment deny the need for additional municipal services and oppose the extension of existing services. In operational terms this means opposition to innovations and tax increases.

To the extent that the last two chapters cover the spectrum of city activities, resistance to innovation has already been treated. That is, one fashion in which caretaker government finds expression is in refusing increased services to residences and business concerns alike. Resistance to change was most easily assessed in those areas of municipal government where new demands were made. In the period following World War II, the impact of increasing numbers of automobiles, suburban growth, and physical deterioration of the core cities, in combination with the new urban policies of the national government, provided the major incentives for policy changes. Not since the days when basic municipal utilities were first constructed had these cities been faced with so many novel problems. Specifically, each city had to respond to demands for public housing, renovation of the central business district, expanded public parking facilities, urban renewal and the necessary planning to carry through on these proposals. We have in large measure already discussed the responses.

A recapitulation of the data of the previous two chapters can give us some insight into the general commitments to caretaker government in the four cities. However, as some proposed innovations were not germane to the subjects in question, a more comprehensive approach is preferable. The referendum results furnish one such basis of evaluation. In them we have a series of official actions, which reflect general community attitudes, as well as the effectiveness of special group actions. Not the least among these special groups were, of course, the city officials, both elected and appointed.

Under the home rule charters of the four cities, referendums were used extensively. Petition requirements were sufficiently liberal to allow voters easily to place objectionable ordinances on the ballot. As referral to the voters by petition was a source of embarrassment to councilmen, controversial issues were frequently placed on the ballot by the councils in anticipation of petition action. This was especially true for ordinances involving any novel measure. Because the charters were specific as to the powers of the council, new policies frequently necessitated amendments and therefore had to be referred to the citizens. Finally, all general obligation bond issues had to have voter approval. For these reasons the referendums were an essential link in the political processes on most matters relevant to the subject of this chapter.

POPULAR CONTROL OF TAXATION

The property tax constituted the major source of local revenue throughout the state in which the four cities were located. Some state funds were distributed to the cities, but these were chiefly for specific purposes, the major one of which being for street maintenance. Most innovations or expanded services had to be paid through higher property taxes or service fees. Although the city charters of each city contained tax limits on the amount of millage that could be levied, none of the cities had reached its legal maximum. Consequently, decisions regarding normal tax increases were still in the hands of the city councils. In the area of mandatory referendums for general obligation bonds, three of the four cities required an extraordinary majority of three fifths of the votes. Gamma required only a simple majority.

Table 23. Voting Results on Selected Referendums

Issue	Per Cent Yes	Outcome
Alpha		
1. Sewage plant construction bonds	86	Passed
2. Storm sewer construction bonds	61	Passed
3. Provide off-street parking	62	Passed
4. Install parking meters	53	Passed
5. Alternate one-way street plan (initiative)	43	Rejected
6. Raise salary of City council ($350 to $1,000)	59	Passed

Beta

1. Set charter tax limit	43	Rejected
2. Set charter tax limit	52	Passed
3. Issue parking bonds for off-street system (initiative)	33	Rejected
4. Storm sewer bonds	56	Rejected*
5. Storm sewer bonds	49	Rejected*
6. Storm sewer bonds	57	Rejected*
7. Storm sewer millage increase for pay-as-you-go	63	Passed
8. Hospital expansion bonds	70	Passed
9. New pension system for firemen and policemen	66	Passed
10. Millage to support pension plan	35	Rejected

Gamma

1. Storm sewer construction bonds	61	Passed
2. Additional storm sewer construction bonds	67	Passed
3. Established off-street municipal parking system	54	Passed
4. Authorize special assessment for parking lots	40	Rejected
5. Improve police and fire pension system	70	Passed
6. Provide health and accident insurance for city employees	57	Passed
7. Reduce working hours of firemen to 63-hour week	41	Rejected

Delta

1. Lower charter tax limit (initiative)	23	Rejected
2. Increase local improvement bonding limit	48	Rejected
3. Authorize water bonds	61	Passed
4. Issue water bonds	56	Rejected*
5. Salary increase for council	36	Rejected
6. Salary increase for council	35	Rejected
7. Salary increase for municipal judge	26	Rejected
8. Salary increase for council	26	Rejected

* Three fifths vote required.

 9. Create independent hospital board and support
    it by one mill levy 46   Rejected

10. Liberalize retirement system for firemen and
    policemen 35   Rejected

11. Liberalize retirement system for firemen and
    policemen 52   Passed

12. Establish housing authority 51   Passed

In Table 22 the experiences of the four cities with referendums during the ten-year period are recorded. The issues selected included all major decisions related either to increased taxes or to the introduction of new functions. (A number of measures of minor consequence have been omitted.) A glance down the columns of this table indicates the differenct disposition of the voters in the four cities. The issues are not of equal importance, however, and some of them are obscure, so a few comments are in order before summarizing the implications of the data. Except for the three issues marked "initiative," all measures were placed on the ballot by council action. Thus, there was at least formal approval by the governing body in each case, though on several occasions it was apparent that the measures had only token council support. Measures were sometimes placed on the ballot out of deference to a council minority or to some group, the police or firemen, for example.

The voters of Alpha had a perfect record of supporting all innovations and improvements. The one item rejected (No. 5) involved a one-way street plan placed on the ballot by initiative petition as an alternative to a council proposal. It would have substantially changed the one-way grid pattern chosen by the council on the advice of the city traffic engineer and an outside consulting firm.

Thus a vote against the matter was a vote in support of the council and of the recommendations of the professional technicians. In considering the voting record in Alpha, attention needs to be drawn to the 86 per cent support of a bond issue for sewer plant construction. This measure carried in every precinct in the city and established the record for public support of a public improvement throughout the study period.

Beta approved only two issues that would have involved increased costs for the city taxpayers. The votes recorded in Table 22 are somewhat deceptive and require explanation. The first two referendums No. 1 and No. 2) actually proposed policies moving in opposite directions. The first vote was taken at a time when the city was operating under a state law that limited municipal taxation. Its effect would have been to allow a higher city tax rate by substituting a ten-mill limit for a lower state statutory limit. Subsequently, the state law was repealed. Thus the second measure, while nearly identical in language to the first, had the effect of imposing a tax limit where one did not exist. It should be pointed out that the first vote was taken at a time when the city was in a severe financial crisis. Every third street light was being left unlighted; branch libraries were closed; and services generally were being curtailed. The need for increased revenue was compelling.

The four sewer-construction issues were voted on over a period of three years. Parts of the city were experiencing severe flooding, a health hazard accompanied each heavy rain, and development of choice subdivision sites was being obstructed. Under the bonding plan three-fifths of those voting (only taxpayers were eligible) had to approve. After three defeats, a seven-year pay-as-you-go plan, requiring a simple majority of all citizens voting, was approved. The hospital bond involved a modest one-mill levy, but here again the issue was complicated. The expansion was part of a plan transferring a municipal hospital district with a constituency larger than the city. The city supported this move, which was partially motivated by a desire to spread the burden of the cost of welfare cases in the hospital. The hospital vote could thus be interpreted as a means of saving city taxpayers money in the long run. Lastly, regarding the firemen and police pension increase, it should be noted that the pension was approved, though the additional funds necessary to support it were voted down. The net result was that the new pension had to be crowded into the regular city budget. In brief, Beta was an unwilling city when it came to voting tax increases.

Gamma's record, though not identical to Alpha's, was certainly similar. In Gamma only one issue that would have resulted in increased costs to the city taxpayers was defeated. This was the firemen's request for a reduced work week (No. 7). The other issue rejected (No. 4) pertained to authorization for the city to finance off-street parking lots by special assessment. There were several peculiarities about this issue. In the first place, the financial burden involved would have fallen on the downtown property owners and not on the general public. Secondly, the city attorney claimed the amendment was not necessary, as the city already had the power to finance the lots. The council apparently placed the measure on the ballot to strengthen its hand in dealing with the parking problem. Councilmen believed that a favorable vote would have been a vote of confidence for a special-assessment parking policy. This it failed to receive, but the council promptly proceeded to initiate a special assessment plan anyway, relying on the legal opinion of the city attorney.

Delta approached Beta in its unwillingness to pass new levies, though the voters did turn down an opportunity to write a lower tax ceiling into the city charter (Item 1). But only one measure involving increased public expenditures (liberalization of the retirement system, No. 11) actually became law. While the water bonds (No. 3) were authorized, the actual vote to issue them (No. 4) failed for want of a three-fifths favorable vote. And although the public approved a public-housing ordinance (No. 12) by a narrow majority, the vote was only advisory in nature. The ordinance was vetoed by the mayor and the public-housing project was never built.

Thus, in the ten-year period, the Delta voters were most steadfastly opposed to changes in local government costing more money. Beta citizens were only a little more receptive to increased costs. The Gamma citizens nearly always approved financial measures and those in Alpha did every time they were asked to. It will be seen that this scaling of the cities roughly approximates the scale for innovations and service levels treated in the last two chapters. The major difference pertains to Beta. Beta was somewhat more amenable to innovations that served the producer interests of the community than this scale would indicate. Industrial recruitment was looked upon as a legitimate municipal function, a view that Delta did not share. The Beta government assumed responsibility for providing municipal parking in the CBD. In providing for basic community needs, Beta eventually did produce needed storm sewers although it took four votes to reach agreement. On the other hand, Delta refused to take care of its water and sewage waste problems, and built a treatment plant only under a court order from the state. Thus, while Beta was nearly as penurious as Delta in authorizing expenditures in the referendum questions, in the overall picture the political system of Beta was somewhat more responsive to certain demands for innovations.

In the previous two chapters we have contented ourselves with scaling the cities according to a particular type and have deferred hypotheses explaining community differences. However, factors peculiar to decision through referendum make it desirable that some preliminary exploration into the question of "why" be interjected at this point. Was the difference in referendum results a function of varied council strategies? Were the differences exaggerated by varied degrees of caution exhibited by the councils? Were the differences attributable to the recruiting process through which councilmen were chosen? To interest group activities directed toward the public? Or were they merely a function of the prevailing economic conditions in the cities? The last question will be treated first.

Table 24. Average Per Capita Property Taxes in the Four Cities, 1948-57*

City	City taxes	School taxes	County taxes	Total
Alpha	$24	$36	$10	$70
Beta	26	34	12	72
Gamma	29	30	17	76
Delta	28	21	12	61

* Based on state taxation reports and annual population estimates. Population estimates were computed from 1950 census and the 1960 preliminary totals, with allowances for annexations.

THE ECONOMIC VARIABLE

Were Beta and Delta poor cities? Were they already disproportionately overburdened with taxes? Was their economic future dim? Were their needs for civic improvements less pressing? The data available on these questions suggest that any economic explanation for the referendum patterns in the two cities must be a qualified one.

First, let us consider the comparative tax burden of the four communities. Because the property tax not only supported city government but schools and county government as well, its burden must be viewed in the context of support for the three governmental units. The figures shown in Table 24 indicate that there was little correlation between resistance to tax increases and the over-all per capita tax burden. Of the two cities showing greatest tax resistance, Delta had the lowest over-all per capita tax rate and Beta the next to the highest.

Table 25.
Per Capita Assessed Valuation of Property, 1955--57

Year	Alpha	Beta	Gamma	Delta
1955	$2,020	$2,410	$3,250	$2,300
1956	2,090	3,050	3,330	2,310
1957	2,270	3,170	3,480	2,330
Average	2,137	2,877	3,353	2,313

However, the burden of a property tax is not evenly spread on a per capita basis. A crucial variable is the ratio of total wealth in property to population. The state provided reasonably comparable total property valuation for the three years 1955-57. In Table 25 the per capita valuations for the four cities have been tabulated. According to this measure of ability to pay, the two cities with the best record for voting capital improvements, Alpha and Gamma, were lowest and highest respectively in per capita wealth. By combining elements in the above computations a more satisfactory index of the comparative tax burden on the individual citizens can be derived. A computation of the total property tax collected in each year as a percentage of total assessed valuation shows how heavily the total tax burden rested upon any given piece of property, assuming equity among the individual assessments. These results are given in Table 26, indicating a picture very similar to the one in Table 23. Beta and Delta, the two cities showing greatest tax resistance in referendums, were midway between the other two cities with reference to the tax burden on each particular property owner. Thus there is no direct correlation between tax resistance and the existing tax burden.

Table 26. Total Property Tax Levy
as a Percentage of Total Assessed Valuation

| Year | Percentage | | | |
	Alpha	Beta	Gamma	Delta
1955	3.84	3.69	3.01	3.20
1956	4.19	3.55	3.04	3.33
1957	4.63	3.68	3.46	3.67
Average	4.22	3.64	3.17	3.40

An important economic variable is the ability to pay. There is no necessary relationship between this and the possession of real property, because property taxes must be paid from income and, for the average family, real property is not a source of income. It is more likely to be a consumption item: a dwelling. Consequently, it is appropriate to examine the income factor in the four cities.

Two measures can be derived from the 1950 decennial census and the 1954 census of manufacturers. The first yields median income and the second real wages per manufacturing employee. Beta and Delta ranked first and third respectively in median income and first and fourth in real wages for industrial employees. But perhaps the closeness of these figures should be stressed more than their rank. The spread can be measured by an index of variation, which indicates the percentage of deviation from the mean. In only one case was this variation greater than 5 per cent: in the median income of Gamma. In this

Table 27. Median Income (1950) and
Real Wages Per Manufacturing Employee (1954)

City	Median income	Index of variation	Real wages per man-ufacturing employee (county)	Index of variation
Alpha	$3,590	102.3	$3,906	99.5
Beta	3,660	104.3	4,027	102.6
Gamma	3,320	94.6	3,985	101.5
Delta	3,460	98.6	3,787	96.5

case the deviation was in the direction opposite the one that would contribute to an economic explanation of the referendum votes (see Table 27).

Prospects for future income may have weighed as heavily on tax decisions as did current income or wealth in real property; consequently, the general economic climate merits attention. Only Alpha had escaped serious economic difficulty in the recession periods that followed World War II and the Korean conflict. Some of this difficulty is reflected in the unemployment figures shown in Table 28. Reliable figures were available only for the years 1949 and following, and only for counties, not cities. Consequently, they reflect the general economic situation in the over-all economic community. As explained before, these cities were centrally located in their respective counties and the county embraced the immediate economic community in each case. As city workers commuted outside the city limits to industrial plants and vice versa, the county figures are probably adequate for our purposes. These figures again document the comparative stability of the Alpha economy.

Unemployment is only one index of prosperity. It is perfectly possible for a community to enjoy some economic growth in the midst of chronic unemployment. In the first place, unemployment is a subjectively defined status to a certain extent. Secondly, there may be increased employment over time, but it may be of a kind than cannot accommodate the available labor supply in a given area. This could result from noncompatibility of the skills of the unemployed with jobs available, or racial discrimination. Consequently, still another measure of increase in the labor force has been used, based upon the assumption that if new industries or businesses are

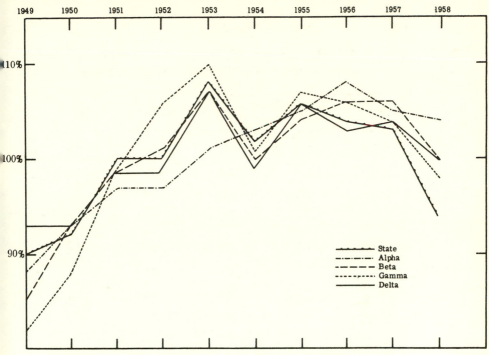

developing in an area they should create additional jobs.
While automation may offset this possibility to a certain
extent, and the ratio of employment to gross receipts
varies by industry, the size of the labor force remains a
fairly reliable economic barometer.

The changes in the labor force over a decade are
reported in Figure 2. This chart was computed by using
the ten-year average as the base of the index. Thus the
pattern and direction of change is recorded, rather than
any comparison of total growth. The graph indicates
several differences among the cities. Alpha had the most
stable pattern, moving generally upward independently
of statewide fluctuations except in the last two years of
the period. Beta and Delta closely followed the fluctuations in the state. Gamma had a tendency to swing in

Table 28. Average Monthly Unemployment as a Percentage of Total Labor Force (County)

Year	Alpha	Beta	Gamma	Delta
1949	6.3	11.2	19.5	7.8
1950	2.4	6.5	9.7	5.4
1951	1.8	3.2	3.6	4.6
1952	2.5	3.3	2.5	5.2
1953	1.6	3.0	3.7	2.9
1954	3.7	4.2	9.0	8.0
1955	2.2	3.5	4.2	4.2
1956	2.1	4.2	6.4	6.1
1957	4.0	5.5	8.9	6.9
Average	3.0	5.0	7.5	5.7

exaggerated arcs starting lower than the state in 1949 and rapidly swinging higher than the state in growth during the period of the Korean conflict. In the best year after World War II Gamma's labor force was high compared to Beta's and Delta's, but in the 1958 decline it dropped lower than that of either by one percentage point.

One final consideration should emerge before we summarize this economic information. A referendum must be considered in the context of the fiscal situation of the particular city. Did any of the cities have an accumulation of bonded debts? Alpha had no outstanding debt at the beginning of the period. In fact, the city had a long standing pay-as-you-go fiscal policy. Though typically such a policy means the postponement of some capital improvements, this probably was not so for Alpha. Since the city enjoyed comparative prosperity during the thirties, it was able to take advantage of cheap materials and labor. It probably had less of a backlog of needed capital improvements in the immediate postwar period than did the other three. Alpha broke its long-standing debt-free policy during the study period and financed a storm sewer and a sewage-disposal plant through bond issues. These were the first such issues on the Alpha ballot in decades.

During the Great Depression, both Beta and Gamma turned to deficit financing. Beta sold bonds even for minor improvements. Gamma plunged heavily into debt in the early thirties to alleviate local unemployment through a home-grown public-works project. Nearly $2,000,000 in bonds were sold for these purposes. In 1947, Beta and Gamma each still had about $1,000,000 debt in general obligation bonds, as well as $300,000 and $500,000 respectively outstanding in revenue bonds for improvements in sewage and water systems. Delta had a small general obligation bond debt of $165,000, but it also had a $500,000 water revenue bond issue dating from 1921. This is an inordinately long time for a debt on such a utility. It indicated slipshod fiscal management at some point in the past. Although these variations existed, none of the cities could be considered debt-ridden, and certainly, none was anywhere near reaching its legal debt limits. The debt-retirement funds constituted a small percentage of the tax bill in each case.

In summary, there appears to be some logic to the tax-resistant stance of Delta and the more receptive one of Alpha. Alpha had low per capita taxes. It had a stable and steadily expanding local economy. The long, debt-free tradition assured no legacy of past disappointments in fiscal management. However, Alpha was also the city with the leanest property base upon which to mount its tax burden. Delta was generally lower than the median in all the economic measures. This may help explain both the low tax scale in this city and the resistance to further increases.

The behavior of Beta and Gamma bore no relationship to the economic variables. Quite the opposite. Gamma was lower than Beta in median income, wages, growth, and higher in unemployment. It also had the highest per capita tax load in terms of both the city and the total amounts. The only favorable factor in the Gamma picture was a healthy tax base upon which to rest the tax levies. However, bonding firms had little confidence in this factor for security on bonded indebtedness: Gamma had the poorest credit rating, according to *Moody's Municipals*.

A strict economic explanation of tax resistance is insufficient to explain tax policy, but economic variables appear to be a significant factor in certain circumstances.

MOBILIZATION OF SUPPORT

In the analysis of referendum voting reported in Chapter V, it was stated that the most consistent supporters for the city councils' positions were persons with higher socioeconomic status. This was the case both with reference to financial issues and proposals for innovations. A heavy concentration of negative votes was found among those with lower incomes or modest and fixed incomes. The negative vote also appeared to have a higher incidence among older people. However, as there were no significant demographic differences among the four cities, differences in the outcomes of referendums cannot be explained by the relative proportions of these groups in each jurisdiction. The question then must become: Were there differences in the political organization among the cities which would have mobilized and activated the latent voting tendencies of certain groups more in one city than another?

In approaching this question we are faced with a methodological problem concerning the establishment of casual factors. Three elements in the political processes distinguished the cities of Alpha and Gamma from Beta and Delta and could have influenced the outcome of referendums. These were the status of the city councils, the role of the newspapers, and the activities of organized groups in opposition to the city council positions. The question is whether these elements differed because the total value structure of the communities differed or whether these were independent variables that reshaped the value expression of the publics in the referendum votes. It is not possible to resolve this question within the framework of the present study. We can only report that voter disapproval of council proposals was accompanied by certain common characteristics in the political process, and in the absence of these characteristics in the other cities, referendum results differed.

The three factors—status of the city councils, the role of the newspapers, and activities of organized opposition groups—all tended to minimize the effectiveness of the councils as proposing bodies. The councils in Beta and Delta were elected by wards. This meant that councilmen, generally, in these two cities were less likely to be men with established city-wide reputations. While there were significant exceptions in Beta, most of the councilmen in both cities became first known to the general public as councilmen. They rarely brought high prestige and reputation to the office. This was reflected in the lower percentage of professionals and nonretail executives elected to these offices in Beta and Delta than were in Alpha and Gamma. Delta councilmen were generally persons of modest education. While the educational level of the Beta council was much higher, the reputation of this group was not enhanced by the constant divisions within its ranks and vacillations characteristic of many of its deliberations. Lack of consensus in the Beta council probably reflected both the absence of a structured politics and conflicting ward constituency interests. Generally, the respondents interviewed in Beta and Delta who were not connected with the city government treated the councilmen with poorly concealed contempt. This was rarely so in the other two cities, and in Alpha the council was generally a source of some pride even among labor leaders.

These images of the councilmen may have been partly the responsibilities of the newspapers. In Beta and Delta, the papers treated the city administrations generally with thinly veiled distaste. This was true of their attitude toward both the elected councilmen and the appointed officials. The newspapers in both of these cities even expressed a certain glee when the council was in an embarrassing position or pinned on the horns of a political dilemma.

In all the cities, the press attended the executive sessions of the council. In Alpha and Gamma the newspapers exercised some restraint in publishing remarks that were off the record. No such understanding existed in Beta.

In retaliation and self-defense the council at times exercised some ingenuity in arranging negotiating sessions without informing the press. The local reporters showed even more ingenuity in finding access to these meetings. In several cases they gave them "star chamber" headlines. As the newspaper had a near monopoly on local news reports, this could not help but have some effect on the community image of the council and city government. If the council was made the butt of a joke, why should people have confidence in its proposals?

The irony of the situation is that the newspapers frequently wholeheartedly endorsed many of the proposals that went down to defeat. The Beta newspaper devoted a large amount of space to feature stories on parking prior to the referendum on that issue. On each occasion, it campaigned vigorously for passage of the storm sewer bond proposal. But as much of its local reporting was devoted to criticisms of the council and the manager the rest of the year, it may not be so surprising that these measures failed to gather public support. The Delta paper generally ignored local matters except for verbatim records of council meetings set in fine print on inside pages. When it was vocal on local affairs it was generally to advocate some general governmental reform.

By contrast, the newspapers of Alpha and Gamma gave the city government a much better daily press. There was, in fact, less material to be exploited for derogatory comments on councilmanic activities. However, the Gamma council certainly had violent factional splits, colorful and outspoken councilmen, and even cases involving allegations of conflict of interest. These matters were all reported, but in a style that did not make the elective officials generally the objects of derision. Thus, the inherent weaknesses of the councils in Beta and Delta for mobilizing support on referendums were accentuated by the primary source of communications on local matters, while the councils of Alpha and Gamma did not have to contend with such a burden.

In Alpha, Beta, and Gamma were organizations active in opposition to the council position on most referendums. These small groups were vocal in espousing values that coincided nearly exactly with what we have called care-taker government. Their membership was never large, the leadership was at times poor, and their funds were usually meager. Their indictment of city government ran to extremes. The government was accused of socialism when it advocated parking lots, the city-manager system was characterized as bureaucratic centralism, the decline of individualism was lamented, and often an indictment was directed toward the local wealthy.

While these groups had their small coterie of followers, their efforts in and of themselves were probably not very important on many issues. However, on particular occasions they were able to rally additional support in Alpha and Gamma. The primary activity in Alpha was in conjunction with urban renewal. The source of monetary support for their publicity was furnished by slum landlords. They attacked at a time when city officials were absorbed in the CBD activities. The scaling down of the redevelopment project partially stemmed from the activities of this group. In Gamma, financial sponsorship came from the opponents of public parking. Members were primarily persons whose property would be taken over and the private lot operators. In their major campaign effort, a referendum authorizing a special-assessment approach to municipal parking development was defeated.

In Beta the organization, the Low Tax League, had a more continuous and successful existence because it had a strong ally—the realtors. Realtors enjoy a national reputation as a conservative force in local politics. While there was an organized realty board in each of the four cities, only in Beta did its political activities reach any prominence.

Ostensibly, realtors have an interest in a low property tax for several reasons. Higher taxes remove potential home purchasers from the market. Any rise in the monthly payment necessary to buy a home removes some families as potential buyers, or forces others to buy less expensive dwellings. With reference to income property, the property tax is a cost item that diminishes the potential profitability of any investment in real estate. In addition, some realtors feel that higher taxes divert individual expenditures from property maintenance, which, in turn, leads to neighborhood deterioration, lowered property values, and eventually to a reduction in the tax base. It is possible, however, to argue the contrary, that higher service standards make a community more attractive, attract population and industry, and hence increase potential customers for realtors. Specific improvements may enhance the value of specific properties; i.e., the improved drainage that prevents basement flooding may increase house sales in a specific area. Thus the interests of realtors are complex in relation to the property tax, and it is not surprising to find that the policies of various city boards were not uniform.

In Beta, the realty board was an unequivocal, self-avowed low-tax interest group. An ex-president of the board declared that the group looked upon itself as the guardian of the taxpayer's dollar. It rarely supported any improvement and vehemently opposed most. On referendum issues it bought newspaper space, issued public statements, and provided speakers for public appearances. Frequently, it operated through the Low Tax League, which was officially a separate body. The use of the front served several purposes. When opposition was being voiced on an issue, such as school bonds, this device took some of the public onus off the realtors. Secondly, there was some division among realtors on various issues. It was easier to get financial contributions for the front organization than it was to place the realty board publicly on record. Thus, a realtor who did not want to associate himself with the position could escape public identification.

The Low Tax League was composed of the more conservative realtors and a membership drawn from other sources. A number of the nonrealtor members were retired persons, usually property owners, a few whom owned slum property. The League, on occasion, engaged in rather forceful propaganda. Its advertisements and handouts employed scare tactics. It would pose alarming questions and use innuendoes suggesting that unknown persons woud benefit from a "yes" vote. On occasion, its tactics became so rough that the realty board refused to help to finance its campaigns, but the League proceeded with individual realtor support.

Beta realtors and their allies never failed in an anti-tax levy campaign. Occasional school levies were successful when the group remained neutral. Once the board— successfully—supported a measure to provide storm sewers. The project paved the way for additional housing starts in the most popular above average income section of the city. The realty interests probably saved the city substantial amounts of money through their opposition to a revenue bond issue for parking. A cheaper means of providing this facility was subsequently discovered. While the referendum was the realtors' favorite weapon, on one occasion they organized a telephone pressure campaign to prevent the council from raising city taxes. They were again successful.

In none of the other cities did the realty board pursue a low-tax policy so openly. In Gamma, the realtors initially opposed municipal parking, partially because, under the plan, no realtor would get fees for land acquisition sales or leases. In interviews several realtors stated that they were reluctant to see expensive downtown land passing forever from the sales market. The Board also applied pressure on behalf of property owners whose values were to be adversely affected by a new zoning ordinance. While there is some evidence that Gamma realtors shared the values of those in Beta, they never employed the same vigorous tactics. In Delta the realtors, as an organization, played no role in local politics. The Alpha group represented the opposite extreme in the spectrum of attitudes toward civic expenditures. It supported nearly every civic project during the ten-year period. It gave open support to several school millage increases. The principal point at which Alpha realtors applied pressure on behalf of their own direct interests pertained to city ordinances which had immediate implications for property sales. For instance, when they felt a subdivision ordinance would curtail development of vacant city land in favor of suburban areas they secured a change that maintained the city standards but made land less expensive to subdivide.

Thus, in endeavoring to explain why Beta and Delta

were more attracted by caretaker government than Alpha and Gamma, we are faced with a web of evidence in which the key strand is by no means obvious. There was no single variable at work. However, if we were to pick from among the factors that appeared to be most important, it would be the esteem that the city council and administration enjoyed in the eyes of the citizens. In Beta and Delta the recruitment process, the newspapers, and the organized political life of the community all seemed to contribute to a situation where it was easy for a citizen to dismiss the recommendations of the city council. While Delta did not have a powerful interest group, such as the Beta realtors, in organized opposition, there was scarcely a need for one, given the behavior of the council. In the first place, the Delta council itself was guided by values that might be considered congenial to caretaker standards. However, the council was occasionally forced by the sheer circumstance of its position to suggest remedial actions for deficiencies in the municipal operation. In facing its responsibility, it did not abet its cause by overloading the ballot with a profusion of ineptly conceived and often confusing propositions.

The Alpha council members had great prestige as individuals and a long reputation for successful municipal management. While Gamma was not able to recruit the same kind of leadership, the council position there was ably supported by well-led business organizations and the local newspaper. There was no effective opposition group. Labor, the potential opposition, was co-opted by the representation it enjoyed on the council.

Chapter XII

Type Four: Arbitration Among Conflicting Interests

As we have defined it, arbitration among conflicting interests is raised to the level of dominant policy when governmental officials are preoccupied with the task of adjusting the varied claims of many interests rather than with combining their energies toward the achievement of specific goals. The chief characteristic of government by arbitration is the accessibility of decision-makers to a variety of claimants and a willingness on the part of officials to honor many such claims.

The idea of a completely "neutral" government is a contradictory concept. Decision-making requires that some claims be sacrifices to others; all governments must act or they cease to fulfill their function. However, it is possible to conceive a scale along which governments could be plotted. On one end of the scale would be governments basically committed to a particular segment of the citizenry, and problems are solved according to the goals of that segment. On the other end of the scale government would approach neutrality. The machinery of government would remain basically uncommitted over the long run. Various segments of the citizenry would win occasional skirmishes, but no group would generally prevail.

It was hypothesized in developing this type that under arbiter government councilmen would view themselves as being essentially *delegates* chosen to act according to the guides of public opinion and constituent demands. However, councilmen who were basically committed to the interests of a segment of their constituency would assume they had been elected because of their views on public policy. Therefore, as councilmen, these persons would maintain that the councilmanic role was analogous to that of the *board of directors* in a corporation and that each member should use his own judgment in deciding issues according to his personal views regarding the interests of the municipal corporation.

The latter outlook implies that the public interest is both ascertainable and indivisible. The good of the city, like the good of the corporation, must be stated in all-encompassing terms. The interests of "all the people" is achieved through a dialogue in council among the elected, whose views have been given a mandate.

The former outlook asserts that the job of the legislator is to do what the people want and that these wants are most accurately expressed on a day-to-day basis. The councilman is a public servant who should entertain the requests and grievances of the citizens and attempt to accommodate their desires, if it is possible within the framework of the law and what taxpayers are willing to spend. As the claims clash, there is no obvious standard by which to judge the merits of each; consequently, the conflicts must be resolved through arbitration.

Councilmen and other informants in the four communities were asked to describe the behavior of the councilmen using these two conceptions of representation. Councilmen were also asked to describe their own attitudes. With few exceptions, the councilmen who rejected the *delegate* role embraced the *board of directors* one. Those who were referred to by others as being delegates spoke of themselves as being representatives of the "little fellow" and expressed ambivalence or hostility toward the board of directors approach. However, a few wanted to embrace both views and refused to see any inconsistency. There was consensus among informants concerning the prevailing approach to representation that existed in each of the municipalities.

Reflection upon the data gathered as a result of this line of inquiry indicated that this measurement of the existence of government by arbitration expressed itself in class terms. The Burkian, or board of directors, concept was embraced by those with higher socioeconomic backgrounds and vice versa for the delegate approach. The councilmen of Delta were self-avowed delegates for their wards' constituents. The Citizens' Committee councilmen of Alpha would not countenance such a role. But on the basis of our previous findings, these were the two communities with the most structured politics and ostensibly their governments were the most dominated by the values of a single segment of the populace.

Thus, it can be seen that the behavior of representatives is an inadequate standard in itself of arbiter government. The actuality of access must be tested not only by traditional practices and the attitude of councilmen, but also by the content of policy. Only a city in which councilmen (1) looked with favor toward the delegate concept, (2) actually practiced this representational function, and

(3) also responded to claims from various segments of the community would conform to our standard of government by arbitration. The activities of the four cities will be discussed according to this standard.

Alpha. The overwhelming majority of the councilmen in Alpha assumed the *board of directors* approach. Most of the councilmen, especially those sponsored by the Citizens' Committee, did not want to be bothered by the chores of representing individual grievances. Indulgence in the practice was frowned upon as breaking the rules. Council members who were important businessmen knew they would have trouble recruiting others to the council if the councilman's job was associated with these kinds of commitments. Of course, there was nothing to prevent citizens from making requests. The standard parry was a polite referral to the city manager, thus discouraging private access through councilmen. In addition, citizens were encouraged to bring their requests before the full council in its public meetings. No more than two councilmen at any one time assumed the role of broker for individual complainants. These councilmen, who asserted they spoke for the "little man," never won a single major battle and could chalk up victories in only a few minor skirmishes. The Citizens' Committee nominees always dominated the city council. Was this domination essentially an expression of a specific segment of the population?

Alpha clearly demonstrated that while the first two categories in the typology logically represent distinct sets of values, in practice they may be largely combined in the program of a given city. The conflict between the producer and consumer interests is clearly evident in many suburbs, but in a small core city that was extending its municipal boundaries to include the residential fringe, a duality of goals was clearly possible, and perhaps necessary. But in combining policies of economic growth and increased amenities, and in selecting alternatives within each of these categories, a pattern of choice emerged clearly. The private and business interests of the more affluent generally prevailed over the less affluent. It was not a case of ruthless choices, of the wealthy exploiting the poor, of discrimination in the distribution of services, or any form of blatant favoritism. Indeed, many prominent civic leaders in and out of office pursued a kind of *noblesse oblige* policy in such areas as racial discrimination or in charitable enterprises. Despite this, the pattern remained.

The downtown renewal project, which topped all other civic projects in its absorption of governmental and administrative attention, would in the long run serve the interests of the largest property owners in the CBD. The traffic, parking, and pedestrian island plans were not designed to help the little merchant. Indeed, with the upgrading of the CBD many of the smaller concerns would very likely be squeezed out. Among the casualties of the overriding interest in the CBD was the urban renewal project. It dwindled from a rather ambitious renewal effort to a modest one, in which council interest declined drastically when the Federal government vetoed efforts to tie the project to industrial and transportation aims.

Other illustrations indicate the same trend. The sale of the power plant was most strongly advocated by the larger business interests. Rent control was rejected by the council despite a study commission report that advocated the opposite course of action. While municipal sewage waste was meticulously cared for, local industries were allowed to pollute the river without any demurrer. When the privately owned utility sought a state-wide rate increase, the city did not protest on behalf of its consumers. (Delta protested vigorously.) The airport was given greater attention than in any of the other cities. Working-class taverns were illegal, but the more well-to-do had their drinking clubs. The salary spread between top and bottom for city officials was greatest of any of the cities. This generally reflected a desire to use government officials for difficult planning tasks and also followed a pattern condoned more by industrialists than lower-income persons. Laws prohibiting overnight, on-street parking were passed to aid street cleaning and snow removal, but effected a hardship on those families without garages and driveways who generally were in the poorer sections. An early casualty in an economic retrenchment move that followed just after the study period was a cutback in recreation, a "frill" that is of most importance to families with limited financial means. Alpha was the only city that prohibited drive-ins, amusement rides, carnivals, and similar forms of working-class entertainment.

Thus a general class bias pervaded many areas of municipal policy. Perhaps a further indication of the refusal to govern through arbitration in Alpha was the absence of a category of incidents that sprinkled the news of the other three cities. These incidents included the many occasions when special advantage through concessions in municipal policies were either sought or granted by particular groups. The prevailing attitude of the Alpha council did not afford access to these kinds of claims.

Beta. By contrast, the councilmen in Beta could not escape from the barrage of requests for private bills.

Because of the ward system, or for whatever other reason, even when a corporation executive of a sizable firm sat on the city council, he was obliged to process complaints about chuck holes in the streets and burned-out street lights. Along with these householder-type grievances, the councilmen were also the object of a different order of requests. Both small and large interests sought to exploit the city government for private advantage and the council of Beta was accessible for these claimants.

The frequent vacillation of the Beta council was symptomatic of this. Vote switching was highly characteristic. Over a five-year period, twenty-one votes were taken on specific extensions of services to fringe areas or on the principle of extension. The votes of over half of the councilmen were erratic. Each incident, of course, involved a different set of property owners. While some of the fluctuation may have been a result of extenuating circumstances, it would be hard to account for all the switches this way. Many interests obviously attempted to exploit the accessibility of the council.

The tavern keepers endeavored to restrict the number of beer retail licenses, contractors attempted to get preference for local businesses on bids for city business, service station managers tried to manipulate zoning to keep choice corners out of the hands of cut-rate competitors, the airport concessions also indicated a pattern of influence: in this case neither a policy of regulated monopoly nor open competition was pursued and there were public accusations of councilmanic protection of a concessionaire.

A review of large as well as small policy questions in Beta reveals no pattern of bias comparable to the one discerned in Alpha. In central business district policies, the council was buffeted by the merchants on one side and the low-tax realty group on the other. The parking issue was largely settled outside the city council. Unlike in Alpha, the one-way street plan was instituted only after many delays and changes. Most adversely affected merchants could find a friendly ear on the council. An ambitious urban renewal project received approval. Its sources of public support were varied, the primary one in the city administration itself. The council could not resolve the issue of Sunday auto racing and placed the matter on the ballot. It neither opposed nor supported rent control; it merely failed to act.

The Beta council rarely took a firm position on general city policies. Other municipal agencies, such as the planning commission or the city administration, sometimes did. Throughout the ten-year period, the inability of the council to hold a position usually served to advantage caretaker interests. At least in the short run, the tax rate seldom increased when the councilmen could not make up their minds. But as a low-tax policy was not in itself desirable to many of the councilmen, such a policy was never openly endorsed, as it was in Delta. The council was sensitive to the pressures of the civic booster, the defender of civic pride, the hard-pressed merchant, and the citizen desiring more services. Perhaps no issue placed the council in more of a quandary than did the matter of the proposed new city hall.

There had never been a city hall in Beta. The municipal offices in 1948 were housed in a group of rented offices over a downtown store. Several years after the study period began the planning commission drew up a long-range capital improvement schedule, which included the erection of a new city hall, though far down on the list. The mayor gave leadership to this particular project, publicly citing the inadequate space for an expanding staff and the need for a city hall to symbolize the city's pride and prosperity. With or without reason, some people accused the mayor of trying to build a monument to his administration, because he intermittently reintroduced the subject and submitted various plans. The mayor's interest was certainly unusual in that he gave little leadership on other issues; however, the need for space was real. A solution seemed to be found when the city was able to obtain an old, centrally located school building for the token sum of $25,000. The small sum was made politically possible by the fact that the perimeters, and hence the constituencies, of the school district and the city were virtually the same.

For the next three years a controversy that overshadowed all other civic questions raged about the question of whether to raze or renovate the school building. During this long period, the subject was constantly raised in the newspaper and figured prominently in the statements of various civic bodies, both official and nonofficial, but it was never a subject of formal council action. Only after the contending parties had practically exhausted themselves did the council make its position known.

The principal protagonists in this drama were the city planning commission and the Low Tax League. The League has already been introduced. The planning commission was generally composed of some of the more important businessmen and professional persons. In social and economic position, the planning commission member ranked well above the city councilman. Generally this body was action-oriented, ready to move ahead on many needed city improvements. The chairman was the manager of one of the largest main street retail stores.

Several weeks after the city acquired the school building, the planning commission recommended that the building be razed. The report stated that the cost of renovation would be excessive. The newspaper was critical of the planning commission's recommendation, asking why it should cost so much to renovate a building that was in daily use as a school. The paper also editorialized that the city needed parking lots more than a city hall, and berated the council, which was reported to be supporting the planning commission proposal. The Low Tax League announced opposition to razing. Two months later the council earmarked $120,000 for the city hall in the capital budget with no recommendation as to its specific use. Estimations by the planning commission for either renovation or rebuilding ran around $450,000, but the figure was not the product of a firm architectural plan.

Through a public meeting and newspaper releases, the Low Tax League hammered away on the general theme, "Why destroy a perfectly good building?" When the planning commission stated that it did not meet the requirements of the fire code, the League produced an underwriter who declared the building one of the best constructed in the city. The planning commission asked, "Why pour money into an old building which will still be old when renovated?" The League replied, "Why destroy a perfectly good building?" A number of planning commissioners privately felt that a school building would make an awkward and ill-arranged city hall. The classrooms, separated by thick masonry walls, were difficult to adapt. A few commissioners dreamed of a new city hall, which might have been combined with an auditorium or other facilities. These hopes were not made public.

While the council remained silent on the subject, the

two-year battle of the estimates began. The League hired an architect who stated that the building could be renovated from $120,000. Six months later the figure had increased to $200,000. Meanwhile the planning commission's estimate for remodeling began to be scaled down. A "poll," which the newspaper sponsored, on the choice between a new and a remodeled city hall, showed the citizens seven-to-one in favor of the latter course. One member of the planning commission complained publicly of pressures being placed upon him and his colleagues. The chairman of the body resigned.

Three years after the opening of the controversy, the city council acted. A contract for remodeling was let for $165,000. The cost at the time of occupancy was over $200,000. Subsequently, additional sums had to be spent. The newspaper was silent on the subject. Many planning commission members continued to insist that the city now had a costly, old, renovated building, which was not worth the investment.

Again caught between opposing forces, the Beta council first sought refuge in delayed action, waited to see which was the safest course, and finally moved cautiously. This summary is not a statement of condemnation. Given their political resources, the Beta councilmen acted in the only fashion they could and still retain their positions. They were never sure what was politically possible. The unknown public reaction had to be tested; consequently, the council had to use the planning commissions as a ploy and buffer to protect its own position on the city hall issue. By contrast, consider a similar situation in Alpha. After the light plant was sold, the city had a sizable windfall for use in capital improvements. The council, in conjunction with the planning commission and administrative officials, worked out a plan. While many private conversations were held on the subject, in the final development the council simply announced the plan to build several civic buildings and a bridge. This plan was not disrupted by organized opposition, the newspaper, or public reactions.

Gamma. Many of the council members in this city had fairly distinct constituencies. For years, the bank had a representative, the chamber of commerce nominated a successful slate twice during the study period, and several labor candidates sat on the body. Other special constituencies included the Dutch ethnic group, the neighborhood merchants, the urban renewal opposition, and the private parking lot operators' organization. In addition, several incumbents assiduously pursued a delegate approach to their job, inviting individual citizens or even city employees to bring problems directly to them. Other council members positively discouraged these unsolicited requests. It appeared to be more possible for a councilman to do this in Gamma than in Beta under the ward set-up. Some councilmen acted as special representatives when first elected but dropped the practice when they felt more secure in their convictions and in their tenure. Once a councilman shouldered a personal request, favor seekers who heard about it often became a severe burden. A few examples may indicate the nature of some requests. One councilman reported an incident in which a citizen complained because the city had moved a street light away from the front of his house. Under the previous arrangement the citizen did not have to burn his porch light, but felt a need to do so in the new and unwanted darkness. The citizen badgered a councilman for eighteen months trying to get the light returned. Another councilman reported being awakened in the middle of the night because a parked car blocked a citizen's driveway. Several years of such experiences often led a councilman to convey the impression to citizens that certain strains of the *vox populi* would no longer be given a willing ear. Thus the Gamma council was comprised of a disparate group, representing various special interests and approaching the job of representation in various ways.

Gamma furnished an example of a city where victories were gained on occasion by most segments of the community during the ten-year period. The council did exhibit periodic internal cohesion. It was capable of taking a position, on a few occasions, so the internal splits did not always lead to *status quo* victories through sheer inability to resolve questions. The council did adopt a new zoning ordinance over the opposition of the realtors, railroads, and various other property interests. The ordinance was written by a professional and it generally followed standards prevailing among planners. When the chamber of commerce and certain realtors tried to locate a chemical factory next to a city park and some residential properties, the residential interests won even though the city was desperately seeking new industries. (The residential area was middle class.)

The downtown merchants benefited from some city parking lots and the street policy favored the CBD. Divisions within the CBD were the primary obstacles to further development, but this very division stemmed in part from a city policy that demanded contributions from the property owners for the improvement program. The reasons for this policy could not be specifically ascertained. However, labor leaders had generally favored having merchants pay and this may have been a concession to them.

Delta. The councilmen of Delta were unabashed, self-avowed ambassadors from their individual bailiwicks. Special representation was institutionalized. Policies affecting one ward were first cleared by that councilman before they were ratified by the entire council. This arrangement applied in the case of zoning changes, street repairs, or other improvements. Councilmen would get their constituents' boys out of jail, order their streets repaired, or find them jobs. The city manager for a time was required to keep a roster of all city employees classified according to their place of residence. This list furnished the basis for filling jobs when vacancies occurred. The councilman with the shortest list was allowed to fill the position.

While most city policies were, in fact, the product of a system of arbitration, all claims were not equally admissible under the system. The prevailing values of the union leadership were essentially those of the residents of working-class neighborhoods. Capital improvements were parceled out just as jobs were. One informant, who frequently attended executive sessions, reported as typical the following fragment of conversation: One councilman shouted to another in the midst of a meeting: "You bastard, you had three more blocks of blacktopping in your ward last year than I had, you'll not get another vote from me until I get three extra blocks." It was impossible for this council to build a sewage-disposal plant, for how could it apportion the benefits along ward lines?

Specific claims from businessmen were completely acceptable. In fact, these working-class councilmen rather enjoyed it when an important businessman came to them to ask favors. However, when businessmen collectively asked for something from the municipal treasury, this was another matter, and off-street parking could not gain support. Delta was also the only city without an urban renewal project. While this lack may have been the function of a nonprofessional bureaucracy, it was also consistent with the council's class values. In the other three cities, it was the laboring persons more than the businessmen who looked askance at these projects.

Despite the political power of the Delta union group, it was not able always to maintain its policies of low taxes and patronage. At times the service claims of the middle- and upper-middle-class citizens could force the union to retreat. The major and nearly only time where this happened was concerned with the municipal hospital.

The municipal hospital was important to all segments of the Delta citizenry because it was the only general hospital conveniently available. As such, its clientele was assured, but so was the fact that citizens from every income level and life-style type would be interested in its costs and level of service. The controversy centered around the relative efficiency of the administration, which was controlled directly by the council. The issue was joined initially over the question of whether or not osteopaths should be permitted to care for patients in the hospitals. The county medical society opposed their admission; the council majority, which had a constituency of working-class people who were the principal clients of the osteopaths, favored admission. The conflict offered an opportunity to raise the issue of efficiency, costs, and employment practices. Soon, for the councilmen and most citizens, this became the real issue.

The hospital was a large employer furnishing a major source of patronage to the city councilmen. The employees' union was torn between the patronage and tax demands of its constituents. While it was vacillating, the upper-middle-class groups in the city were activated.

The first proposed solution, developed by a variety of

citizen groups, was to place the hospital under an independent board and to finance its operation with a one-mill tax levy. In a referendum with an unusually high voter turnout, the proposal was defeated. The Republican wards gave strong support to the plan. The rank-order correlation between the Republican ward voting pattern and the affirmative referendum vote was .950. Although the union group was victorious, it was left with the problem of the financially insolvent hospital. Under a subsequent plan, the hospital was to be leased to a private corporation without the millage support. At this point the union capitulated. It lost patronage, but prevented a tax increase. After the union abandoned control of the hospital, wholesale firings were made by the new administration.

This case offered a rare instance of a middle-class victory in Delta. A professional hospital administration, with no patronage obligations, was installed. The original controversy was settled in favor of the medical doctors, who had strong middle-class support, and against the osteopaths, who had much less. The osteopaths, the "workingman's doctors" as one informant described them, did not lose completely, though. A volunteer group agreed, as part of the settlement, to help raise funds for a small hospital for these physicians, and this was done.

This middle-class victory was largely won over the union organization, not over the working class. The union organization gave up patronage and the working-class residents did not have to accept a tax increase. However, to the extent that this loss of patronage loosened the political hold of the organization, it may have been a reverse for both. This can certainly be said about the defeat on the issue of the osteopaths.

The other major defeat suffered by union organization and its constituency was dealt to it by the state. Delta procrastinated for years on building a sewage-disposal plant adequate for its needs. Finally, the state, acting through court order, sold the bonds and ordered the plant built at the city's expense.

In summary, we note which city governments were most controlled by segments of the population and which displayed more open systems, where government approached being a neutral instrument arbitrating among conflicting claims. The most "open" system appeared to be in Gamma, where policies assumed no pattern. The council was easily accessible. The Beta council was also accessible, but its very accessibility seemed to neutralize it as a decision-making body. As a result, in actual performance the government of Beta actually favored the low-tax bloc—an alliance composed of property owners, persons on fixed incomes, and some lower-income groups.

Delta and Alpha were at the other end of the scale, and in that order. Policies in both of these cities were highly consistent. The policies of the working-class union organization were occasionally untenable and a few defeats were suffered. The council majority of Alpha never had to retreat from a stand once it was assumed. Coincidentally, there was no evidence that the larger property interests ever were disadvantaged by a municipal policy. This cannot be said about the other three cities.

Part IV

Conclusions

Chapter XIII

Community Differences and Policy Variations

Why did the communities differ in their responses to similar issues and problems? This question has been a major preoccupation of the latter part of this study. Two variations of the question will be considered in this chapter. First, in what ways did the basic characteristics of these generally similar cities actually vary, and how may these variations be related to the typological differences? Secondly, in what way did the political processes vary so as to cause or reinforce differing tendencies in the

A Typological Profile of the Four Cities

	low	medium		high
Economic Growth	Delta		Gamma	Alpha
			Beta	
Life's Amenities	Delta	Beta	Gamma	Alpha
Caretaker	Alpha	Gamma	Beta	Delta
Arbiter	Alpha	Delta	Beta	Gamma

cities? The typological chart presented previously is re-
peated here for convenient referral in this discussion.

Before proceeding to the two tasks a caveat must be
interjected concerning the limitations of that which follows. The purpose of the typology is to provide a framework for developing a theory of political decisions at the
local level. The yield to be reported is a far more modest
product. Instead of a theory of community policy differences, we derive only a set of observations of correlated
instances, which should be of use in the construction of a
theory.

Helen and Robert Lynd suggested that the difference
between local and national government is the difference
between concern with how income is earned and how
income is spent. Obviously this is an oversimplification,
but it may suggest a distinction helpful in explaining the
differences in political behavior reported here. All levels
of government are involved in policies having implications for both producers and consumers. However, even
in an age of an emerging social service state, local government is more a consumer-service-oriented agency than are
government systems at the higher levels. It is less involved
in regulation than in providing consumer commodities
in a socialized fashion: commodities such as water, sewerage, streets, fire and police protection, parks and health
services. While all citizens consume these services and may
desire more of them, the wealthy individuals are more
capable of paying for them and appear to be more desirous of having them. City services are a necessary part of
their style of life. As a result, these persons exhibit concern regarding the administration of them. The data on
voting responses on tax referendums reported in Chapter
V lend support to this theory.

Our data also indicate that the consumption-oriented upper-middle class is often also favorably disposed toward policies of economic growth. Economic growth and amenities, when stated in general terms, can be made to appear compatible. "The city which is an attractive place to live is also the city attractive for new industries." But on specific issues, the values may clash as they affect individual citizens. In Gamma the choice had to be made between the two when a chemical manufacturing firm wanted a site adjacent to a residential neighborhood. Alpha made a choice between a renewal project and downtown revitalization. But in these middle-sized cities only occasionally were the two sets of values thrown into direct competition. More commonly, the choice was whether or not to initiate a specific measure, such as municipal parking or creation of a new park. When raised in an *ad hoc* fashion, the decision was likely to turn on the momentary strategic position of particular interested parties.

While both economic growth and increased amenities were frequently political expressions of the more well to do ranged against the caretaker sentiments of the less well to do, this does not furnish us a theory to underpin the typology. There was little indication that the distribution of persons in the economic levels varied significantly from one city to another.

COMMUNITY CHARACTERISTICS

The relative distribution of income levels did not provide a sufficient explanation, but variations in the economic structures of the communities proved more fruitful. Alpha exhibited the most steadfast adherence to policies that have been identified with the preferences of higher-income citizens. It emphatically rejected caretaker government. The most distinctive feature of the economic structure of this community was its higher percentage of home-owned industries. It was the home office of several large national firms. It had many other small but substantial locally owned industries. The founding families were still prominent in the management of most of these industries, with the Brinton-Lowe family the leading example. In this respect Alpha was a survival from the American past, a past where local indigenous capital, rather than national capital, controlled industry and executives did not look longingly toward life in some distant metropolis. If the executives wanted to control their living environment they had to do it in Alpha. They were not persons with a "limited liability" in the community. Consequently, management was willing to free top talent for local politics. Shortly after the close of our study period, one of the leading sons of the Brinton-Lowe family was elected mayor. Upon the occasion, he resigned a position of prominence in his firm, announcing that he would henceforth give full time to civic affairs. Thus Alpha had a "fifty-thousand-dollar" executive serving as mayor—for one thousand dollars.

The longevity of local ownership may have in turn resulted from the stability of these local industries. The two industrial mainstays, paper and pharmaceuticals, were comparatively depression-proof. Mergers for purposes of diversification were not an essential for these industries, as there was no compelling necessity to seek stabilizers to cushion against fluctuating economic fortunes. Wages were not especially high in these industries, but employment was stable. During the Great Depression when other cities continually cut back capital improvements or plunged into debt, Alpha was able to maintain its municipal plant and at the same time maintain a debt-free city. Partly as a function of its economic position and partly as a result of a professional administration Alpha provided services compatible with upper-middle-class consumption demands and, at the same time, did not tax the lower-income groups severely. (Alpha also benefited from a legal arrangement in the immediate postwar inflationary period. From the end of the war until 1949, Beta and Gamma operated under a statutory low-tax ceiling forcing them to cease all capital outlays. Alpha was not subject to this ceiling, which could only be removed by the state legislature.)

In the analysis of the referendums, it was seen that Alpha drew broad support for civic improvements from all but the very poorest sections of the city. A sewage bond was ratified by 86 per cent of those voting. While the Citizens' Committee political organization was undoubtedly one factor in evoking this response, the economic stability of Alpha would seem to be another. The working people of Alpha had no legacy of experience with prolonged unemployment during which the property tax had pressed heavily on home purchasers. Security of employment at least is a reasonable hypothesis to explain the broad support reaching into lower income groups.

Beta, Gamma, and Delta had similar economic structures and a bulk of the industries were, or were rapidly becoming, absentee-owned. These same industries were more sensitive to national economic fluctuations. Heavy concentrations in durable goods created a need on the part of management to merge with other firms. Public apprehension concerning the future was engrained into the local culture. Gamma and Beta had seen many large industries leave and fewer enter. Delta had not lost any major industries, but neither had it gained any, and the existing larger industries had widely fluctuating labor forces. The average incomes for the four communities appeared to be the same, but the average hid the fact that Alpha had lower, though stable, wage rates; in the three durable goods centers, incomes for those employed may have been higher, but many did not work a full week, or did not work at all.

The old economic elites of Beta, Gamma, and Delta were gone in the flesh and remained only enshrined in the stone of philanthropic monuments erected in the past. In Gamma, many public buildings and parks were decorated with the names of old lumber barons, largely extinct by the turn of the century and completely gone as the Great Depression began. Beta sported a large park, the product of similar philanthropy in the 1920's. Interestingly, hardly an additional acre had been turned to park use since and, as a result, the recreational facilities remained disproportionately piled in the wealthy corner of the city, where residents already possessed parklike lawns and backyards.

Unfortunately for the sake of research, none of the four cities was both economically stable and dominated by industry with absentee ownership. The problem for our analysis is whether the more important factor is the ownership pattern or mere economic prosperity. A second problem is posed by Gamma. While this city suffered all the economic privations of Beta and Delta, it consistently rated higher with respect to amenities and did not display the same intransigence on tax referendums.

Besides variations in the economic structure, gross community differences were also present with respect to ethnic composition. The source of difference may have contributed in a small way to an explanation of Gamma. Beta and Delta historically and contemporarily possessed large ethnic blocs, internally more cohesive than those in Alpha and Gamma. The most important of these groups was the Poles, a bloc which has been credited with retaining a certain separateness by Thomas and Znaniecki.[1] Though we are dealing with a later generation, some of these characteristics continued to characterize the political activities of the Poles in these two cities. In neither city were they a numerical majority; however, their influence was in part a legacy from past actions, which saw the creation of ward systems. In Delta, this effect can be traced to a specific incident: in the 1920's when the Poles, in conjunction with the French-Canadian and German neighborhood blocs, successfully worked for the reinstatement of a ward system after a brief trial with at-large elections. In the 1950's these same neighborhoods contributed heavily to the defeat of a new proposal for at-large elections.

In both cities the Polish population was largely working class and lower-middle class. None of its members had penetrated the economic elites of the cities. One found no Polish bank officers, editors, industrial executives, or prominent professional men. There were a few successful entrepreneurs, especially in retailing and construction. In both cities, frequently the losing mayorality candidate belonged to a major ethnic bloc, usually Polish. In both cities, but especially in Beta, the Polish neighborhoods gave a constant negative vote on proposals for civic improvements. Thus, there is some evidence that these ethnic blocs, especially the Polish ones, were still concerned with a politics of status. This appeared to affect their political behavior with regard to traditional political issues of city government. They represented a public difficult to mobilize for the "broader" community aims implicit in policies directed toward economic growth and expanded amenities.

The most conspicuous ethnic groups in Alpha and Gamma were the Dutch. The initial arrival of the Hollanders preceded that of the Poles in Delta and Beta by about a generation. Either as a result of this earlier arrival or because of a different cultural outlook, the Dutch entered into the civic life more as individuals than as ethnic spokesmen. Many became prominent among the economic elites. Indeed, it was part of the public lore in Alpha that the local civic pride and concern for amenities were fostered by Dutch cultural traditions. "Why is Holland so clean? Because everyone sweeps his own doorstep." This riddle was often heard in Alpha as an explanation of the local civic virtues.

To the extent that the ethnic blocs of Beta and Delta helped to maintain a ward system and to stress a politics of neighborhood interests, they contributed to a political system that recruited and strengthened the forces within the cities which were attracted by caretaker government and were often hostile to policies of economic growth and increased amenities.

THE POLITICAL PROCESS

Political institutions may reflect stable value preferences in a community and thereby make the form of the decision process merely a function of dominant values. However, political forms and traditions may develop to fit one set of circumstances and at a later time their very existence may influence the course of decisions in a manner unanticipated. A manager may be chosen for his traditional managerial skills, but once in office he may act as a rallying point to further goals that were not considered at the time of his selection. A charter commission may choose ward elections to achieve "well-rounded representation," but the consequences of this choice may be to favor a particular view. Once the ward elections are in use the redistribution of strategic positions in the political process may prevent a recall of the decision. In this sense, variations in the composition of the political process may be an important factor in explaining policy variations and may not necessarily be simple reflections of dominant value preferences in the communities. In this section, the character of the municipal bureaucracy, the council-manager form, nonpartisanship, and electoral arrangements will be considered in this light.

A major element that distinguished the governments of Alpha and Gamma from those of Beta and Delta was the strong professional traditions in administration existing in the former. The presence of a structured politics gave strong support to the bureaucracy of Alpha, but in Gamma the bureaucracy was more exposed and had to seek its own support. However, the manager was a long-time incumbent and had earlier served as manager of one of the satellite suburbs for nearly a decade. The manager of Gamma combined great political knowledge of the community along with his professional skills. During the years when the council was dominated by men who assumed a broker's approach to their jobs, the manager was under constant attack because his values were directed toward goals associated with economic growth and ameni-

ties. Although the council could place obstacles in the way
of the manager's program and even control areas of
personnel policy, it never succeeded in dismissing him.
Elections would be held, the manager would receive a
more favorable council, and his program would continue.
For instance, the manager kept plugging away for over
a decade for the construction of a major four-lane, limited
access highway into the very heart of the city. In this
case, his accomplishment was a function of his knowledge
of state politics as well as of local conditions.

By constrast, Beta had a tradition of short-term managers. During the later half of the study period a professional manager arrived on the scene who initially
experienced many of the defeats by the caretaker elements
that previous incumbents had also experienced. After
approximately five years of tenure the manager began to
achieve more of his goals. Gradually department heads
were replaced and a professional staff was assembled. The
developments subsequent to our study period indicate
that if the typology were applied now, Beta would have
to be placed in a different category. The question is: Did
the manager create the change or did the political climate
of the community change? There were changes emerging
in the political organization of the city. The weak old
Association for Sound Government expired and a new
businessmen's group began covertly recruiting and electing councilmen. The new recruitment method showed
some promise of affording organized support for the manager. But a manager who was experienced in the community and who had a program for change arrived on
the scene before formation of the new organization. This
suggests, but does not prove, that this latest manager was
the significant factor in explaining community change.

It must be added, even though it only complicates analysis, that professional managers could not survive in Delta long enough to develop personal sources of support. Thus, our four cases indicate that a manager is only one force in remodeling policy even where the political process is not already highly structured. On the other hand, the existence of a strong manager may obviate the necessity for groups agreeing with the manager's policies to organize. They never did in Gamma, except sporadically when the manager was in trouble.

It has been implied in the foregoing that the council-manager form of government is not neutral regarding city policies, that it favors one type of policy over another. Considering the importance of this subject to the students of local government, perhaps it deserves additional comment. In the first chapter three basic assumptions underlying the council-manager plan were set forth. These were: (1) that the council should represent the city as whole, rather than discrete interests, (2) that administration should be conducted by professionals, and (3) that the council should control policy; the manager, administration. It is not our intention to disinter the arguments in public administration that have led to drastic qualification of the third point. But while the politics-administration dichotomy is now poor public administration theory, it contains an element of practical wisdom. Probably the language used by early administration theorists was too stark, but nevertheless the council-manager plan does require a certain mutually satisfactory delineation of functions between the council and manager. The line is not between policy and administration, but rather between policy supported by community consensus and policy that has not yet achieved this consensus. Furthermore, if there is not some stability in the content of these mutually agreed-upon spheres, the manager will experience difficulties. This is one reason for the first principle, which requires at-large elections. In the terminology of this study, the manager plan is incompatible with a brokerage approach to representation. Of the four types, arbiter government would seem to be the least likely to produce an adequate framework for mutual understanding between professional administrator and lay councilman.

Arbiter government is characterized by the absence of a fixed standard in allocating city resources and favors. If each councilman is a delegate of neighborhood interests, or acts as a channel of access for shifting interests and disparate groups, the manager is robbed of a standard by which to guide his administration. Pressure will continually be placed on the manager to fix *that* street in *that* ward. If services or policy is dispensed to obtain political support, the council, not the manager, is the source of allocations. If allocations are on a rough rotation system, as was the case in Deta, the skills of the manager are greatly downgraded.

But in Gamma, and to a lesser extent in Beta, the manager retained an important administrative and policy role, despite the degree of arbiter government, because the sanctions of the individual councilmen were not so great. There was never any organization that could completely challenge the manager and his professional standards. Even so, the manager was at times administering policies that he felt were undesirable. But he never faced a political organization that looked to the elections as a time of crisis. There was always the prospect of change in councilmanic membership if he bided his time.

The other three types of policies—amenities, economic

growth, and the maintenance of traditional functions—ostensibly provide a consistent basis for action. However, caretaker government is in fact, if not in theory, even more in conflict with the council-manager plan than is arbiter government. It must first be recalled that the city manager considers himself a member of a profession. He is a person skilled in the art of doing. But the manager is not simply an administrator, for his profession incorporates a sense of mission. The city manager's code of ethics asserts that "The city manager . . . has a constructive, creative, and practical attitude toward urban problems and a deep sense of his own social responsibility as a trusted public servant."[2] Thus the manager is a problem-solver by trade. It is against his professional code of ethics to let the city's physical plant deteriorate for the sake of low taxes.

The clash between the manager plan and caretaker government does not stop with professional values, however. Career advancements for managers are based upon concrete achievements, not simply satisfied councilmen. The profession-oriented manager is outward-looking toward his peers in the International City Managers' Association. He may sometimes be more interested in their opinions of him than he is in those of his councilmen. Their judgments, rather than those of local citizens, tell the manager whether he is a success or failure. In a study of city manager attitudes it has been reported that managers believe they should do things that will enable themselves to "move up" to more desirable cities. Ability to move is an indication of professional status. Any action on the part of the city council to rob a manager of the opportunity for mobility should logically prompt the manager to resign.[3] Beta and Delta, the two cities that embraced caretaker principles, also had the greatest difficulty in retaining city managers. Indeed Delta could not (or would not) retain anyone with professional experience. The managers who did remain in office for several years were ex-politicians who had risen through the patronage system. These Delta managers had no potential for mobility in the professions. Their managerial careers began and ended in that city.

The amenities and economic-growth types are much more appealing to city managers, for these concepts of government provide a basis for manager initiative. Furthermore, the likelihood of manager-council clashes is reduced under them, because administrative policies have guidelines. In addition, managers have greater opportunity to further themselves professionally. Civic monuments reflect to their credit in the form of storm-sewer systems, industrial parks, shaded thoroughfares, and pedestrian malls. It is not surprising to find that in Alpha and Gamma the tenure of the city managers was usually long and the incumbents were men highly regarded in the profession. These two cities illustrate the kind of city toward which managers aspire. Alpha, especially, was one of the prized assignments.

Increased amenities and economic growth provided a congenial policy framework for the ambitions of individual managers and simultaneously the goals of such values demanded professional leadership. While the council-manager plan is not the only way of obtaining this aid, it is a convenient and familiar alternative.

Similarly, the question may be asked whether non-partisanship favors any particular type of policy orientation. The answer is a qualified yes. Our study has indicated that fewer people on the lower end of the socioeconomic scale vote on the nonpartisan than on the partisan ballot. Even when partisan and nonpartisan elections were held simultaneously, as was the case in Gamma, this was true. An exception to the pattern appeared in Delta, where the union organization apparently stimulated the turnout of lower-income persons. The inquiry into tax referendums and urban renewal suggested that caretaker government had broad support in lower-income areas. Thus, to the extent that the nonpartisan ballot reduces voting among lower-income persons, it favors the achievement of policies concerned with amenities and economic growth. One may only wonder what the consequences would have been in Alpha, Gamma, or even Beta if the voting turnout in low-income precincts had been matched by the record of similar precincts in Delta. Perhaps this is another way of saying that as long as civic improvements are based upon the *ad valorem* property tax, they will be achieved only because of self-disenfranchisement of a large number of tax-sensitive citizens; conversely, political organizations drawing support from lower-income groups will not embrace economic growth or improvement in amenities as the primary function for local government.

Regarding at-large and ward elections, there was a parallel between the kind of representation and the policy orientation of the cities. The fortunes of the Delta union organization under at-large conditions may have differed substantially. The conspicuous failure of the union in mayoralty elections was probably only partially a function of union interest in the office. The whole political organization and its techniques were geared to the scale of small wards. It is equally difficult to picture the Citizens' Committee of Alpha maintaining its hegemony under the ward system. The bulk of its councilmanic recruits were drawn from three precincts out of a total of thirty-two to forty. If the Committee had to work through pawns recruited from various sections of the city, it is doubtful if the council would have enjoyed the same kind of civic repute as did the existing councilmen.

Again, however, the ward versus at-large question is one factor among many. Gamma and Alpha both had at-large systems. Both did shy away from caretaker policies. But this is a very small sample on which to build bold assertions. Beta and Delta had ward systems and both were lower on the scale in regard to the provision of local amenities. Perhaps the strongest statement that can be extracted from this evidence is that the claims civic reformers have made over the past half-century are not contradicted by the data in this study. At-large elections are a necessary but not a sufficient condition for enabling upper-middle-class values to prevail. Similarly, the objections of labor union leaders to at-large representation appear valid, given their value assumptions. In Gamma, even with sustained action, the labor unions could gain no more than one representative. In Delta, ward organization brought control of the council. However, without organization there is no guarantee that the ward system would produce victories for working-class interests. To be sure, Beta had a partial ward system, and the prevailing low-tax policy probably pleased the low-income families. But this policy was probably not a self-conscious recognition of the interests of the less well-to-do citizens.

The success of a policy very likely will have a reciprocal effect on other policies. The ability of Alpha to annex large suburban areas dramatized the similarity between the consumer-service orientation of that core city's policies and those which are frequently associated with suburban areas. (This does not imply that residential suburbs are able to afford such policies, but only that amenities are the preferred goals.) Alpha's political style, dominated as it was by business and university leadership, avoided the core-city stigma of lower-class status, poor amenities, and raucous disputes. Thus, the ability to annex probably meant that the political traditions would be maintained through the transfusion into the political system of new citizens likely to support the Citizens' Committee tradition. The disparity between the political values of Beta and Delta, on the one hand, and their suburbs on the other, precluded similar annexation in those cities. (Gamma's special metropolitan problems made this test largely irrelevant there.)

SUMMARY

Our data have yielded some insights into the factors underlying preferences for the first three types of policy orientations, but little has been said about the fourth. The difficulty is that the political structures in these communities long predated our study period; the origins of the Citizens' Committee and the Delta union organization lie buried in the past. Our comments on this subject must be confined to the implications of structured politics for the political process generally. This will be given attention in the last chapter. The following generalizations are borne out by the data about the first three types:

1. To the extent that policies of economic growth and amenities call for increased expenditures, support generally comes from the higher income groups and opposition comes from lower income groups.

2. Conversely, the strongest supporters of caretaker government are centered among low-income citizens.

   a. to the extent that nonpartisanship reduces the working-class vote, it also weakens the forces for caretaker government.

   b. Contrarily, ward elections strengthen caretaker policies.

   c. The existence of cohesive ethnic blocs generally adds to the political strength of working-class citizens and thereby strengthens the forces for caretaker government.

3. Professional city managers favor values associated with both economic growth and amenities.

   a. The effectuation of manager values are associated with long tenure.

4. The economic climate of a city is insufficient in itself to determine the value orientation of civic policies.

5. High incidence of home-owned industries is correlated with high rating in the scale of preferences for amenities and economic growth.

6. Caretaker values are more in direct opposition to policies of increased amenities than are those providing for economic growth, for the latter are less frequently associated with costly expenditures.

7. In middle-sized cities, producer-consumer conflicts are rare.

NOTES

[1] William I. Thomas and Florian Znaniecki, *The Polish Peasant in Europe and America* (Chicago: University of Chicago Press, 1918), Vol. I, Introduction, esp. pp. 152-156.

[2] From The City Manager Code of Ethics, as revised in 1952.

[3] See George K. Floro, "Continuity in City-Manager Careers," *American Journal of Sociology*, Vol. 61 (November, 1955), 240-246.

Chapter XIV

Political Institutions and the Structure of Politics

City governments, while dwarfed by the activities of state and national governments, still retain jurisdiction over important political decisions that have great significance for the lives of urbanites. Decisions on industrial development, urban redevelopment, utility expansion, zoning, and planning affect life styles, the economic base, job opportunities, and business sales. The amenities of everyday existence are affected by traffic regulation, parking facilities, street maintenance, parks and recreation systems, and land-use policies. The home-purchasing consumer must look to the city for protection through the various housing and fire codes. Fluoridation, an ample and satisfactory water supply, sewage disposal facilities, inspection of food-dispensing establishments and, sometimes, municipal hospitals, all contribute to the health of citizens. The cultural life of a community depends, in part, upon libraries, museums, art galleries, civic auditoriums and community colleges. The future character of a neighborhood—whether it stabilizes or deteriorates—may depend upon zoning, planning, and inspection practices. In addition, city politics includes a miscellany of other matters, such as those concerning bus service and rates, taxi service, elaborateness of school plant, housing for low-income groups, racial discrimination patterns, flood threats to basements, and fluctuating property values. All this would seem to imply the existence of competitive politics involving nearly everyone. But it does not, judging from the experience in our four cities.

There are a number of reasons which may explain this lack of political participation. One has been suggested by Morris Janowitz in his concept of "limited liability."[1] Most citizens can express serious dissatisfaction with a neighborhood or community by moving. The volume of mobility among urbanites is eloquent documentation that many do just that. Only a minority of citizens, for business reasons or close personal ties, cannot change domiciles as a means of expressing political dissatisfaction with city policy. Other factors are undoubtedly involved in low participation. For those who cannot move or do not choose to do so, past civic performance may represent an accumulation of frustrated hopes. There is evidence that some voters in urban settings especially—though the phenomenon is not confined to them—feel "alienated" from the political process. Much nonparticipation is probably related to the existence of consensus in socially homogeneous communities—it is simply an implicit expression of confidence in or acceptance of those who are politically active. Perhaps the institutions of city politics simply do not provide a convenient mode of participation or viable sets of alternatives.

Several of these possibilities are beyond the scope of this present study. No attempt has been made here to probe the attitudes and values of the citizens. However, we are in a position to comment on the institutions in the political process and the functions which they perform.

While the policies of the governments did exert the kinds of influence described above on the lives of their citizens, the impact on any group was rarely oppressive. City politics was not responsible for grinding hardships on any large number of citizens. When problems did arise that threatened property or health, some kind of workable compromise policy was usually provided. Municipal government did not obviously affect the income of *most* people, except in the negative form of taxes, and even here the property tax had only a moderate effect on the redistribution of wealth.

Local politics, therefore, floats along the edges of the mainstream of domestic issues in the nation and, when written largely in terms of state or national considerations, expresses itself in a qualitatively different style of politics. There is a great disparity between public housing as a local, as compared with a national, issue or, for that matter, between housing policies generally at the two levels. Considerations that go into a state highway policy are qualitatively different from those that are involved in a municipal street policy. The issues are the same, but they are politically exploited in an entirely different fashion. Finally—though the sources of information are more meager here—there is a qualitative difference between policy development in a large metropolis and in a middle-sized city.

COUNCIL LEADERSHIP

Judged by the behavior of the city councils in our study, municipal legislative bodies—with perhaps the largest cities excepted—are faint and modified copies of those at the level of state and nation. By the simple fact that they were manned by amateurs conducting city business in their spare time, it was difficult for them to supply active leadership. Attention to routine business, in itself, tended to absorb all the spare time and energy that most individuals could afford to devote to the position. Rule by amateurs is likely to mean that, under most conditions, persons outside the legislative body must be depended upon to make the essential policy decisions in all but a formal sense.

The role which councilmen played in the various cities was directly related to the structure of politics. There was a substantial difference between the character of legislative decisions in Alpha and Delta, where there was a considerable degree of organized recruitment and campaigning, from those in Beta and Gamma, where government was largely institutionalized arbitration. In these latter two ctities, it was rare that either individual councilmen or the council collectively was identified with any policy or set of policies over a span of time. Occasionally, an individual did stand out, but with hardly an exception these men were associated with causes that failed or with opposition to proposals for which they offered no definite alternatives. In Beta one councilman led a fight to force annexation of fringe areas by refusing to extend services. While he was able to recruit occasional majorities for his position, the ultimate goal of annexation was never reached. Another councilman led an abortive revolt against the city manager. A third member became identified with the building of a new city hall, a project which failed. A Gamma councilman led an attack on the city manager and his personnel policies with initial success and ultimate defeat. Another member was the unsuccessful champion of public housing. A third fought a losing battle for ramp parking. These individual efforts were never able to mobilize consistent majorities.

Accompanying this lack of councilmanic leadership was a characteristic unpredictability in policy decisions. The typical pattern of policy development was for a group outside the council to take the initiative, with the council reserving judgment until very late in the negotiations that took place between the group and the administration, or between the group and other groups. The Beta council would often vacillate on an issue even at the voting stage. The Gamma council was sometimes no more decisive. An illustration is provided in the case of the urban renewal project. Even after the planning staff had worked for several years developing a project acceptable to the Federal authority, the professional staff was unable to estimate with confidence the council's position up to the very night of the formal vote.

Under the more structured systems of Alpha and Delta the position of the councils was more predictable. In part, this was a function of the fact that the councils in these two cities were much less accessible to all groups in the community. Groups that had not been identified with the councilmanic recruiting organization could not expect the same type of access as those that had. Under structured conditions, then, the council was less broadly representative, but councilmanic leadership was much more possible.

In the case of Alpha, we found successful individual and collective leadership. For example, a collective policy was successfully pursued in relationship to annexation and fringe policy, an accomplishment never possible in

Beta, the other city where this issue was prominent.
Leadership for the downtown redevelopment project was
clearly identified with the mayor and one councilman.
The fight over sale of the light plant was led on both
sides by councilmen. Similarly, individual councilmen
were active leaders in such matters as fair employment
practices, capital improvements and urban renewal.

No single individuals stood out as leaders in Delta, but
continuity of policy was definitely present. Because the
councilmen were men of modest education, neither very
articulate nor capable of conducting public deliberations
in an effective fashion, leadership was collective in
character. The possibility of a more open public stand,
however, was also curtailed by the fact that the local
newspaper bitterly opposed the union organization. Had
councilmen been inclined to exploit news coverage in
mobilizing public support for their goals, they may not
have received cooperation from the press. Furthermore,
as the orientation of the dominant council group was
generally predisposed against innovations, the need for
personal leadership was less here than in Alpha. A diminished role played by elected leaders in the development
of issues probably also had a depressant effect on interest
in city politics.

Unlike representative assemblies at higher levels of
government, the city legislature does not provide the
public forum to bare the character of disputes among
groups. The legislative processes are certainly obfuscated
in both the state and national chambers, but there are
still publicly identifiable spokesmen who do achieve headlines or who do attempt to exploit issues for the further-
ance of political careers. Such approaches could not be
further from the minds of most amateurs on the city

council. There were occasional individuals who enjoyed combat in the public limelight, but these men were rare. Consequently, most councilmen were quite willing for the drama of city policy formation to be played off-stage where they and their colleagues were scarcely identified as participants.

Again Alpha was exceptional, since councilmen did commit themselves publicly, with more regularity than elsewhere. On some issues, this was encouraged by the greater consensus that enabled individuals to know with some degree of accuracy the predisposition of the council. But the practice was also a function of the character of the individuals on the council. Undoubtedly, a corporation president is more prepared by his occupational experience and status in the community for speaking out than is the corner grocer and the real estate salesman.

THE MAYOR

The role of the mayor under the council-manager arrangement has been given little attention by the supporters of this plan of government. Should he be simply the presiding officer? The first legislator among equals? The ceremonial head of the city? Or a policy leader? One thing is clear: He is not supposed to be the chief administrator. And in none of our four cities did he approach that role. The mayors in these four cities never threatened the position of the city manager. However, they did differ as to their roles in policy leadership. Differences were, of course, related to personalities, but more importantly to political structure.

As we saw in Chapter VI, the mayor was an important policy leader in Alpha. In this city the charter designated the individual receiving the highest number of votes for city council as mayor. This usually meant the mayor had a constituency that included the supporters of the Citizens' Committee, but was also broader. He was thus usually acceptable to the majority on the council. In a policy-oriented council, the mayor fell heir to a position of leadership by the very set of circumstances in which he found himself.

In Beta and Delta the mayor was the only councilman elected without reference to ward lines and in both cities the office was completely ineffective. In Beta some mayors attempted to focus public attention on particular problems but were repaid for their troubles by losing their offices. One mayor became identified with the proposal for a new city hall. Following failure on this issue, he retired from office and there were indications his action was not voluntary. A second mayor worked for two terms toward a solution of the metropolitan problems of the area. He received constant criticism from inside and outside the city council. On his third try for office he ran a poor third and the office fell to a man who had earned a reputation for voting against every tax increase and almost every city capital improvement.

The difficulty of the Delta mayor stemmed from a somewhat different source. The controlling city employees' union never contested the office vigorously. They held a councilmanic majority and the mayor had a vote only for breaking ties, although he also had a veto. As a minority member, the mayor was even excluded from many deliberations. The only noteworthy action of one mayor was to veto a public housing ordinance. His successor was no stronger and (in a private interview) he characterized his own administration as devoid of accomplishments. He had no rapport with the union group and spent his time trying to expose what he considered to be its machinations. He was rarely successful and retreated to defensive tactics. He retired to run for the council, believing that he would have a greater voice as a ward alderman than as mayor. A third mayor, apparently taking a cue from the experiences of his predecessors, devoted his time to chamber-of-commerce-type activities in advertising the city.

The Gamma mayor was chosen by the members of the council from their own ranks. This encouraged a seniority system and a reduction of the role to a ceremonial one. It is extremely doubtful if even citizens who were conversant with local affairs were sure which councilman was acting as mayor at any given time.

It seemed quite clear that leadership without organized backing was most difficult. An individual who was elected without any particular mandate took a hazardous plunge when he began to associate his name with issues.

THE ADMINISTRATION AND THE STRUCTURE OF POLITICS

The role of administrators as policy leaders varied inversely with that of the councilmen. In game theory, this was a zero-sum game. The professional administrators, especially the city manager, the planning director, and the chief engineer, in certain respects filled the vacuum left by the council in Beta and Gamma. In Alpha and Delta the administration was definitely in a subordinate position to the council. However, as the existence of structured politics was not the only variable affecting administrative leadership, this observation must be qualified.

While the bureaucracy was definitely subordinate to the council in Alpha and Delta, the political organizations were completely different. The Alpha Citizens' Committee held views largely consistent with those of the professionally trained administrators. In addition, the experience of many of the Alpha councilmen in business bureaucracies furnished them with a model for the division of labor between council and administrators. The analogy was easy to draw between the engineering standards of subordinates in industries and the professional standards of the specialists in the city bureaucracy. Consequently, when the city administrators made traffic decisions based upon traffic volume counts, or scheduled street repairs on the basis of inventories of use and conditions, such criteria were familiar and acceptable to the council. To the extent that the council accepted professional standards, it might be said that the administration and the council formed the ideal partnership envisioned by proponents of the manager plan.

Furthermore, the council shared certain other general values with the administrators. The administration is generally a force for raising service levels, goal also shared by the Alpha council majority. To be sure, the council policy was one of gradualism, never of haste, but there was usually no attempt simply to ignore problems. There appeared to be an affinity between the views of the professionals and the upper-middle-class membership on the council.

In Delta professional standards were largely rejected by the controlling group. Guided by considerations of low taxes and a distribution of services designed to insure continued political control, the council could not use the professionals except in certain limited areas. Over the period of a generation, the city manager was normally a nonprofessional. When a councilman shifted to the managership or other administrative post, his salary increased and his political influence declined.

However, in Beta and Gamma the professionals played a different role. The administration came closer to assuming active leadership in the sense of setting the agenda. The loosely knit councils in these two cities could never set general guides for the course of city policies. Rather, the administration worked out a proposed program to which the council would then react. To be sure there was a certain pattern to the council reactions and certain strong interest groups which gave cues to the administration.

A major example of administrative agenda-setting was supplied by urban renewal. Not only did the administration develop the plans, but it also took over active leadership in developing public support. In Gamma this was true, too, for the downtown plans, the rewriting of the zoning ordinance (with solid planning-commission assistance), the development of a freeway, as well as most major and minor improvements. In Beta, the administration played an active role in the early stages of central business district readjustments policies, the storm sewer issue, a water revenue bond program, and, in a guarded fashion, on the city hall. Because of the tradition of parsimony in Beta, the administration had to take account of the anticipated reactions in each case. In Gamma, where resistance to expenditures was not such an omnipresent limitation, the administration could pursue a more aggressive leadership role.

Often the council would be ignored by the administrators until late in the development of a particular policy.

One administrator admitted that he paid little attention to the council when he first launched a project. He dealt directly with citizens whom he felt would "pick up the ball." The same person admitted it was possible to move too quickly in this fashion and that time was often consumed at a later date in trying to inform the council on the considerations that had gone into the development of a policy. But commitment of the council was not the first step in policy development. In our interviews with councilmen in these two cities, ignorance of current policy areas was frequently apparent. Councilmen often simply waited to be informed by the administrators on policies.

In brief, in the absence of structured politics the administration filled the gap of leadership. However, the administration was not alone in stepping into the vacuums. The other principal entrants were the interest groups.

INTEREST GROUP ACTIVITY AND THE POLITICAL STRUCTURE

Interest groups need to be divided into two categories: those that must mobilize substantial public backing in order to accomplish their goals and those that only need access to those in positions of authority. The primary distinction is between those groups needing the support of the resources of city government to accomplish their goals and those wanting a priority of benefits within the framework of the city's normal expenditures, or that want concessions in the regulatory phases of the city operations. The demands of this latter group of interests are usually small in terms of the full range of city policies. Its efforts are largely conducted in private and the procedures involved are barely researchable.

We are primarily interested here in the former group of interests, those which endeavor to enlist major resources of city government to achieve a group goal. Some consideration of the use of the term "interest group" must be entertained here. If the term is confined to formally organized political activity, it would exclude many direct citizen actions. The most obvious clusters of interests do have their organizations. But the problem is with the term "obvious." They are more obvious because they are organized, not because they ultimately define and channel the course of public decisions. This is especially true when direct democracy gives a means of expression to some voters who therefore need not organize at all. The opponent of civic improvements is likely to have his day at the polls. Unless we bracketed the recalcitrant public as a "potential group" in accordance with Truman interest-group theory, we would fail to explain much civic policy. But the advocate of change usually does have to organize as a necessary step in the mobilization of public support. Indentifiable interest groups do appear in relationship to programmatic politics.

The organized groups were essentially of two types, those which attempted to influence policies through the election of officials and those which attempted to influence officials after the elections. According to the normal breakdown of political organizations, the former groups might be considered parties in that they attempted to control the total government. It is something of an axiom in politics that the task of organizing a successful election campaign leads to a moderating influence on group goals. In order to mobilize a majority it is necessary to develop broad identifications and avoid being stigmatized as the agent of any particular minority interests. We have no data on the public perceptions of the two prominent groups in Alpha and Delta. However, both of them endeavored to keep their activities secret. So we have the anomaly of the only party-type organizations existing in the four cities endeavoring to mask their true identity.

But there was a qualitative difference between the groups that worked through elections and those that did not. Neither the Alpha Citizens' Committee nor the Delta union organization was simply a front group for particular organizations. It is true that the latter group was primarily interested in working conditions for city employees, but the process of winning elections transformed its operations into something much more than the extension of the union organization. It, as in the case of the Alpha organization, came closer to being a class-based political-action organization than an interest group.

The class base of these two political organizations furnishes a key to the interest groups having access to the councils elected by them. The Alpha council was more accessible to the business community than was the one in Delta. The downtown merchants, the service clubs, the chamber of commerce had ease of access because the councilmen were actually members of these groups. This did not mean that individuals purchased access through constributions, but rather that entrepreneurs and professionals generally had a commonality of interest with the council majority. There was every indication that specific claims for zoning changes, traffic matters, or license applications were processed in a standardized and public manner.

The character of the council minimized the necessity for the kinds of organized pressure present in the other cities. Indeed many businessmen who were interviewed looked upon the whole Citizens' Committee operation as a kind of device for the conservation of resources. As long as the "right" men were on the city council, political organization in addition to the Citizens' Committee was of little necessity. The principal function of interest group organization was to achieve internal consensus, not to develop more effective pressure on the council, as was most obviously shown in the case of downtown redevelopment. This is not to say that Alpha was devoid of normal associational life; merely, that the energies employed in influencing the city council differed in pattern from our other cities.

The class base of the Delta union organization required business groups to use entirely different political procedures in order to influence the council. The character of interest group activity in Delta was close to that in Beta and Gamma: In order to obtain action on any problem of major dimension, initiative had to come from sources outside the council. This often meant the administration in Beta and Gamma, but in Delta this was less the case. Here business interests dealt with councilmen on a personal basis. General organizations, such as a downtown association, were not effective.

The standard ploy for masking the activities of major interest groups is the appointed "citizens' study group." Usually those persons most interested in such matters as parking, area-wide cooperation, or taxation make up the study committees investigating the problem. Consequently the study committee reports incorporate the claims of particular groups and give them quasi-public status. The same condition exists in relation to the lay bodies provided by the city charter, such as the planning commission, the zoning board of appeals, or the tax review board.

Even groups such as the chambers of commerce or manufacturers' associations frequently work through citizens' committees rather than seek self-sufficiency. The Chamber of Commerce is very conspicuous just because it is the principal organized business group in the community. The Chamber professional leadership is anxious to receive credit for any accomplishments, but it must also avoid the stigma of appearing to want to run the city. Probably the most powerful political force in Gamma was the Chamber, but it usually worked in combination with other groups or through the citizens' committees.

Although the citizens' committees probably abounded in about equal numbers in the four cities, they assumed especially important functions in Beta and Gamma. In many respects the city councils in these two cities were review boards, which alternately pondered the proposals of the administration and those of citizens' committees. For long periods, however, the negotiations between the contending parties would completely bypass the city council. In Beta, the downtown development organization negotiated directly with the realtors to revise the parking plan. On the urban renewal project the bargaining assumed a complex pattern among the realtors, the administration, the planning commission, and the financial institutions. Bus franchise negotiations primarily involved the chamber of commerce, the administration and an appointed study group. The pay-as-you-go storm sewer proposal was suggested by the Chamber of Commerce. The city hall issue was largely a battle between the realty group and the planning commission. Industrial development was, for the most part, handled by a citizens' group and the chamber of commerce.

In Gamma, industrial development was handled by a nongovernmental body. Area consolidation policy was promoted by the Chamber of Commerce, the manufacturers' association, and a variety of citizen study committees. Negotiations leading to a new zoning ordinance involved the planning department, the planning commission, the Chamber of Commerce, the manufacturers' association, and the board of realty. The housing problem was adroitly parried at one time by the council, which shunted the problem to a study group comprised of the unlikely combination of labor union leaders and the realty board members. The Chamber of Commerce controlled harbor policy in a virtually unilateral fashion. While complex negotiations over central business district policies were carried on between the administration and the downtown organization, the council must also be listed as an active party-at-interest.

The council was not excluded from the policy process, but was more an organization giving legitimacy to the results of the negotiations of other groups. Spare-time councilmen could not possibly be in the center of the whirlpools of interest that circle around all policies. However, in Alpha and Delta the council did provide limits or a framework within which negotiations by other groups could take place. When decisions appeared to be going beyond these boundaries or were failing to live up to council expectations, the councils would often take over direct supervision of legislation. This appeared to be less true in Beta and Gamma. Here, the council lashed out occasionally to reassert its legal prerogatives but then would retire without indicating a clear set of purposes.

THE MANAGER

In three of the cities studied the manager played the social role expected of him by his professional organization. In each case, he avoided taking a public role of policy innovator, except at the specific request of the council or in cases involving matters on which he could be considered a technical expert (e.g., on the effect of allowing a bank to install a drive-up window or of a proposed shuffling of administrative agencies).

The manager presented and sometimes strongly defended policy proposals that had originated largely from one of his own agencies (e.g., the police department on parking policies), from an advisory group (e.g., the planning commission that developed urban renewal plans), from study committees of lay citizens (e.g., citizens seeking to prevent the breakdown of public transportation), or private groups (e.g., downtown merchants interested in off-street parking.) There appeared to be a psychological advantage to the manager if he could place himself in the position of defending a policy developed by these individuals or groups. He would take a strong stand, but would use the protective coloration of saying, "professional planners tell me . . ." He would, in other words, take a public position of *leadership* in policy matters, but preferred to attribute policy *innovation* to technical experts or citizens' groups.

Although managers in the three cities appeared to exercise considerable skill in avoiding a public appearance of being the tail that wags the dog, in two cities they were accused of seeking to "control" the mayor or council. In Gamma, the manager had to overcome major opposition which, for a short while, actually held majority control of the council. The manager chose to wait out the opposition, almost succeeded in keeping from being quoted in the newspapers concerning his own views on the conflict, and eventually weaned the mayor over to his side, thus making a majority of his supporters on the council. (The manager had to take a leave of absence as a result of illness. During his convalescence the mayor acted for him. This brought the two together from time to time in private conferences. When the manager returned to the city hall, the mayor was his friend.) In Beta, two councilmen once accused the manager of policy domination and voted against proposals having his blessing, but there appears to have been no support for the two from other councilmen. In a later election, a little-known candidate, seeking to join them, failed to secure nomination.

In Delta, the manager was different in almost every way from those in the other three cities. Over several decades, Delta had hired only one professional non-resident as manager, and he had been dismissed after he sought to assume a leadership role. The job was viewed as a patronage appointment of the highest importance, but the incumbent was expected to be little more than an office manager. Councilmen expected—and were accorded —the right to distribute ward patronage in the naming of personnel. They dealt directly with department heads and lesser administrators. They prepared the budget. They did not ask for or expect policy recommendations from the manager. If they needed technical advice, they turned to department heads. The manager, in turn, did not identify with the profession of managership, had no ambitions beyond his present job, did not try to impose his opinions or preferences upon the council, and played almost no part in the municipal decision-making process.

It might be noted that only in Alpha did the manager come close to playing the part expected of him by the original theory of the council-manager plan. That theory assumed that the manager would merely carry out policy after it had been established by a council of able, respected leaders of the community. The important policy and leadership role of the manager and his administration in two of the cities would have represented, in the early image of the plan, an invasion of the council's prerogatives. The pattern in Delta would have missed the expectations of the model even further, for while the manager there was not a policy leader, he was not the chief administrative officer either; indeed, he was not even a professional administrator, either by training or by psychological identification.

We find, then, that in our four cities the role of the manager did not fit a consistent pattern. In Beta and Gamma, the manager was a key leadership figure and a policy innovator. In Alpha he had a vigorous council, which itself sought to lead, and which shared policy-making with him. In fact, his role as a leader was preserved there mostly by the deliberate intent of a council that was strongly committed to the principle of professional administration. In Delta, the council would not permit the manager to serve as either a leader or innovator. Its Jeffersonian philosophy emphasized the desirability of decentralized decision-making and minimized the role of the professional administrators, including the manager.[2]

At the outset of this study the question was posed whether the council-manager form was compatible with the political processes in the middle-sized city. The conclusion is that it is not size, but rather the value structure of the community and institutionalization of political values that are the significant considerations.

THE APPOINTED BOARDS

Earlier we noted that interest group representation takes many forms, including the quasi-official study commission and also the official advisory bodies such as the planning commission, the zoning board of appeals, and other units prescribed by city charters. This point needs both elaboration and qualification. The planning commission is the principal advisory body in the sense that planning commission decisions must be approved by the city council. On the other hand, the board of zoning appeals and the board of tax review are usually chosen by the council or mayor, but any review of their decisions is handled in the courts.

Of these citizen boards, the planning commission played the most significant role. It also attracted the most prominent citizens to its ranks. Typically, however, an interest group representation scheme was the basis of choice. Interests most commonly represented were those of real estate, the downtown merchants, construction, banking, and industry. A union official, white-collar, or social welfare worker was a rarity.

We asked our informants in each community which persons were most likely to be leaders in their own right prior to holding office—members of the city council or of the planning commission. In Alpha and Delta they were rated on a par, while in Beta and Gamma the planning commission members were more apt to be considered community leaders independent of their public position. The planning commissioners in Alpha, Beta, and Gamma were drawn from top professionals and executives. In Delta, they were persons of modest means, education, and reputation.

The functions of a separate, appointive planning commission are several. This agency relieves the city council of a burdensome task, thereby helping to save the amateur standing of that body. It recognizes the political character of physical planning by placing a citizen's body in review of the decisions of the professional planning staff, and it provides a device for the legitimation of professional convictions. As a nonelective body, it is especially valuable in making decisions that are not popular. This function shields the city council from a good deal of political pressure. The council can solemnly report that it is following the commission's recommendations ("They are trying to do a good job. We have to back them up.") It also provides a source of access, removed from the limelight, for interested parties. Clearly, all these are not likely operative at the same time, but with most planning commissions each possibility is realized at one time or another.

The pattern of planning commission behavior and its relationship to the city council did not, in our study, appear to be closely related to political structure. The professional planning staffs were strongest in Alpha and Gamma. In these two cities the planning commission also had the greatest success in gaining support from the city council. One planning commissioner in Gamma credited the success of his group to the strength of expert testimony. The staff could always give "good sound planning" reasons for any action. This was often persuasive.

In no city did the city council merely rubber-stamp the planning commission recommendations, however. If there were citizen objections in Alpha, the council would often reconsider the matter *de novo*. Most frequently, the matter would be resolved in favor of the *status quo*. The same pattern occurred in Beta and Gamma on the smaller matters such as zoning changes. The pattern of access was not the same for the council and the planning commission. A person who was on friendly terms with a majority of the council could occasionally sway the outcome on appeal. This type of activity was more likely to occur at the councilmanic level than in the planning commission, probably because of the close association of the planning staff with the latter. In Delta both the commission and the council were vulnerable to personal lobbying and the planning staff was weak.

The most frequent clashes between the planning commission and the council took place in Beta. The planning commission was always more eager than the governing body to push forward on a public improvement program. But the council had to face the caretaker forces demanding that the line be held on taxation.

Thus, in three of the four cities, the planning commission was the preserve of the informal leadership of the community. It was usually made up of executives in industrial firms, leading merchants, persons from the professions. Only in Delta, where these persons had few claims on the city council, was this condition absent. The success of the planning commissions in Alpha, Beta, and Gamma in realizing their aims was not simply a function of organized political action. It depended upon the strength of the professional staff as well on the vulnerability of the council to individual influence, and the dominant value system of the community.

The zoning boards of appeals and the tax review boards were largely removed from public scrutiny. The principal means of imposing responsibility on these bodies was through state law. This is the most archaic form of achieving administrative responsibility. Some respondents claimed several of the zoning boards indulged in practices approaching spot zoning. In one city the board of tax review was controlled by the manufacturers. As the board's prime function pertained to assessment of personal propetry, this meant that the property owners holding the greatest amount of personal property controlled the assessment process. These facts were revealed through superficial probes, and they did not involve all four cities. We suspect that a full study of these institutions would reveal deficiency in accountability and equity.

SUMMARY

It has been the general proposition of this study that the loci of leadership are directly related to the form of political structure. Organized recruitment and campaigning for city council members leads to the concentration of much decision-making in the council. Without such organization, the professional administrators and the interest groups fill the void.

While the Chambers of Commerce, the realtors, the downtown merchants and, occasionally, the neighborhood merchants were the principal organized groups, these and other major economic interests often influenced city policy through citizen study committees and the formally appointed citizen bodies. The study committees usually included those directly interested, and provided an institutional means for compromise among the strongest voices, but there were other interests that remained unrepresented on them.

Thus one of the continuing problems of both leadership and representation in the middle-sized city concerns the institutional means by which the marginally affected individual can influence the policy process. If we return to the list of significant community policies given in the first paragraph of this chapter we find that there are many areas of municipal life in which citizens are interested as consumers. We found that interest groups did not center around the many consumer services supplied by municipal governments. Our findings indicate that a parking-study committee will likely include the merchant, the banker, and the realtor, but not anyone representing the parker. The political institutions probably closest to representing the whole spectrum of interests of broad blocs of citizens were those embroiled in the election process. Although the values of the Alpha Citizens' Committee and the Delta union organization were poles apart in their objectives, the activities of these two groups shared the function of making politics in their two cities easily comprehensible. Responsibility for public policy was assumed by the elected officials and important policy decisions actually were made by them. These would seem to be necessary conditions for a viable system of local democracy.

We are under no illusions that the task we set out to accomplish has been completed. We have described the way four cities differ. We have described some of the community characteristics and institutional arrangements that appear related to these differences. Yet there remains much that has not been explained. A certain amount of luck was involved in the choice of the four cities. Much of what we have said that seems significant to us has been extrapolated from the experiences of the cities at the extremes, Alpha and Delta. The lingering doubts and dissatisfactions inevitably accompanying any work of this character are largely related to the other two cities. Had all four cities been similar to Beta—or especially to Gamma—we cannot help but feel that our findings would have been more meager.

Perhaps one final observation can be wrung from this

same impression. A commonplace about local politics is that decisions are made on personalities, not issues. Perhaps it is in the Gammas that personalities do have greater force in local politics. When the political process assumes an amorphous character, the political interests of an editor, the civic conscience of a local business executive, the ambitions of a planning director, or an inappropriate remark by a councilman, may loom large in determining the direction in which policies will drift. In brief, conditions that are most difficult for the researcher may also be the conditions under which the public has the greatest difficulty perceiving its own role. Similarly, public reactions may take on an aura of mystery to the researcher.

The patterns of politics in the four cities, as we have seen them, are almost uncomfortably disparate. The irrational, episodic, almost unpatterned behavior in Gamma might well give cause for concern to any supporter of liberal democracy: if the stakes were higher, and if state and Federal governments, superimposed upon that of the municipality, did not serve both as checks and as alternative routes to the achievement of public policy goals of the dissatisfied. The negativism of the electorate and the caution and lack of self-confidence of those in power in Beta were more a demonstration of persistent nondecision on the part of a community than of a viable problem-solving mechanism. This might be interpreted in many ways in terms of its meaning for contemporary society. Not the least important possibility is to see Beta as indicating the weakness of the municipality as a decision-making institution, if it is based upon the general-property tax for financing, and if the taxpayers are largely industrial workers. The parochial, nonprofessional, sometimes myopic governing body and administration of Delta seemed an anachronism in the mid-twentieth century and might well have been dismissed as such, if it were not that, impressionistically at least, we felt that here was something akin to a system of government providing the ordinary burgher with access to the decision-makers and a method of representation that made him feel comfortable. Alpha, with its economic leadership clan strong in the tradition of *noblesse oblige,* with its system of virtual rather than direct representation of many segments of its population, with its strong commitment to professional administration, community uniqueness, and high service levels, came close to the prototype of the ideal middle-sized American city as it might be seen by a Chamber of Commerce secretary, or a "civic-minded" organization man and his wife—but its economic base, which probably made its governmental achievements possible, was so atypical of a middle-sized city today that it could offer few communities the hope of serving as a lodestar.

The cities were all different, but they were a part of contemporary American local government. The institutions, procedures, habits, and values might not be found in the same combinations in other cities of the nation, but the same phenomena are surely abundant elsewhere in their many permutations. The communities examined were fitted into a typological framework for analytical purposes. Other cities could be as well, thus providing the basis for a comparative analysis of local public-policy making and execution.

NOTES

[1] Morris Janowitz, *The Community Press in an Urban Setting* (Glencoe: The Free Press, 1952).

[2] Portions of this section borrow from Charles R. Adrian, "Leadership and Decision-Making in Manager Cities: A Study of Three Communities," *Public Administration Review*, Vol. 18 (Summer, 1958), 208-213 and are used by permission.

APPENDIX A

Percentage of Manufacturing Employment in Durable and Nondurable Goods for Selected Years

	Durable			Nondurable		
	1940	1950	1955-57 average	1940	1950	1955-57 average
Alpha	35	35	40	65	65	60
Beta	83	85	80	17	15	20
Gamma	85	88	90	15	12	10
Delta	82	79	81	18	21	19

APPENDIX B

Municipal Wages and Salaries, 4 Cities, 1950–1958

Common Labor
Dollars per Hour, Range

	Alpha	Beta	Gamma	Delta
1950	1.07–1.22	1.10–1.26	.95–1.15	1.00
1952	1.25–1.35	1.27–1.44	1.10–1.43	1.46
1954	1.38–1.57	1.37–1.58	1.19–1.59	1.51–1.61
1956	1.46–1.60	1.56–1.93	1.44–1.74	1.61–1.71
1958	1.62–1.72	1.62–1.88	1.84	1.78–1.88

Labor Foreman

1950	1.45–1.55	1.31–1.50	1.30	*
1952	1.55–2.17	1.50–1.70	1.48–1.58	1.68–1.76
1954	1.71–2.01	2.06–2.16	1.61–1.71	2.18–2.32
1956	2.04–2.20	1.85–2.30	1.89–1.94	1.91–2.28
1958	2.25–2.74	*	2.05–2.15	2.20–2.58

Patrolman
Annual salary, range, dollars

1950	3120	3100	3040	3026
	2975–3276	2908–3304	2880–3200	*
1952	3620	3510	3440	3430
	3470–3879	3303–3729	3200–3680	3300–3567
1954	*	*	*	*
	3870–4538	3456–3972	3800–4200	3879–4012
1956	4420	4330	4200	4239
	4020–4824	3856–4792	4000–4400	*
1958	4670	4480	4400	4540
	4252–5092	4160–4810	4200–4600	4405–4754

Firemen
Annual Salary, range, dollars

1950	3130	3100	3000	3020
	2975–3276	2908–3304	2880–3200	*
1952	3670	3510	3440	3480
	3470–3879	3303–3729	3200–3680	3407–3567
1954	*	*	*	*
	3870–4538	3456–3972	3800–4200	3879–4012
1956	4180	4320	4200	4239
	4020–4355	3856–4792	4000–4400	*
1958	4720	4480	4400	4590
	4252–5092	4160–4810	4200–4600	4400–4780

Electrical Inspector
Annual salary, dollars

1950	3656	3500	3420	3410
1952	4429	3900	4500	3951
1954	4850	4300	5000	4300
1956	5100	5150	5200	4550
1958	5400	*	5200	5370

Superintendent, Water Pumping Stations
Annual salary, dollars

1950	*	5100	3500	5906
1952	6036	5600	5800	6700
1954	6090	5800	6200	7300
1956	6900	6200	6200	*
1958	*	*	*	*

Superintendent of Streets
Annual salary, dollars

1950	4598	4400	4800	4300
1952	5726	4500	5800	4850
1954	6500	4700	6400	5100
1956	6800	6100	6000	5500
1958	6950	6800	6200	6200

Purchasing Agent
Annual salary, dollars

1950	5100	3650	3600	4400
1952	6100	4050	4700	5000
1954	7300	4500	5400	5200
1956	7000	5100	5600	5500
1958	8700	6100	6200	6050

Park and/or Recreation Director
Annual salary, dollars

1950	6966 P.	*	4800	3950†
1952	5416 P.	*	*	4500†
1954	8120 P. 7920 R.	4700 P. 6500 R.	6200	4900†
1956	9056 P.	7800 P&R	6600	5500†
1958	10,050 P. 9,700 R.	8774 P&R	8500	6000† 5500–6660†

City Assessor
Annual salary, dollars

1950	5800	5150	4800	4900‡
1952	6798	5700	5700	5000‡
1954	7852	6200	6400	5500‡
1956	7500	6500	7200	5700‡
1958	8450	7860	7000	7060‡

City Attorney
Annual salary, dollars

1950	12,000	4500§	4500	4800
1952	15,500	5000§	4980	5367§
1954	14,000 includes fee for asst's. & clerical help	5800§	7200	5800§
1956	*	5000	7200	6028
1958	*	6000§	7800	*

Personnel Director
Annual salary, dollars

1950	*	*	*	Assessor
1952	*	4500	4100	Assessor
1954	2400**	City manager	5200	Assessor
1956	6160	City manager	5850	Assessor
1958	7600	6200	6300	Assessor

City Planner
Annual salary, dollars

1950	6500	3600††	4800	*
1952	7210	4100††	5800	4200
1954	6500	5800	6400	4400
1956	7500	6400	7200	5300
1958	8800	7100	8800	6100

Director of Public Works and/or Engineer
Annual salary, dollars

1950	*	*	*	*
1952	8300‡‡	5000	*	6500
1954	9900‡‡	7700‡‡	6500‡‡	7100‡‡
1956	12,600‡‡	8500‡‡	7000‡‡	7600
1958	13,500‡‡	9700‡‡	8800‡‡	8400

City Manager
Annual salary, dollars

1950	*	*	*	*
1952	*	*	*	*
1954	16,000	11,000	15,000	10,700
1956	17,500	11,800	15,000	11,000
1958	18,000	12,500	17,000	11,500

* Data not available.
† Parks & Cemeteries. No Recreation Division.
‡ Also Purchasing Agent and Personnel Director.
§ Part-time.
** Part-time.
†† Part-time.
‡‡ Chief Engineer.

APPENDIX C
Percentage of Foreign-born Whites, by Country of Birth,
Selected Countries, 1940

Country	Alpha	Beta	Gamma	Delta
Poland	0.71	1.81	0.71	1.88
Germany	0.64	0.74	0.84	1.45
Netherlands	3.85	0.05	2.05	0.04
Sweden	0.14	0.09	1.27	0.26
French Canada	0.07	0.09	0.31	0.44
Total, Foreign Born	8.35	6.61	8.78	8.30

Native White, With at Least One Parent Foreign-born,
Selected Countries, 1940

Poland	0.89	4.62	1.63	9.71
Germany	3.72	5.61	4.60	7.64
Netherlands	8.89	0.34	7.73	0.29
Sweden	0.41	0.37	3.76	0.63
French Canada	0.42	0.37	1.92	4.10
Total	23.13	23.67	29.45	34.57

Negroes

1940	1.94	3.34	1.46	0.30
1950	4.29	5.34	3.97	0.62

Age Composition of the Four Cities in 1950

| | Percentage of total population | | |
	21 and over	60 and over	Median age
Alpha	70	16.2	32.6
Beta	69	15.7	33.6
Gamma	65	12.7	30.9
Delta	64	13.4	30.0

Median Years of Education, Based upon 1950 Census

Place	Years
Alpha	10.7
Beta	10.7
Gamma	9.7
Delta	9.2
State	9.9
State urban	10.2
U. S.	9.3

APPENDIX F

Church Membership, Based on 1936 Census of Religions

	Percentage of Population		
	Protestant	Roman Catholic	Jewish
Alpha	82	16	2
Beta	58	41	1
Gamma	64	35	1
Delta	37	61	2

Index

Accessibility of council, 267

Administration in four cities, 201-06; professionalization of, 279-88; *see also* City Councils; City Manager

Adrian, Charles R., 40, 86, 103, 315

Advisory boards, 309-12

AFL-CIO council, 117

Age composition in four cities, 324

Alpha: amenities, 34-36, 199-221, 271; arbiter government, 34-36, 271; caretaker government, 34-36, 249-50, 271, 274; economic growth, 34-36, 192, 194-96, 255, 271, 273-74; city hall, 44-45; economy of, 45; differences from other cities, 46-47; lack of primary, 55-56; civic tradition, 58-64; occupational makeup of council, 62-63; civic awards, 63-64; home-owned industries, 63, 148; role of business community, 63-65; selling of municipal power plant, 65-69; recruitment of officials, 69, 76; occupational categories of candidates, 80-82; nonpartisan elections, 89; voting patterns, 90-93, 96-99, 108, 124; politics of consensus, 101-03; referendums, 105, 229-31, 236, 275; downtown program, 127-32, 169, 273; wages, 147, 201-03, 237; role of organized labor, 150-51; public housing, 155-56; urban renewal, 167-68, 246; reliance on public forum, 174; annexations, 177, 183, 286-87; planning dept., 205, 309-11; police service, 206-08; traffic prob-

lems, 210-11; fire protection, 211-14; sewage, 215-16, 256; water system, 217-18; streets, 218-19; recreation, 220-21, 256; fiscal policy, 240-42; newspapers, 244-46; role of councilmen, 254-56, 267, 292-95; class bias in council policies, 255-56; ethnic blocs, 278; administration, 279-80, 297-300; city manager, 279-80, 305-07; mayor, 295-96; interest groups, 302, 312-14; pattern of politics, 315

Amenities: securing of, 25-27; assessment of city interest in, 33; in four cities, 34-36, 199-221, 271; defined, 199-200; administration and personnel, 201-06; planning departments, 203-06; police service, 206-08; traffic problems, 209-11; fire protection, 211-14; sewage treatment, 214-16; water system, 217-18; street systems, 218-19; recreation, 220-21; as goal, 255; upper middle class attitude toward, 273; support of, 287-88

Anderson, Elin C., 39

Annexation, attitude toward, 12, 176-83; state law on, 176-77; in Alpha, 286-87; relationship to political values, 286-87

Annual Inventory of Traffic Safety Activities, of National Safety Council, 209

Appalachians, 188

Apple Valley, 188

Arbin, 54

Arbiter government, 28-29, 31, 251-

326

Alpha; Beta; Four cities; Delta;
Gamma
Citizens Committee in Alpha, 58-
59, 65, 70, 71, 81, 124, 129, 253,
275, 285, 287, 313; opposition to,
62; role in power plant sale, 67-
69; slates of, 90; domination of
city council, 254; relationship to
administrators, 298; as interest
group, 302-03
City assessor, salary data, 320
City attorney, salary data, 321
City councils, 15; occupational representation of, 56-58, 62-63;
handling of controversial matters,
105; role in downtown development, 127-43; attitude toward
urban renewal, 164-65, 167-68;
attitude toward public housing,
170, attitude toward zoning, 174-
75; handling neighborhood problems, 174-75; annexation attitudes, 177-81; status of, 243; organized opposition to, 246-50;
negotiations with interest groups,
305; as aid to city manager, 308;
see also Alpha; Beta; Councilmen; City manager; Delta; Gamma
City government, attitude toward
shopping plazas, 12; pressures on,
12; interest groups in, 21, 300-05;
policies, 289-91; *see also* City
councils
City hall, in four cities, 43-45; issue
in Beta, 258-60
City manager, characteristics of
plan, 18-21; size of city as relating factor, 19; role in urban
renewal, 160, 166; attitude toward
annexation, 178; salary data, 203,
321, 322; why chosen, 279; in
Alpha, 279-80, 286; in Gamma,
279-80, 286; in Beta, 280; and
city policies, 281-87; effect of
arbiter government on, 282; policies of, 288; relationship to
council, 297-300; role, 305-08; dif-

ferent role in Delta, 307-08; *see
also* Alpha, Beta; City councils;
Councilmen; Delta; Gamma
Civic awards, 63-64
Class stratification, 15
Code of ethics of city managers, 20
Community differences: characteristics of, 11, 271-78; political, 278-
87; *see also* Alpha; Beta; Delta;
Gamma
Company towns, 22
Consensus, politics of, 100-03
Consolidation: *see* Annexation
Consumer services; *see* Amenities
Councilmen: classified by occupation, 78; educational data, 85;
role in referendums, 243-44; in
arbiter government, 252-53, 256;
as delegates, 252-54, 262, 264; as
board of directors, 252-54; accessibility of, 257-58; in Gamma, 262-
63; role in Delta hospital controversy, 265; leadership qualities,
291-95; relationship to administrators, 297-300; and interest
groups, 303; *see also* City Council;
Council-manager system.
Council-manager system, 18, 43; attitude of labor toward, 145; in
city policies, 280-87; in caretaker
government, 283; role of mayor,
295-97
Cultural facilities in four cities, 63-
64
Curley, James M., 16

Dahl, Robert, 16, 40
Dearborn, Michigan, 26
Decision-making, 16, 251; *see also*
Arbiter government
De Grazia, Alfred, 86
Delegates, councilmen as, 252-54,
262, 264
Delta: amenities, 34-36, 199-221,
271; arbiter government, 34-36,
264-67, 271; caretaker govern-
ment, 34-36, 249-50, 271; econo-
mic growth, 34-36, 271; city hall,